THE
POTTER'S
MANUAL

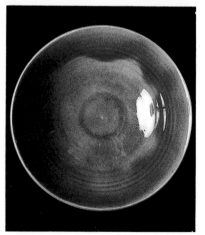

THE POTTER'S MANUAL

Kenneth Clark

CHARTWELL
BOOKS, INC.

A QUARTO BOOK

Published by Chartwell Books Inc
A division of Book Sales Inc
110 Enterprise Avenue
Secaucus
New Jersey 07094

This book was designed and produced by
Quarto Publishing Limited
32 Kingly Court, London W1

Art Editor: Moira Clinch
Editor: Emma Johnson-Gilbert
Assistant Editor: Lucinda Sebag-Montefiore
Editorial Director: Jeremy Harwood
Art Director: Robert Morley
Photography: Ian Howes
Design: Nick Clark, Joanna Swindell
Special thanks to: Alex Arthur, Caroline Courtney,
Sabina Goodchild, Peter Huck, Ted Kinsey, Hilary Krag,
Julian Mannering, Nigel Osborne, Nicola Thompson,
Liz Wilhide.

Typeset in Great Britain by QV Typesetting Limited
Printed in Hong Kong by Lee Fung Asco Limited
Origination by Hong Kong Graphic Arts Services Centre

CONTENTS

FOREWORD

In 1964 I wrote my first book *Practical Pottery and Ceramics*. In this I attempted to show that thrown and reduced stoneware, and trailed slipware, however admirable, were not the only valid forms of studio ceramics. This notion would seem strange to those working today because the spectrum of work produced internationally is now so wide. At present potters are able to experiment and practise in a wide range of ceramic materials and with a variety of techniques for making and firing ware. There has also been a broadening of the criteria for judging both techniques and idiom. In recent years ceramics have invaded the world of fine art. The validity of an object is no longer seen to be dependent to such a degree upon the material used and the function of the article, but upon artistic and aesthetic qualities also. For me the key figure in this change of attitude was Picasso, and his work at the Madoura Pottery at Vallauris in the late 40s reflects this. In the 60s and 70s many potters reacted against what they felt to be the restrictions of thrown symmetrical forms. At the same time there was a renewed interest in early industrial techniques. The early industrial English potters, inheritors of our vital mediaeval tradition were very able and independent craftsmen. They had been stimulated by the sudden increase in skilled labor, technical innovation and an expanding market for pottery, and their ideas became the basis for labor intensive quality production in factories. While I was aware of what Picasso was doing in Vallauris, in contrast to it I was fortunate to work in several country potteries where earning a living from making pots was the daily routine. This was followed by periods of work in a factory in Stoke-on-Trent where I acquired a knowledge of industrial techniques.

In one way *The Potter's Manual* has been an attempt to fill some of the gaps left by my first book and to suggest ways in which potters can extend their techniques of production to meet the needs of changing markets and conditions, and in doing this I have tried to keep a balance between the work of the artist innovator, and the production potter or ceramicist. Having worked with my wife Ann for over thirty years on commissions demanding many different types of ceramic media and techniques, I have endeavored to include as much of this technical information as space would allow. Much of what has been written and illustrated would have been impossible without the generosity of all those included in the book who have given their time and knowledge and to whom I am greatly indebted. The complete lack of secrecy regarding information on materials and skills has been refreshing. Where once knowledge of materials and techniques were closely guarded secrets, in today's climate of accessible information what one does with it is of primary significance. The illustrations have been chosen either to demonstrate particular techniques, or to show an interesting use of materials with the idea of providing stimulus and encouragement for others.

Kenneth Clark

1
CLAY AND POTTERY BODIES

There are few countries in the world where there is not some form of clay available. It is often very near the surface and can be seen when roads are cut through hillsides, in the banks of rivers or streams and in outcrops on beaches and cliffs. It appears as seams which are smooth and compact compared to the layers of sand, gravel, earth and rocks that often surround it. Most clays began as felspathic and granitic rocks which were decomposed millions of years ago by hydrothermal action and weathering agents.

Clay is a highly malleable substance and its most important quality, plasticity, enables it to retain a given shape when molded, leaving the surface smooth and unbroken. The bulk of most clay bodies is made up of the minerals alumina and silica, together with small amounts of other minerals. It is the proportion of these two minerals, together with small percentages of the other minerals acting as fluxes, which assists the fusing and then melting of the clay body during the firing process. This is a process in which the clay is baked in a kiln at a given temperature, causing it to change chemically and become hard and tough when cool.

The two main groups recognized by geologists are primary or residual clays and secondary, or sedimentary, clays. Primary clays are those which have remained in their forming grounds, but these are comparatively few throughout the world. The most important to the potter is china clay, or kaolin, which is mined using high pressure water techniques to wash the fine clay into suspension, separating it from the gravelly rock and fine sand mixture. It is then treated, and settled in vast tanks for drying out and preparing for its many uses.

China clay is very pure, but due to the large particle structure, it is non-plastic. China is thought to be the only country with a plastic china clay. Because of its purity, primary clay is not suitable for working in its natural state and can only be used as an ingredient with other clay bodies. It is used in a prepared body for its strength and whiteness and is an essential ingredient of porcelain ware. Bentonite, a mineral similar in composition to primary clay, is often added to a clay body to aid plasticity.

Secondary clays are those which have been eroded and carried away by water and earth movements to be deposited in sedimentary layers. In this process of weathering the clay particles have become extremely fine, laminatory in structure and some, such as ball clays, very plastic. Impurities which are picked up as the clay moves will affect the color of the clay and its degree of shrinkage on drying out when fired. Ball clays are blue to black in their natural state due to the presence of decomposed vegetable matter, but when fired they become white to buff-colored. When it was first mined and transported to Stoke-on-Trent in England in the early days of the pottery industry, it was convenient to shape the clay into balls for carrying by packhorse- hence the name 'ball clay'

Ball clay is pure, very plastic and vitrifiable and is commonly used in stoneware and earthenware bodies for these qualities. Many other secondary clays have combined with other minerals and organic matter during their formation process. Red clays, for example, contain a high proportion of the mineral iron oxide which is the most common coloring agent and gives us all the red clays found throughout the world. Red clays are fusible and high in plasticity which makes them excellent for throwing on the potter's wheel. They have a low melting point and are used for building bricks, flower pots and other terracotta ware. Another secondary clay is fire clay, so called because it is found close to coal seams, is very refractory (high-firing), often coarse in texture and is used in high-fired prepared bodies, such as stoneware. When it is calcined and reground, fine clay is a common source of grog. This is added to clay bodies to give them added texture and to lessen shrinkage; it can also be used to create color.

Within these broad classifications, there is obviously an extremely rich variety of clays, each with its own individual texture, color and working quality. The possibilities are almost endless, which is all part of the appeal of pottery as an art form. Never be afraid of experiment; provided that the basic rules are followed, such experiments will be successful more often than not and you can learn even from mistakes.

Stoneware vase
Ewan Henderson, UK
Height: 16 in (41 cm)

Ewan Henderson has a strong personal involvement with landscape and natural objects and spends a great deal of time, when he is not working with clay, painting watercolor landscapes This vigorous pot evokes the ruggedness and rich variety of rock faces. Several clay bodies and glazes have been used in layers to create the laminated effect. A bone china body is used over a stoneware core and many of the nodules result from the mixing in of red earthenware clays, which bloat and expand at stoneware temperatures. The pot was fired in an oxidizing electric kiln and taken to a temperature of 1260°C (2300°F).

Natural and prepared clay

NATURAL PLASTIC CLAYS are those primary or secondary clays which can be used with the minimum of cleaning or treatment after being dug and weathered. The weathering process is important as it allows the elements, particularly rainwater, to penetrate between the fine particles of the clay and hence aid its plasticity. The most common of the natural clays are red clays, ball clays, fire clays and some stoneware clays.

Few natural clays are used on their own as, for most purposes in pottery, the mixing with other bodies or ceramic compounds is necessary to give the desirable qualities for working the clay. It is important to remember when using a natural clay that its degree of shrinkage from plastic to fired state should not exceed 10 per cent. If it has a higher shrinkage than this and is very plastic, a non-shrinking ceramic mineral or a less plastic clay can be added to bring it to the right plasticity.

Apart from any suitable natural clays the potter can use, the bulk of available clays for potting are specially prepared by blending different raw materials. One clay can be added to another to combine their working qualities and ceramic compounds can be added to change the color, texture and fusibility of the clay body. Ready-made bodies can be purchased from a supplier, but many studio potters prefer to make up their own.

The basis of most prepared clays is the highly plastic ball clay, with the addition of ceramic minerals such as felspar, alumina and silica or non-plastic materials such as kaolin clay, china stone or whiting. A coarse body can be obtained by adding some form of sand or grog to a fairly plastic clay. The choice of ingredients for any clay body is dependent on what use it is being put to, what type of ware is being produced and what method of decoration is applied to the pottery. Each clay body has a different mechanical strength, color, texture and resistance to heat and the essential differences in pottery ware results from the individual qualities of the clay bodies and the heat to which they are subjected in the kiln. Only with experience and experimentation can the potter choose the right ingredients in the right proportions

Commercially available clays

The reason for purchasing prepared and cleaned clays direct from a supplier is to maintain, as far as possible, an ac-

A selection of different clays in their dry powdered state

Bentonite A highly plastic mineral with the same formulae as a primary clay. It is used to give plasticity to bodies such as porcelain and bone china as well as to give suspension in glazes. Additions are between 1 and 3 per cent.

Black ball clay One of the many highly plastic ball clays. The black clays contain a range of fluxes and vitrify at a temperature between 1100°C (2010°F) and 1200°C (2190°F). Their composition varies greatly and they are broadly categorized as silicious or aluminous. They are too plastic to be used alone, but are used as an ingredient in prepared bodies.

Kaolin A non-plastic high firing primary clay used in bodies and glazes. When vitrified and ground it gives a range of grogs called molochite, which have a constant refractory quality.

Powdered red clay This clay contains iron oxide, silica and alumina as well as small quantities of fluxes which, together with the iron, help vitrification.

Fireclay This clay forms the basis of many grogs once it has been fired and ground, and it is usually found close to coal seams. Fireclay is a refractory clay which is used for fire bricks and it is high in alumina. It fires to a pale buff color and can be used alone or mixed with other clays in a prepared body.

Stoneware clay Most stoneware clays are gray in color but they vary in composition. They are seldom found as natural clays, but are prepared from ball clay and minerals.

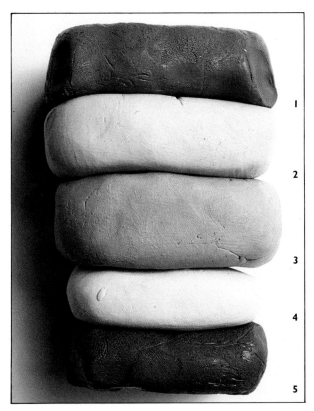

1

2

3

4

5

Clay bodies (left) are normally categorized according to their firing temperature. For potters who wish to work in all fields of ceramics a wide knowledge of the different clay types is important. Although numerous variations exist there are four main types of clay. Red clay (1) the world's most common clay, is used in earthenware. Its high plasticity makes it ideal for throwing. Bone china clay (2), low in plasticity and greenish-blue in color, is mainly used for casting. Stoneware and white earthenware clay (3) are both gray in their raw state and difficult to distinguish while the cream colored porcelain clay (4) is the whitest of prepared bodies after firing. Here (left), all these four types of clay are shown plus a black clay (5) prepared after mixing red clay with a black stain. The chart (below) indicates firing temperatures and different body characteristics.

CLAY BODY	FIRING TEMPERATURE
Earthenware: Red in natural state and after firing	1000°C - 1080°C (1830°F - 1980°F)
White, cream, pink in natural state and when fired; other colors when stains added (mainly to a white body)	1060°C - 1180 °C (1940°F - 2150°F)
Stoneware: Gray in natural state, buff-colored when fired	1200°C - 1300°C (2190°F - 2370°F)
Porcelain: White to cream when raw, white when fired	1280°C - 1350°C (2340°F - 2460°F)
Bone china: White when raw, and when fired	1240°C - 1260°C (2260°F - 2300°F)

ceptable level of consistency and quality in the clay you use.

Some merchants specialize in a particular type of clay, but most endeavour to offer a wide range for maximum scope. If you are buying direct, do not order too much because, however well wrapped, clay tends to dry out, and the time spent dampening and preparing it can rapidly equal the cost of buying fresh clay ready for use.

A good supplier will offer all red to white earthenware clays, grogged red and white earthenware clays, smooth and coarse stoneware clays, at least one porcelain body, possibly a bone china body and a dark chocolate body, and perhaps a black as well.

Most suppliers have a wide range of bodies in powder form which will include one or more types of ball clay, and several now supply prepared, ready-for-use, casting slip. This is mainly for earthenware, but occasionally for porcelain and bone china. Plastic clay is usually supplied in 25kg packs for easy handling.

Choosing and preparing clay

Whether you prepare the clay yourself or buy a ready-made body will depend on the purpose and output of your work. A production potter who is earning a living at producing hand-made domestic stoneware, using a limited range of clays, will probably make a large quantity once, or several times, a year and store it until needed. The potter will then have the necessary clay bodies, and will not have to rely on uncertain deliveries from a supplier. If you acquire the basic equipment of dough mixer and pug mill (or blunger, filter-press and pug mill) the cost of preparing

your own clays should be considerably cheaper than buying it ready-made.

A professional potter with a wide range of activities and techniques may find it more satisfactory to buy prepared clays from one or several suppliers in small quanitities, according to the various needs. It is likely that the expense of purchasing in this way will be covered by the higher fee demanded for more specialized ceramic work. The raw materials for a clay body can also be bought in powder form from a supplier and can be mixed with water in a dough mixer (bought second-hand from a baker).

For beginners it may be interesting to find and dig a local natural clay as part of the learning process. It is particularly important if you plan to work in a wide range of ceramics, from throwing and press molding to casting making murals and coarse clay panels. If a natural local clay is being used, alone or with dry ingredients, it should be filter-pressed to clean it thoroughly and then pugged before storing. It is desirable to filter the clay if it is to be used for throwing, or if a fine clay is needed for the ware. For storage, the clay should be wrapped in plastic and covered, if possible with damp sacks.

Preparing local clays

If you have access to suitable deposits, you can dig your own natural clays, but more time and effort is involved in preparing them for use. Only if prepared clays are not available or are excessively expensive is it worth preparing your own clay from natural sources all the time. However, if you are just beginning to make pots, the finding, digging

Preparing clay bodies

Though clay bodies are available commercially, many potters like to make up their own. Some easy recipes are given (right). Some make them up in bulk, once they have thoroughly tested them to make sure they fulfill the requirements of a particular use or type of work. Others may make up small quantities to achieve a specific color or quality of clay that is unavailable commercially. The basic raw ingredients for an earthenware body are shown below.

It is also the practice to make up casting slips, using powdered ingredients. The slip is mixed in a blunger and sieved before use

	Earthenware			Stoneware		Porcelain	
Recipe	1	2	3	1	2	1	2
Ingredients	%	%	%	%	%	%	%
Ball clay	65	30	48	25	35	-	17
Kaolin	14	20	25	25	20	55	50
Flint	11	35	4	-	-	-	-
Whiting	10	-	-	-	-	-	8
China stone	-	15	23	25	-	-	25
Sand (silver)	-	-	-	25	-	-	-
Felspar	-	-	-	-	20	25	-
Bentonite	-	-	-	-	-	5	-
Quartz	-	-	-	-	-	15	-
Firing temp	1080°C - 1120°C (1975°F - 2050°F)			1260°C - 1280°C (2300°F - 2340°F)		1280°C - 1320°C (2340°F - 2410°F)	

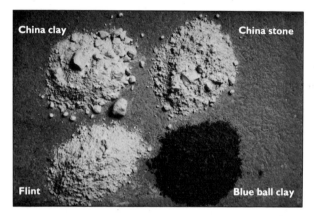

China clay — China stone — Flint — Blue ball clay

and preparation of a small quantity is an invaluable and rewarding experience and will give you a certain understanding of the qualities of clay.

The simplest way to prepare a sample is first to dry it out thoroughly, place it in a shallow container and cover it with water. Within half-an-hour it will have broken up and taken on the consistency of thick cream. To prove the sample, sieve it through a 80-mesh sieve to mix it and remove any impurities. Dry it on a plaster slab until it becomes malleable and plastic. Roll a coil 11 in (28 cm) long and flatten it with a rolling pin until it is ½ in (1 cm) thick, and trim it to make a test strip. Scribe a 4 in (10 cm) line in the middle which will be used to measure percentage shrinkage from plastic to bone dry, and then to fired state (shrinkage should not exceed 10 per cent). Observe any twisting or warping when the sample is drying.

When it is dry, fire one piece to 1060°C, then another to 1120°C and a third to 1280°C observing the color change, shrinkage and porosity at each stage. Next throw a small bowl or vase to prove the throwing qualities and then when biscuit fired test a transparent glaze and an opaque glaze for fit.

Preparing a special body

If you wish to prepare your own clay body, using powdered raw materials obtained from a supplier, first make a small test batch to prove, as for the local clay sample. For a large quantity weigh out the dry ingredients first and cover them with water. Leave until thoroughly soaked, before mixing and sieving them, as with local clay. If you have a dough mixer, put all the dry ingredients into the container and add water while the mixing is in progress. This way you will achieve the correct plasticity and softness. It can then be left to dry sufficiently for putting through a pug mill (or it can be wedged by hand) for final mixing before storing. When the clay is dry enough, store it in a concrete or brick bay, wrapped in a sheet of plastic and covered with damp sacks.

The following recipes are suggestions for prepared bodies which you can mix and test yourself. Each example shows the percentage of raw material used.

Colored clays

These are best made by adding body stains to powdered clay so that you get a more even distribution of the stain through mixing and sieving. It is prepared as a fairly liquid slip and allowed to dry to a workable stage. The proportion of stain may vary from 2 - 10 per cent, but potters seldom make large quantities of colored clay due to the high cost of prepared stains. It is therefore used for articles which command a high profit return on financial outlay. Three basic colored clays — chocolate, black and blue — are made up as follows.

Black body
100gms red clay
5gms manganese oxide, manganese dioxide or black stain

Brown body
100gms red clay
2gms manganese oxide or black stain

Blue body
100gms white clay
1 - 2 gms cobalt oxide or blue stain

Handling clay

It is only by handling clay that you can decide what its most desirable qualities are for a particular technique or type of ware. For example, will it respond well to being rolled out in a slab and handled, rolled into coils and used for building or being pressed into a mold? How does it expand and hold its shape when thrown? Does it retain its strength and shape as the form gets thinner or does it produce a broken textured surface when shaped? Few clays have all the desired characteristics so that much proving will be necessary before you settle for your favorite bodies.

The handling strength of a prepared clay will greatly depend on the ball clay or bentonite content of the mixture, which gives plasticity and adhesion to the ware.

PREPARING A SAMPLE

The same method of testing is applied to a natural, dug clay or a body made up from selected raw materials. Once the sample has been tested and found suitable, large batches may be prepared using the necessary equipment. Having prepared enough clay for the sample, it will be subjected to the standard tests for plasticity, shrinkage and firing, to ascertain vitrification temperature, glaze adhesion and how it reacts with different types of glaze. You may even test its properties as a suitable clay to use for slip casting, as well as how much fine or medium grog it will take and still remain workable. If it fires satisfactorily to stoneware temperatures, subject it to both an oxidizing and reducing atmosphere. Many earthenware clays will stand firing to stoneware temperatures.

1. Clay which has been dug from a clay pit, ready for breaking up, drying out and slaking or soaking.

2. The clay is pounded into small pieces, ready for soaking.

3. Just enough water is added to cover the clay. The soaking time will vary for the different types of clay.

4. The clay is left to soak until all the water is absorbed and it has become very soft. A clay with grog will take less time to soften than a more refined clay.

5. Surplus water is poured off and the clay is mixed to a thick paste. If necessary add more water for easy sieving.

6. The slip is sieved through a 100-mesh sieve (as shown) using a rubber kidney to push the slip through and clean as much as possible from the sides.

7. The slip is poured out onto a plaster or wooden bat to stiffen a little. It is turned frequently to prevent the clay hardening too much.

8. The clay is lifted from the plaster slab when it has stiffened enough for wedging.

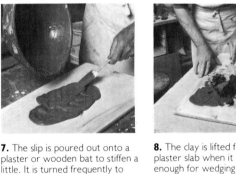

9. The clay is wedged thoroughly until the consistency is even throughout. It is then ready for testing.

Testing for shrinkage The clay is rolled to approximately ¼ in (1 cm) thick, 4 in (10 cm) long and 1 in (3 cm) wide. A line 4 in (10 cm) long is scribed in the surface of the clay and it is left to dry. Most clays shrink approximately 10 per cent from raw to fired state. If the shrinkage is greater than 10 per cent, add some non-shrinking ceramic raw material to the body to reduce shrinkage. Remember, however, not to reduce the plasticity too much or the clay will not be workable. The highest shrinkage takes place from the leather-hard to the bone-dry stage.

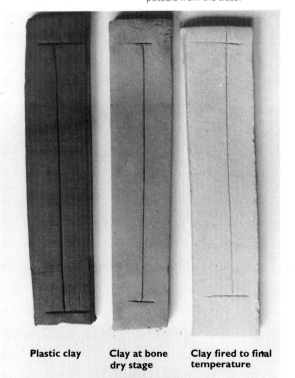

Plastic clay　　**Clay at bone dry stage**　　**Clay fired to final temperature**

Types of ware

THROUGHOUT THE HISTORY OF POTTERY, individual types of ware have been given their own specific names, which are now generic descriptions. Terracotta, for instance, comes from the Italian and means 'baked earth'. This section outlines the chief types, categorizing them according to definition. Of all the various types of clay, terracotta red clay is probably the easiest to throw for a beginner.

Terracotta red clay

The low-firing earthenware clays, particularly the red, are what are known as terracotta clays. Most people associate the term with red clays only, but the word comes from the Italian, meaning simply 'baked earth'. This clay is found in large deposits in many parts of the world and is commonly used for bricks, drainpipes, roofing tiles, flower pots, garden ornaments and domestic ware. For some of these purposes it is quite suitable to use as found, but for others it will be necessary to prepare it more carefully. When fired, it can acquire a white scum on the surface which is due to soluble salts of lime being deposited as the moisture in the

clay evaporates. This can be neutralized by adding approximately one per cent of barium carbonate to the clay mixture during preparation. Small nodules of lime can be cleaned out by filter-pressing or mixing, sieving and drying the clay out in troughs. Red clays contain between 8 and 10 per cent of iron oxide which determines its low firing temperature (between 1000 - 1080°C/1830 - 1980°F). With the addition of sand or grog it will fire up to stoneware temperatures (1200 - 1300°C/2190 - 2370°F).

Terracotta red clay is one of the cheapest clays to buy and it is the easiest to throw with, making it ideal for beginners. However, when decorating it is not necessarily the most suitable color for all types of ware. The best effect is obtained by making the most of the red quality instead of covering it with opaque glaze or light colored slip.

White and buff earthenware

While terracotta red clay is the most common earthenware clay, most other earthenware clays are white or buff when fired, having been prepared from a basis of ball clay with

TERRACOTTA

Most people think of terracotta as the red earthenware which ranges from flower pots and architectural ornaments to figurative modelling or sculpture. However its use for both decorative and functional ware is constantly being extended.

Terracotta planter
John Huggins, UK
12 in × 14 in (30 cm × 36 cm)

This thrown relief form has a relief roulette band of decoration which includes symbols of the sun and rain. The handles were made from extruded strips and the pot fired to a temperature of 1040°C (1900°F).

Decorated pot from Niger
Height: 16 in (41 cm)

This pot was hand-built and decorated with slips and pigments. It is a contemporary pot, but is traditional in style and symbolic decoration, and is reminiscent of Australian aboriginal designs which use a well-balanced use of black, white and halftone in the coloring and decoration of ceramics. Indigenous clay and colors were possibly used, and the pot is unglazed to emphasize the textured surface decoration.

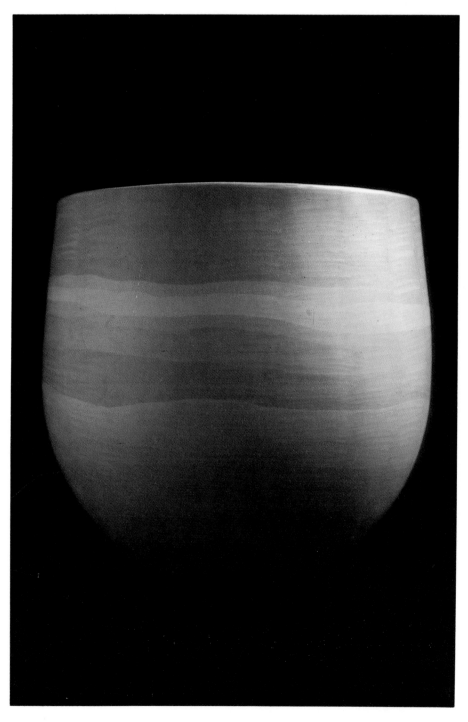

Coiled and burnished pot
Ann Harris, UK
Height: 9 in (23 cm)

A subtle and attractive use of three colored clays — chocolate, red and orange. The coils have been joined freely and are well balanced with the contour of the pot and the quality of the texture of the burnishing. This is one of the oldest and most basic techniques for treating a clay surface, and it is increasingly used on individual ceramics, using terracotta clay.

Burnished and decorated smoked dish
Siddig El Nigoumi, UK
Diameter: 7 in (18 cm)

This press-molded dish has been burnished with red slip and the decoration scratched through. It is a bisque fired to 800°C (1470°F) and then the dish is inverted and supported while it is carbonized (using burning newspapers). The resin and carbon in the smoke quickly penetrate and seal the surface. The decorative design was inspired by the directional signs in a car park adjacent to the potter's studio.

EARTHENWARE

Throughout history, earthenware clays have been used for domestic ware, although toys, figurines and articles connected with religious practice were also produced. Today earthenware is used for both decorative and functional ceramics. The body is usually white, buff, pink or red and is fired at a temperature range of 900°C - 1060°C (1650°F - 1940°F).

Meringue vase
Betty Woodman, USA
16 in x 8 in (40 cm x 20 cm)

This piece of earthenware is hand-shaped, with strips of clay and sprigging applied to it with a cake icing tool. The vase shows imaginative handling of the form together with a direct, fluid use of clay applications. It could either be thrown and then shaped, or slab built, with extruded strips and other embellishments added when the clay is soft.

Silver luster camel coffee pot
Roger Michell and Danka Napiorkowska, UK
Height: 8 in (20 cm)

This decorative piece is made with fine earthenware clay. It is thrown and turned with the additions (spout, lid and handle) made by press moulding. The glaze is a low solubility lead glaze, fired by a biscuit and glaze combined firing to a temperature of 1080°C (1980°F). A two-hour soak is allowed for the glaze. The decoration is white gouache, used as resist, and the pot is brushed over with platignum luster and fired to 750°C (1380' F)

Hand-made tile panel 'Plaza'
Alan Lloyd, UK
6 ½ ft x 5 ½ ft (198 cm x 160 cm)

The pieces for this panel are cut from slabs made in a slab roller. The clay is then laid out on boards and the design composed in the leather-hard clay. The burr from lines scratched in the surface is either smoothed or left until dry to obtain a clean edge for drawing the motifs. Texture can be given to the smooth, rolled surface if required. The tiles are fired to earthenware temperatures (850°C/1560°F - 1200°C/2190°F). As the panel is not glazed, various surface qualities can be obtained by burnishing before the clay is fully dry. Colors are obtained with basic oxides, sometimes reburnished after firing.

Terra sigillata, decorated hand-built vase
Fiona Salazar, UK
Height: 15 in (38cm)

An extremely fine colloidal slip, prepared by precipitation, is applied by brushing, pouring or spraying onto a leather-hard clay surface. It is then burnished so that the fine grains are compacted and, on firing, give a shiny and almost glaze-like surface. Coloring oxides or stains can be added at the liquid slip stage and applied one over the other. Adjoining areas can also be scratched away. Color slips are also used to decorate the top of the vase.

Hand-pressed earthenware dish
Idonia Van der Bilj, UK
Diameter: 18 in (46 cm)

The stained clay motifs are shaped and flattened into squares and then pressed onto a raised hump mold, or into a recessed mould. A rolled sheet of clay is then placed over them and pressed and smoothed down, so that the motifs become embedded in a layer of the rolled clay. The colored motifs are drawn in colored clays, the design for them having been planned first in pencil and transferred from the paper to the mold.

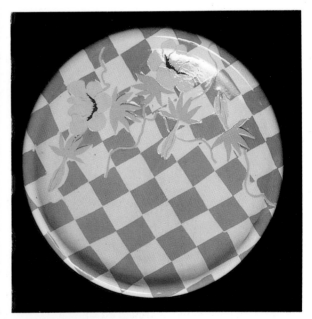

Traditional slipware cradles
Mary Wondransch, UK
Height: 4 in (10 cm)

These small pottery cradles illustrate the use of different colored clays as well as the techniques of slip trailing and sgraffito. They are a traditional present to parents on the birth of a baby and the name of the child and the date of birth is applied to the side or end of the cradle.

STONEWARE

While rich, brightly colored glazes are possible at stoneware temperatures, this area of ceramics is more commonly associated with subdued subtle grays, pale greens, rich blacks and speckled bodies. This is particularly so in reduction firings. Additional attractiveness is given to stoneware by its tendency to mattness and dryness in some glazes and clay surfaces.

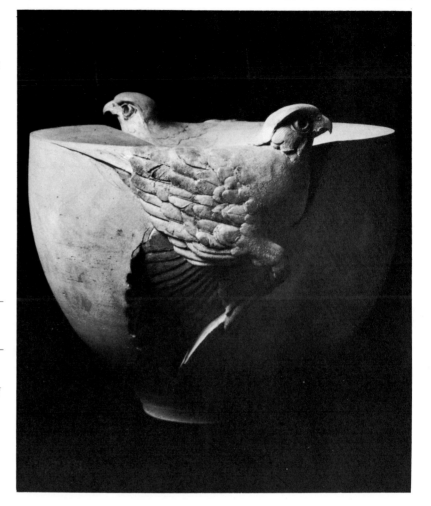

Double-walled thrown and modelled form
Kenneth Bright, UK
Height: 16 in (40 cm)

This form combines the techniques of throwing and modelling to create a relationship between the two surfaces. The clay for modelling is joined to the outer wall of the thrown form and the birds are modelled onto the surface. The clay body is a combination of Moira clay, fireclay and buff grog. The article is brushed with willow ash (which reacts with the iron in the fireclay) and given an oxidized firing to 1280°C (2340°F). Similar pieces are brushed with ocher, ash glaze and kaolin to give a dryish matt yellow-brown color.

other ceramic mineral additions. Because they have less strength than stoneware clays they need to be fired almost to the point of vitrification. This occurs when the body begins to fuse and the fine holes or spaces between the firing clay particles close so that the clay becomes solid and non-porous. All good clay suppliers will give firing ranges for their clays and white or buff earthenwares range from 1060°-1180°C/1940-2150°F. If it is used for domestic ware the higher the temperature the less likely it is that the applied glaze will craze or stain. When rich and strong-colored glazes and pigments are being used for decoration, or for their decorative effects, light-colored earthenware clays are the most suitable to work on.

Stoneware

Stoneware is similar in mineral composition to stones, both having been exposed to similar heat treatment. They are both dense, non-porous and on occasion alike in color and texture. The main difference is that stones are formed naturally while most stoneware clay is made from selected ceramic minerals and a proportion of plastic clay. The firing temperature is between 1200-1300°C/2200-2370°F and, while glazing improves the surface for domestic use, it

is not always essential.

Stoneware bodies can be fine or coarse, but their final state depends on the temperature of firing. Domestic stoneware pots are generally heavier than their earthenware or porcelain equivalent and are best made with a fine stoneware body. Coarse bodies can be reserved for large containers or garden pots which may have to withstand heavier treatment and greater stresses in firing. The two most common types of firing for stoneware are oxidized and reduced. In oxidation the flow of air into the combustion chamber of the kiln is unrestricted and complete combustion of the fuel takes place as the temperature steadily rises. However, in a reduction firing the air intake is restricted and, instead of fully combusted fuel giving off carbon dioxide, carbon monoxide is produced. As this is an unstable gas it quickly combines with oxygen atoms in the clay body and glazes of the pots, thus changing their chemical composition and giving changes of color to the clay and the glaze.

Porcelain

Porcelain clay is fine in texture and white and tough when fired. It can be either opaque or translucent according to the

**Decorated thrown
stoneware jug**
Michael Casson, UK
Height: 24 in (61 cm)

This robust jug shows the result
of vigorous throwing and a rich,
wood-fired salt glaze. Both shape
and decoration have a
spontaneous quality. The handle
is pulled on the pot and appears
to grow with tension from the
neck of the form. The
distinctively shaped spout is
designed for ease of pouring.

**Thrown and glazed
stoneware plates**
Estelle Martin, New Zealand
Diameter: 10.2 in x 11.8 in
(26 cm x 30 cm)

The decoration of these plates
has a soft, sensitive quality of
brushwork which blends well with
the texture of the glazes. Both
plates are ash glazed and fired at
1280-1300°C (2340-2370°F).
Metallic oxides in the body can
enrich the glaze if it is given a
good firing.

composition and density of the clay. Porcelain bodies are
not easy to throw or handle as they have a critical moisture
range and can easily be too soft or too dry. Prepared
porcelain bodies can be bought from a supplier, but many
potters mix their own body.

A whole range of colored, matt or opaque glazes may be
applied to porcelain, but the true quality of the body is most
apparent under a clear glaze. Because of the difficulties in
handling porcelain, it is not used widely for domestic ware,
but is more commonly used for individual pieces,
modelling and casting.

Porcelain can be raw-glazed, but the standard practice is
to give it a low bisque, or first firing, to at least
1000°C/1830°F. This will make it easier to handle and
reduce the risk of breakage as it has a very poor mechanical
strength in the unfired state. When the body and glaze
reach maturation during firing (between 1280-1300°C/
2340-2380°F) the glaze is no longer a layer of glass fused
onto the surface of the pot, but has combined with the body.

Bone china

This is a specially prepared body or paste with the special
characteristics of thinness, translucency, whiteness and

David Leach porcelain recipe

		Bentonite	2%
Standard porcelain china		(pure South African)	
clay (see suppliers)	56%	Maturation point: 1250°C	
Potash felspar	25%	(2280°F)	
Quartz	17%		
(sieved through a 200-250 mesh sieve)			

This fluted porcelain pot by
David Leach was made using
the special recipe (above). The
regular, rhythmic fluting
emphasizes the form, which is
further enhanced by a
transparent Y'Ching celadon
glaze. The pot is fired to a
temperature of 1280°C
(2340°F).

PORCELAIN

Porcelain is cool white and very hard. The body, when fired, can be either translucent or opaque, depending on the thickness or composition of the clay. In the last decade porcelain has undergone a renaissance, with potters throughout the world extending and exploiting its qualities, often with excellent results.

Hand-shaped form
Agalis Manessi, UK
Height: 12 in (30.5 cm)

The making of this form is a combination of coiling and pinching techniques. Pinched pieces of clay have been added to the surface of the pot to achieve a low, soft relief which is then decorated by brushing and incising at the dry clay stage. Color is sometimes scraped and repainted using a mixture of copper, rutile and nickel. Chrome is also used to give pink under a tin/dolomite glaze, which is given an oxidised firing to 1250°C (2280°F). The body is made from a David Leach prepared porcelain recipe (page 19).

Sculptural form
Eileen Nisbet, UK
Height: 16 in (41 cm)

The clay body used for this ceramic sculpture is the David Leach recipe (page 19). The porcelain clay is rolled into extremely thin sheets before cutting. The pieces are then carefully scraped to reduce the thickness gradually towards some of the edges. Decoration is applied by brushing or inlaying colored strips to the raw clay. An oxidised stoneware firing is to a temperature of 1240 - 1250°C (2260 - 2280°F). When firing is complete the various shaped parts are glued together with cylindrical spacers to keep them apart.

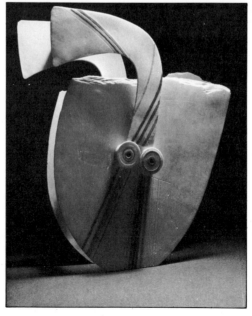

Krater porcelain vessel
Robin Hopper, Canada
Height: 9.8 in (25 cm)

Thrown form with thrown clay
additions. It is glazed with an
alkaline slip glaze with additions of
copper and rutile. The pot is
once-fired to porcelain
temperature.

Lidded porcelain vessel *(above)*
Rudy Autio, USA
Height: 1 ft 10 in (56 cm)

The form of the vessel roughly
indicates the curve of the figures,
and this is further emphasized by
the brushwork of the drawing.
The vessel is decorated with a
fritted glaze when it is bone dry
and once-fired.

Hand-shaped porcelain
David Brokenshire, NZ
Diameter: 8 in (20 cm)

These press molded and hand-
shaped bowls have been inspired
by flower forms. They aptly
convey the frailty and delicacy of
flowers, a subject most
successfully expressed through
the skilled handling of translucent
porcelain. The clay body is David
Leach's porcelain recipe (page 19)
and it is first bisqued and then
gloss fired to 1300°C (2370°F) in
a reducing atmosphere. They are
colored, before the glaze firing,
using soluble metallic salts.

BONE CHINA

Bone china is a ceramic body of great strength and delicacy when thinly made and fired. It fires to a cool-white color and is usually glazed with a transparent glaze in order to emphasize these particular qualities.

Slip cast and pierced bone china beaker
Sandra Black, Australia
Height: approximately 4 in(11 cm)

This delicate piece is made from an extremely pure basic material — Eckalite no. 1 china clay (Australian kaolin). The deflocculent used for the casting slip is Dispex. The beaker is cast in a one-piece mold and pierced at the leather hard stage. It is bisqued to 800°C (1470°F) and the bisqued piece is soaked in water and then polished with wet and dry sandpaper. The second firing is at 1280-90°C (2340-60°F), with half-an-hour for reduction at the end of the cycle. The beaker is unglazed. Recipe for clay body developed by Dr Orwin Rye, Canberra Art School

Eckalite no. 1 kaolin	30
Bone ash, natural	45
Potash filspart	22.8
Silica	2.2

Bone china lamp
Pamela Green, UK
Height: 8 in (20 cm)

This slip cast light sphere has hand-shaped applied features. These give subtle variations of light which contrast with the symmetry of the spherical form.

Thrown and carved bone china vase
Kenneth Clark, UK
Height: 3 in (7.5 cm)

Bone china is difficult to throw and turn due to the texture of the body and the very limited plasticity of the clay. The finer the quality of the ingredients, the easier it is to throw. The body used for this vase is Potterycrafts bone china. Carving is best done at the bone dry stage and the ware must be handled with great care until fired.

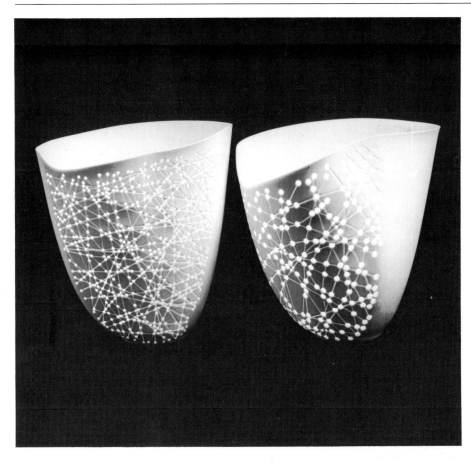

Slip cast pierced and scratched forms
Angela Verdon, UK
Height: 4 in (10 cm)

The thinness of the ware is achieved in the casting, by filling the mold with slip and immediately emptying it. It is then left for several hours to dry and shrink away from the mold. This gives a casting of eggshell thinness. The first firing is to 1080°C (1980°F), after which the form is drilled and pierced and refired to 1220°C (2230°F), with a two-hour soak completing the firing. When fired the articles are hand polished.

extreme strength. Most of these qualities are provided by one of the constituents, calcined bone, which acts as a flux to the body, making it fuse into a tough glass-like substance at temperatures over 1240°C/2260°F. Because it has a poor mechanical strength before firing and has a limited top-firing range (after which it quickly loses shape and collapses) bone china is usually only used by potters with considerable experience in ceramics. It is only recently that artist potters have used bone china to any extent and great skill is needed in handling it. When used industrially for domestic ware a complete technological process is employed in the making and firing.

Bone china bodies are biscuit fired to their maturing temperature and glaze fired at a temperature between 1040°C-1080°C/1900-1980°F. A suitable recipe for a china body is 50 per cent calcined bone, 25 per cent china clay and 25 per cent china stone or felspar.

Because of its smoothness and whiteness it is an ideal clay for many techniques of fine quality decoration using a wide range of colors. It is particularly suitable for litho transfers and for ground-laying.

Raku

Raku is a particular type of ware or ceramic body developed by the early Japanese potters. It was glazed and fired at their tea ceremonies then the bowls were used by participants.

Recently Raku has become extremely popular elsewhere in the world. One reason for this is that it can be produced from fired bisque to the finished glaze state very rapidly. It is also possible to get a wide range of variations in color and effect from different glazes and bodies. In recent years the quality and type of ware made by the Raku method has been developed far beyond that employed by the early Japanese potters.

You may wish to prepare your own Raku body, there are now several manufacturers who will supply a suitable one. Because of the sudden extremes of temperature which the fired ware will need to withstand, the clay body must contain a high percentage of sand or grog. The pieces should first be bisque fired to a temperature of about 900°C/1650°F. If you wish to increase the strength of the ware you can raise it to 1200°C/2190°F, but you must leave the pots sufficiently porous to withstand severe thermal shock. The glaze firing can be carried out in anything from an electric kiln to a coal, wood, gas or oil-fired kiln built in your own back yard. The pots are placed in the kiln and extracted when the glaze has melted. This will depend on the nature of the glaze and can range from 30 minutes to one hour. The average temperature for firing Raku is between 750 - 1000°C/ 1380 - 1830°F, but it can be higher.

When the glaze is set and the pieces removed, they can be subjected to a number of different treatments. The final result is affected by the cooling and oxidizing period and the

RAKU

Raku is a very popular technique and material with wide ranging possibilities for developing surface qualities and colors. It is sually a low-fired, coarse-grained body with a soft plain glaze which produces interesting designs and textures. As a medium it is more expressive and decorative than it is utilitarian.

Thrown Raku bottle
David Miller, UK
Height: 14 in (35 cm)

This bottle was made using grogged Raku clay, with talc added to improve the tensile strength. It was bisque fired to a temperature of 980°C (1800°F). It was then given a thin layer of copper slip, before rapidly firing to 1000°C (1830°F) plus. The fired article was removed quickly from the kiln and smoked in a metal container. This gives a beautiful, highly incandescent luster to the warm, buff clay surface.

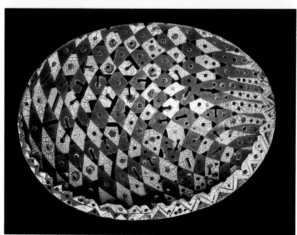

Pierced and decorated Raku dish
Ian Byers, UK
Length: 10 in (26 cm)

This dish has a fresh vibrancy of colour, and shows a control of decoration which is not usually associated with Raku lusters. The decoration is done by applying a red and white glaze.
The black is achieved by reducing the article in a special lidded brick box containing dry, soft wood sawdust, after it has been removed from the kiln. The firing is between 900 and 1000°C (1650 and 1830°F).

Multi-fired Raku vase
Harvey Sadow, USA
14 in x 12 in (35 cm x 30 cm)

A full, vigorous form with rich
flowing colors and a luminous
layered surface. This interesting
texture is achieved by repeated
firings and sand-blasting between
the application of colored slip.

BLACK CLAYS

Black can be a very striking color when used in a clay body, if it is contrasted with a red or yellow glaze, or a white tin glaze. Depending on the temperature of firing and the thickness of the glaze, the result with be either a soft pale white (where the stain permeates the glaze) or, if thick white, it will give a sharp contrast when scratched through. Areas of clear glaze and a matt, vitrified body give a subtle contrast.

Thrown decorated black bowls and vase
Kenneth Clark, UK
Height: vase 7 in (18 cm)
Diameter: bowls (4-6 in (10-15 cm)

All these pots were spray glazed after bisque firing with a ten per cent tin glaze composed of low solubility lead and borax. Body stain from the black clay has permeated the thin glaze of the bowl on the left, giving it a soft warm brown color. The glaze of the pot, has been scratched immediately after glazing. When scratching, if the glaze is too thick or lacking in glue it will flake.

type of reduction used, which can range from burying the article in wet or dry sawdust, garden vegetation or other combustible organic matter. It is common practice to plunge the pot into a bucket of cold water after the reduction process while the article is still hot in order to preserve the particular quality of the ware at this stage of cooling. For maximum reduction the red hot pots should be placed in a container and covered with sawdust or vegetable matter. A drum or can should be placed over the top to prevent any further oxidation and the escape of smoke and fumes.

Raku glazes are naturally high in flux, such as lead, lead frit, alkaline frit or a combination of both. The lead or frit content must be in the region of 80-95 per cent, the further 5-10 per cent being made up of kaolin, flint or ball clay. A typical recipe for Raku would be: 90 per cent lead basilicate, 6 per cent kaolin and 4 per cent flint.

Glazes may be brushed with oxides or have oxides added to them. They can also be applied over colored or plain slips and, in the case of alkaline glazes, used to get rich copper reactions of turquoise or green, according to the strength. Rich luster effects are also common with certain oxides — their application or addition ranging from 1 per cent to 15 per cent for iron, copper, tin or manganese; never more than 1 per cent if cobalt is used. Copper reds can be obtained with up to 0.5 per cent copper and an addition of 2 per cent ferric oxide will give a fine yellow color.

Black clays

Black clays range from earthenware to porcelain. The ware was in vogue in the nineteenth century, but black clay has only been used intermittently since then. A black clay body lends itself to attractive designs and decoration, such as the subtle contrast of a vitrified body with areas of transparent glaze. However, as with red clays, the disadvantage is that any chips to the ware are very noticeable if a contrasting tone of glaze is applied.

Most black earthenware bodies are made by adding either five per cent black stain or manganese oxide to a red clay. For special bodies a little cobalt can be added, but this is an expensive ingredient. Other colorants include black iron, iron oxide and copper oxide. Chocolate-colored bodies can be made with the addition of one per cent manganese or black stain. For a stoneware or porcelain black body it is essential to start with a sufficiently refractory clay, before adding the stains, as most black bodies mature at a temperature over 1100°C/2010°F.

Egyptian paste

This is a specially prepared body in which the glaze is supplied by soluble salts of soda, drawn to the surface of the ware as it dries. Great care must be taken in handling the clay in order not to disturb the soda or rub it off. The outer layer of soda crystals react with the body during firing to form a glaze coating with gives color to the pigment or stain present in the body. An attractive example of Egyptian paste is the Egyptian style beads which acquire a brilliant turquoise from the soda and copper reaction. Most of the basic oxides, such as iron, manganese, cobalt and chrome can be used in this way with a wide range of colored body stains.

Egyptian paste is not a material that lends itself to func-

EGYPTIAN PASTE

Thrown and turned Egyptian paste
Dick Studley, USA
Diameter of bowl: 13 in (33 cm)
Height of bottle: 10 in (25 cm)

Because of its low plasticity and high alkaline content, Egyptian paste has a very critical moisture tolerance level for throwing. The body is prepared by mixing it with hot water and a little vinegar and leaving it to age for as long as possible. Wedging by hand improves the paste for throwing.

Recipe for the body fired to 1060°C -1100°C (1940°F - 2030°F)

Sodium bicarbonate	1	Macaloid Plastic kaolin or ball	
Dolomite	4	clay	25
Soda ash	1	Mullite	2
Whiting	4	Flint (200	
Frit 3134 (ferro)	4	mesh)	20
Soda felspar	15	Flint	
Bentonite	2	(326 mesh)	20
		Add hot water	30

A mask should be worn when preparing the body, and rubber gloves as a precaution.

tional ware; it is used almost exclusively for its decorative effects. By adding minerals which give greater strength and durability to the body you would invariably counteract the particular qualities of color. Because it has a poor mechanical strength while being formed it is only used for small articles or objects, such as beads, small decorative dishes, and features for mirror frames, clocks and similar articles.

Care must be taken in the firing to ensure that the glaze does not adhere to the kiln shelf. Beads should be supported on straight lengths of element wire to prevent contact with the kiln shelves, and each other. The ware is most successful if fired once, in the region of 1000°C/1830°F or below. A recipe for Egyptian paste is as follows:

Firing Temperature	°C 850 °F 1560	850 1560	850 1560	955 1750	955 1750	1000 - 1060 1830 - 1940
Nephyltine syenite	30	34	39	-	39	-
Soda ash	6	6	4	-	6	6
Sodium bicarbonate	6	6	4	6	6	6
Potassium carbonate	-	-	-	6	-	-
High alkali frit*	5	10	-	-	-	-
Kaolin	-	5	6	10	6	15
Flint	38	35	37	20	37	20
Bentonite	4	4	2	2	2	-
Copper oxide	3	3	3	2	3	2
Ball clay	10	-	-	5	6	5
Lithium carbonate	4	-	4	-	-	-
Whiting	-	-	-	5	-	5
Fine silica sand	-	-	-	8	-	8
Felspar	-	-	-	40	-	-

* can be obtained from Podmore (no. P2250) Ferro (no. 3134).

2
TECHNIQUES OF MAKING

Although a general knowledge of methods and materials is acquired through the experience of processing and handling clay in its many forms, before attempting to produce a finished article or design it is first necessary to discover as much as possible about the techniques of making pottery. Otherwise few pieces will be wholly successful. Instead they will become vehicles for experiment and discovery rather than complete objects. Knowledge of a particular process will enable you to execute your idea or design with confidence, while remaining open to the many possibilities that may develop as the work progresses. Adequate research and development should proceed any project so that it can start from a broad and sound base.

Pottery making falls into three categories: hand-making techniques, wheel techniques (a combination of the hand and machine methods), and machine production or reproduction by mold-making techniques. Learning how to prepare clay by kneading and wedging so that it has an even texture is a prerequisite for successful construction. The various methods of manufacture by hand include the modelling of figures, birds and animals, pinching and coiling pots and building techniques such as weaving and slab construction. Hand shaping is a tactile skill which is

developed through handling the clay and is a medium which allows plenty of scope for personal expression.

The hand and machine approach deals with throwing and turning objects on the potter's wheel or using a slow or fast turntable for decorating the ware. This is a technique which enables the potter to control the clay with the aid of a machine. Successful potters combine an exploitation of the wheel's circular motion with skilful manual manipulation of the clay so that the exercise becomes automatic, allowing the potter to concentrate wholly on the design and shape of the object being created. Although machines are used there is still plenty of scope for personal expression, particulary when decorating. Pottery made in this way can often be totally embellished by hand during construction or clay may be added to the finished form.

In machine production and reproduction by mold-making techniques a prototype form is precisely and deliberately originated and built by the potter. The model is then reproduced by machine, either automatically or with some intervention from the potter. Alternatively it is cast in a mold. The finished item can be very distinctive, but frequently lacks the individual quality which personal handling of the clay gives to the ware.

Raku broken and reassembed pot
Rick Dillingham, USA
Height: 14 in (36 cm)

This is an unusual technique which gives attractive results. The pot is Raku fired and then broken up to make a series of sherds. These are then decorated with gold, or pigments and stains, and refired. After this the pieces are reassembled and glued together. Many of Rick Dillingham's shapes are based on the basic geometric forms, such as cones, triangles and spheres. When decorating the pieces he works intuitively, without a preconceived idea of how the whole will look when assembled. He is creating individual works of art which are simple and have a very definite strength. In this he is influenced by the work of Indian and pre-technological cultures.

SHAPE AND FORM

A sense of and feeling for shape and form is an essential hallmark of all good pottery. For some, this is easier to achieve than for others, but much can be learnt by application and perseverance. The aim should be to make the continuous conscious effort to be aware of the possibilities of various shapes, come to understand their character and so use this knowledge, which can be both tactile and visual, to make a personal statement in your pottery. Study the way artists of the past have tackled the problem, by seeing how they recorded the way shapes are formed. Man-made objects and artefacts can often be a source of inspiration, as they have been for many designers, craftsmen and artists over the centuries.

What is form? It is defined as having various aspects, balance, proportion and the relationship of the constituent parts being the most important. The best way of coming to an understanding of these intricacies is either by throwing on the wheel, a valuable way of creating forms and experiencing their qualities, and through modelling in three dimensions to extend awareness and appreciation. Always remember that shape is the key to immediate recognition, followed by color and detail with context, surroundings or associations being the third consideration. Above all, always feel free to give rein to your imagination, since this will enable you to give personal expression to your pottery and to your ideas about the shapes and forms you want to create. Do not be disheartened if your initial efforts are less than successful — you will learn something new from each attempt.

straight neck.

sketching shapes contrasting body with neck.

Thrown porcelain shell forms
Robin Hopper, Canada
Height: approx 6-7 in (15-17 cm)

These thrown and shaped forms were inspired by sea shells. They are made from laminated blue and white porcelain clays, fired unglazed to porcelain temperature. In their creation, Hopper has managed to retain all the plastic and decorative qualities of his medium.

Slip cast shell teapot
Early industrial European
Height: 6 in (15 cm)

This practical, yet unusually shaped, teapot uses a modelled shell for a knob. It was cast using a cream-white earthenware body and richly decorated with copper, manganese and iron oxides in combination with a lead-based glaze. The metal handle has a cane wrapping.
Collection of Kenneth Bright

Thrown forms in porcelain and stoneware
Lucy Rie, UK
Height: 11 in (28 cm); 6 in (15 cm) 14 in (36 cm)

Rie's individual and distinctive forms are skilfully-thrown mixtures of contrasting clays. The combinations enrich the colors of the pots, as well as emphasizing both shapes and the spiral quality of the throwing technique. The dark spiral in the small pot was created with a red clay with iron additions. When using such combinations, it is important that the contrasting clays are compatible and have similar rates of shrinkage.

Porcelain handle and spout pot
Nicholas Homoky, UK
6 in (15 cm) x 4 in (10 cm)

This pot was thrown and then shaped by beating the clay body with a flat wooden spoon. By deliberately altering the conventional symmetry of the thrown shape, Homoky created a completely different quality of form. The decorative drawing was inlaid with a black slip and, when dry, the pot was fired to 1260°C (2300°F) in an electric kiln. The final polishing was with carborundum paper.

Preparing the clay

THE FIRST STAGE in the process of making pottery is to prepare the clay for use. Because it must expand evenly during any making process, it is essential that it should have an even consistency throughout. Clay cannot be worked effectively unless any lumps or air pockets have been eliminated and it has been thoroughly mixed. Wedging and kneading are two ways of mixing plastic clays by hand, while still retaining a compact shape.

Kneading

This is similar to dough mixing in bread-making and is the best method for pieces of clay of a manageable size which are sufficiently soft. Firm, rhythmical pressure is applied to the clay with the palms of the hands.

Wedging

This method is used if the clay is uneven, or if different clays are being blended together. One method, from which the name probably came, is to place the clay on the edge of the bench and cut it in half, at an angle, to form a wedge shape. This piece is lifted, twisted and slammed down onto the other half of the clay on the bench and the action is repeated until the mixing is complete. Although it is a slow method, it is more suitable than kneading for large pieces of clay.

A second method, also used for large pieces, is spiral wedging. The clay is pushed and lifted with a rocking motion in such a way that a spiral movement is set up and it is gradually mixed to an even consistency.

Uneven clay can be wedged by cutting horizontal slices from an upright lump of clay, laying the slices on edge and flattening them, one on top of the other, with the palm of the hand. The slices are then kneaded together before the process is repeated.

MIXING THE CLAY

Preparing clay by hand is known as wedging. This is always easier to do if the clay is slightly softer than needed for working; it can always be kneaded on a dry bench, or a plaster slab, to bring it to the required firmness. If the clay is too hard, slice it into small pieces and place these loosely in a large bowl. Sprinkle with water and cover with a wet cloth. Repeat the process two or three times over the next four to five hours and then drain off any water in the bowl. Remove the clay and wedge until ready for use.

Points to remember
● Always store clay wetter than needed, as it inevitably tends to dry out.
● For large pieces, mix for a time by the wedging method, cut into smaller pieces and knead until thoroughly mixed.

Mixing the clay/kneading I. The clay to be kneaded should be placed on a slightly absorbent surface, such as wood. Both hands are placed firmly on top of the lump of clay, to cover the top, at the angle shown in the picture above.

2. The clay is kneaded with downward pressure, as with dough, using the wrists of both hands to flatten the lump.

3. The lump of clay is lifted from the back and pulled forward to a vertical position.

4. The kneading process is repeated approximately 10 times, with the clay rhythmically pressed in a circular movement of pushing and lifting.

5. The clay is then turned through 90° and the whole operation begun afresh until the piece is thoroughly mixed.

Mixing and cleaning 1. Uneven, dirty clay can be mixed, checked and cleaned when soft by palming it. This reveals irregularities and breaks up lumps.

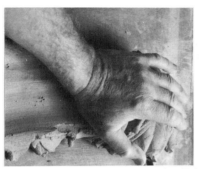

2. Spread the clay thinly with long strokes. This makes it easy to see and remove hard pieces of clay, or foreign particles.

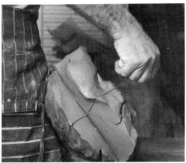

Wedging 1. A large lump of clay is mixed by ramminglone piece down on top of the other, turning the lump and repeating this action. The clay is placed upright, and at an angle, on the edge of the bench. A wedge-shaped piece is then cut from the whole with a cutting wire.

2. The top wedge is lifted up and turned through 90°.

3. The top half is then thrown down firmly onto the other half of the clay on the bench.

4. The clay is lifted from the right and twisted through 90°. It is then rested on the edge of the bench, cut again and the sequence repeated until the clay is thoroughly mixed and homogeneous.

5. Lift the lump of clay and place it at an angle on the edge of the bench. Repeat the process.

Spiral wedging 1. Lift the clay up ready for downward pressing, with a rhythmic rocking and twisting motion. The clay should be reasonably soft.

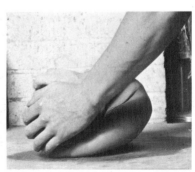

2. After completing the first stage of spiral wedging, lift the clay and repeat the process on the other side.

3. Lifting the clay up ready for pressing down to continue the movements of spiral wedging. This should be a continuous flowing process.

Mixing two colored clays 1. The two different colored lumps of clay are placed on the bench and the cutting wire is drawn across to slice pieces from each one.

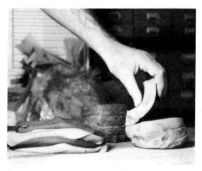

2. Alternate slices are placed one on top of the other, and pressed down firmly as you proceed.

3. The pieces of clay should be turned on their side so that the edge is pressed down firmly onto the slice underneath.

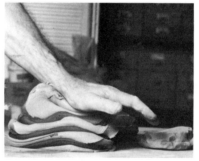

4. When you have built up several layers, press downwards and forward with the wrists of both hands to flatten the lump of clay.

5. The clay is kneaded until it is thoroughly mixed. The cross-section (above) shows how the two clays are mixing during the kneading process.

Checking the clay To make sure that the clay is properly mixed, cut the piece in half and run your finger over the inside surface. You will be able to see any air bubbles (or feel any lumps) on the surface which indicates that the clay is not yet thoroughly mixed and needs further wedging. Store clay which has been kneaded or wedged in a damp atmosphere if you are not using it immediately. It will keep for several months, wrapped in plastic and stored in an airtight container. If clay is stored in its plastic state, it will actually improve over a period of time.

Hand-making

ALL METHODS OF HAND-SHAPING a plastic clay involve squeezing and pressing the clay, whether you are making a pinched pot or producing an article using the coiling or throwing technique. These slow, hand-shaping methods are essential for developing tactile sensibility and manipulative skill. When making a pinched pot you will discover the relationship between the weight of the clay and the size of the finished object and how the shape of the hands can effect the shape of the pot; in coiling or slab-building you learn how to control the clay on a larger scale. For these methods there is plenty of time to think and observe the development of the form as you progress with the work.

Hand-shaping and pinching.

One of a child's first instincts when given a piece of clay is to pick pieces off the lump and squeeze and press them together. In order to develop and explore this method, you can make a mosaic or pattern of clay on a piece of board with two different colored clays. The technique can be extended to make a dish on a hump mold or you can use the inside of a bisqued dish as a support mold for modeling another dish (see Making and using molds, page 66).

Having explored the pinching and squeezing of clay the next stage is to take a lump of well-kneaded clay which fits comfortably into the hand and is not too soft or too hard. Begin to squeeze and press with the flat of the fingers from the center of the clay with a rotating movement. This must not be done too slowly or the warmth of the hands and the atmosphere will dry the clay very quickly so that it becomes too stiff for handling and will begin to crack before shaping is complete. As the clay is rotated the angle of the fingers will guide the form of the clay to create an open, wide shape or a deep, enclosed bowl shape. To avoid cracking at the

PINCH POTS

The following illustrations show, in cross-section, the stages of making for three different shapes of pinch pot. These pots can be made from any type of clay, as long as it is physically strong enough to withstand handling and forming to the required shape. Clay is pleasant and satisfying to handle, whether it is gritty and coarse or smooth and fine, and making pinch pots is a good way of getting to know these individual qualities and the treatment which they demand.

1. While revolving the ball of clay in the palm of your hand, use your thumb and the flat areas of the fingers to start shaping the pot. Support the form with the other hand as you do this.

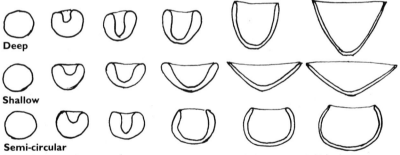

Deep

Shallow

Semi-circular

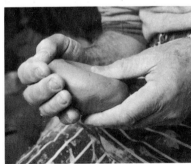

2. This picture shows how one hand supports the piece of clay while the thumb and fingers of the other hand press and squeeze it into the desired shape.

3. Always work from the center of the piece of clay, pressing out to the edges. Many potters have difficulty controlling the edges of the pot in the final stages of making, although irregularities can be made into a feature (page 154).

4. This reverse view of step 3 shows the fingers pressing flat against the outside surface, while the clay is gently revolved, squeezed and shaped between the thumb and finger.

MAKING A COIL POT

The clay for coiling should not be too plastic and should ideally contain some fine sand or medium to fine grog. The clay is wedged first and the coils can be rolled by hand or extruded from a wad box. Equipment will include a turntable or banding wheel, together with a cutting wire, modelling tool and scrapers. An atomizer may be useful for spraying the pots when they get too dry. Symmetrical and asymmetrical shapes can be coiled as well as figures, heads or animals, but avoid sudden changes in form or profile and reduce overhang to a minimum.

Points to remember
- Coils may be slightly thinner as the height of the pot increases, but they should be well luted to avoid cracking or springing when fired.
- They must be soft for easy joining.
- When complete allow them to dry slowly at an even temperature.

1. Flatten a ball of clay from which to cut a base. Make the base the same thickness as the coils.

2. A circular base is cut for the pot. Make sure it is wide enough in proportion to the form. Many beginners make bases for elegance, so that they are too small to support the pot.

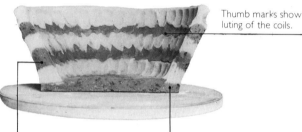

Thumb marks show luting of the coils.

Cross section showing how each coil is luted to the previous one. The surface can be smoothed later on.

The first coil, luted to the base, is the largest for maximum support.

5. The hands move outwards as the clay extends and stretches. Rolling could be described as a squeezing technique.

6. The first coil is positioned on the edge of the base. If the clay is moist enough, no water is needed when joining coil to coil.

A wad box (left) is a piece of machinery for extruding coils of clay. The soft clay is slowly forced through a template at the base of the box to give a continuous length of clay of a predetermined size. The size and shape of the coils can be varied by changing the plate. Templates need to be strong enough to take the pressure of the clay, but can be made from metal, plastic or wood.

9. The pot is turned slowly on the banding wheel to check the required outward curve.

10. A coil is cut off and joined. This should be in a different place each time. The luting marks can be seen on the outside of the pot.

edges, they should be thinned at the earliest stage of making and before the clay begins to dry too much. While pinched pots can be made from any type of clay, each one has its particular characteristics and these must be understood.

Coiling

A pot of any size can be built using the coiling or hand-building technique. It is best to begin with a large shape, even if it is never fired or is too big to go into the kiln. In the process of making you will begin to develop a sense of scale and learn to control the clay at a speed which allows you time to think and adjust. You will also learn the mechanics of handling clay, how to control dampness and you will have the satisfaction of making a pot of large dimensions.

In all work with clay you must first make sure that the clay has been thoroughly mixed and wedged, so that it will expand evenly whether you are rolling or squeezing it. The clay should not be too plastic or close in texture, but should have about 20-30 per cent of medium grog or sand added to it to make it more refractory and able to withstand the weight and handling involved in making a large coiled pot.

The choice of red or white clay for your pot may determine your treatment of the surface when the pot is complete. The surface may be textured or smooth. If smooth it may be more satisfactory in some cases, and with certain colors, to use a white clay for decoration with slip, coloring pigments or glazle. Once the clay has been prepared, cover or wrap it in plastic to prevent uneven

3. A largish lump of clay is shaped into a thick sausage, ready for rolling by hand.

4. The coil is rolled on a smooth, absorbent surface. The hands should be at a slight angle to the coil, moving outwards as you roll. Roll lightly and gently with a continuous movement.

7. The first coil is luted to the base with the forefinger. Any luting pressure is resisted by the fingers, so that the pot does not lose its shape.

8. The outside of the coil is luted to the one underneath, while the inside is supported with the fingers of the other hand.

11. The growing shape should be supported firmly as the coils are luted together. Luting marks can be left for texture, or smoothed when the pot is a little firmer.

12. This picture shows the positon of the hands for luting the inside of the pot, and supporting the outside.

13. The coils are smoothed when firm and then scraped when the pot is leather-hard. It may be left in this state, or decorated with pigment or slips. It can be biscuited and glazed and the pigments applied to the glazed surface before firing. Any excessive lean of the pot can be corrected at the leather-hard stage by lifting it and gently, but firmly, striking the base onto the bench at the correct point. The last coil for the top of the pot is a very important part of the overall character of the pot and can make or mar the form. The thickness, the angle and the shape of it are all determining factors.

drying and only uncover it to remove handfuls of clay for rolling into coils as needed. First roll a large sausage shape between your hands and then place it on the bench and begin rolling from the center outwards. It is essential to work with a gentle continuous outward movement when rolling or the clay will become oval in section, rather than round, and will be difficult to build. Several coils can be made at a time and lightly covered with a damp cloth or piece of plastic until needed. The thickness of the coils will be determined by the size of pot you want to make. For the base, cut a flat circular piece of clay from the rolled slab and place it on a wooden bat or a banding wheel.

The first coil should be the largest, to act as a foundation for the rest, linking the base and the developing walls of the pot. If the shape is to grow outwards, each succeeding coil should have a slightly larger circumference than the previous one and conversely, when you want the pot to begin to curve inwards the coils should be smaller. Large pots can only be made in stages. Allow the lower section to become firm in order to stand the overall weight of the clay, but at the same time keep the top edge damp with a moist cloth. This ensures that the edge is ready for building on when drying has progressed sufficiently.

It is very important that each coil, when wound round, should be well luted to the one below. This is done by supporting the outer edge with the palm of the hand and pressing down firmly and rhythmically with the thumb of the other hand to join the inside coils. For smoothing the

ROLLING CLAY

For many hand-building ceramic techniques, it is necessary to first roll the wedged or kneaded clay on a firm bench or table. Begin by flattening the clay into approximate dimensions for the final shape. Clay is best rolled on a piece of thick, absorbent medium weave canvas or similar material. The clay and the cloth can be carried together when rolled, and the clay placed over a hump mold. This can be done by laying it across your arm and hand and lowering it over, or into the mold.

Points to remember
● At every stage of rolling keep the clay free and lift it regularly from the work surface.
● The rolling pin should be smooth and even, but of medium to hard wood with sufficient absorbency.

1. A lump of clay is flattened by hand, in preparation for rolling. Note how the clay is lifted at one end to allow quick and easy expansion.

2. The slab is roughly thinned out by patting the surface to flatten it.

3. Using a rolling pin, roll the clay from the centre so that it moves out easily and the undersurface does not stick to the canvas. The clay should be released after each rolling. If it is too wet it will tear when lifted.

4. Wooden slats or battens are used to determine the required thickness of the clay. If the clay is too stiff it will crack at the edges and be difficult to roll.

5. It is extremely important to keep the clay lifted and free of the canvas throughout the rolling process. A rolled clay slab can be used for dishes, slab pots, free shaping or for a combination of coiling and slabbing.

outside of the pot, support the inside wall with your fingers and blend the outside of the coils with your thumb.

When several coils have been added any adjustments can then be made to the shape or surface. The pot can be revolved slowly on the turntable, passing it between the thumb and forefinger of both hands. This will control both the profile and evenness of the clay. The clay form can be open, such as a bowl or dish, or enclosed as for vases or containers. Treatment of the surface, and applied decoration, is fully described in Chapter 5, Techniques of decoration, on page 108.

Weaving

The clay should be smooth, plastic and moist for weaving and, if possible, have a low shrinkage from plastic to dry state. A quantity of coils should be thinly rolled and kept covered with a damp cloth or thin plastic sheet until ready for use. Techniques of making, shaping and handling the clay can only be learnt through individual research and development of the skill. Clays may vary in color and, once made, the articles need to dry as slowly as possible.

Slab building

Making slabs for building is similar to preparing pastry for baking. The clay needs to be, as before, thoroughly even in texture — not too wet and not too hard. You must first flatten the wedged lump of clay with the palm of your hand or fist into a thick, even slab. It is now ready for rolling on a heavy piece of cloth or canvas. Rolling should be done in

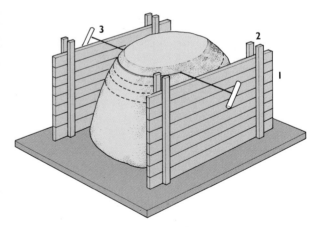

Cutting slab When you require a quantity of slabs for building, or for identical dish molds, it is easier and quicker to slice them from one lump of clay. Place the piece of wedged clay between two columns of wooden slats (**1**) which are held loosely between vertical dowelling (**2**). Cut across the lump of clay horizontally with a cutting wire (**3**) until you have used it up. If desired the slices can be lightly rolled or smoothed after cutting, but make sure they are leather hard before you start using them.

SLAB BUILDING

The equipment you will need for slab building includes a rolling cloth, a rolling pin, wooden battens, a steel rule for measuring and an edge for cutting clay. You should also have a suitable knife, wooden modelling tool and any necessary card or hardboard templates. There are two types of slab: firm and semi-dry slabs for forms with flat surfaces, and rolled plastic slabs used in free-form building dishes in press molds, pots and sculptural forms.

1. The outline of the template is lightly scribed on a soft rolled slab (the measurement includes shrinkage). The slab is left to firm before cutting.

2. The slab for the wall of the container is cut out with a straight-edged rule and a thin bladed knife.

3. The edge to be joined, and the matching surface of the horizontal slab on the bench, are wetted with a sponge.

4. The two moist surfaces are then rubbed together to create a film of slip which will act as a bonding agent to adhere the two surfaces together. The best method of aligning the edges is to slide one along the other until they are in the correct position.

5. A thin coil is applied between the walls to strengthen the join.

6. The horizontal and vertical edges of the third side are wetted to make a film of slip for joining the other walls of the pot.

7. The wet edges are now worked together to create a bonding slip. One hand rubs the walls together while the other supports the outside wall.

8. One of the end slabs is fixed firmly in position.

9. The inside corners and joins are reinforced with coils of soft clay, luted to the surfaces.

10. The last wall of the container is attached.

11. A boxwood spatula is used to seal and smooth the outside area of the joins.

12. A spacer template is marked and cut from a slab the same thickness as the construction slabs. Other spacer strips are placed in the bottom.

13. The spacer template is placed in position to keep the sides of the container apart during drying and firing.

Points to remember
● When constructing the container, the slabs should be firm and slightly flexible — not stiff — and all should have the same degree of dampness.
● Allow the slabs to dry in a cool atmosphere away from draughts, or cover lightly with thin plastic sheeting.
● Sometimes, slabs can be cut immediately after rolling, but in this case they must be left flat on the bench to dry and stiffen before they can be moved.
● Most forms of decoration can be added to slab forms.

alternate directions, starting from the center, and the clay lifted regularly from the canvas so that it moves out easily and quickly as you roll it. The slabs, when ready, are placed on a flat board. Cardboard templates can be cut for each section of the pot and lightly outlined in turn on the surface of a rolled slab of clay. The clay can then be left to dry until leather-hard when the shape can be cut out and left ready for building. Try to have all sections of the pot of equal dampness, but if some appear too hard, cover or wrap in a damp cloth until they become softer. Alternatively, spray a little water from an atomizer to moisten the clay.

The best joins are made when only a thin film of slip is used. This is done by dipping a finger in water, wetting the two surfaces and then working them together until a thin film of slip (combination of clay and water) is formed. This will provide adequate slip for adhering the two surfaces. When the surfaces are almost ready for joining, wet them slightly again so that they do not suddenly bond together before you have lined the slabs up in the desired position for final fixing. Once the shape has been formed, very thin coils of clay should be added to the inside corners and joins and smoothed together to strengthen the pot. The outside joins should be smoothed over with a flat boxwood spatula and any unevenness filled in.

Shapes can be supported internally as they dry to prevent distortion. This is done using pieces cut off the original slabs. These will then dry out at the same rate as the pot and thereby prevent distortion. A template is used to control the top of the pot during shrinkage. When the slab pots are leather- or cheese-hard they can be placed on a thin layer of sand on a kiln shelf until drying is complete. Pot and kiln shelf can then be lifted together into the kiln for firing and this will prevent damage or cracking from further handling.

SLABBING AND WEAVING

This technique combines slab building with intricately woven coils of clay. Firstly a slab is prepared, as for a slabbed pot, using the same equipment and tools. The coils to be woven should be thinner than used in coil pottery and frequently dampened with a fine plant sprayer or atomizer to keep them moist for handling. If different colored coils are required the clay should be stained at the powder stage, made into slip, sieved and dried out and, after it becomes plastic, wedged ready for coiling.

Points to remember
- Keeping the whole construction damp enough is the main problem with this technique.

1. Very thin coils are rolled from the center outwards, keeping the hands at an angle to the coil. A fluid but gentle rolling movement is necessary to prevent the coils from breaking.

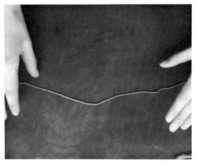

2. Repeat this operation until the coil is of the desired thinness. When making the coils, roll them carefully, so that they are true rounds and not ovals, as the latter are difficult to work.

3. The first layer of coils is laid across the soft, rolled slab at an angle, and the second layer is laid straight across these. Each layer of coils can be multi-colored or the same color, according to choice.

4. The end of each coil should overlap the edge of the slab at one end and can either reach to the top of the slab or just short of it at the other end.

5. When all the layers have been placed onto the slab, the surface is covered with a cloth and the coils are gently rolled into the surface of the slab. The slab is cut into a rhomboid so that when the pot is shaped and joined it becomes cylindrical.

6. The surplus clay is cut from the end of each side, prior to forming the pot.

7. A scalpel is used to cut around a template to form the base of the vase. The clay should be rolled to the same thickness as the main body of the vase.

8. The slab is now turned face down on the bench and the edges are scored or textured with a sharp tool. The base of the vase is also scored around the edges for joining to the cylinder.

9. Liquid slip is brushed onto the scored surfaces to be joined together, to assist adhesion.

10. The base of the vase is placed on the banding wheel and the edge is prepared with a coat of slip, ready for joining to the body of the pot.

11. The slab is wound around the base, prior to joining the edges, to form the walls of the vase.

12. The two edges are brought together to make the cylindrical body of the vase.

13. The edges are pressed firmly together and adhered to each other with the previously applied slip.

14. A boxwood modelling spatula is used to smooth and compress the join. The pot should be allowed to dry slowly to prevent cracking or springing of the join during firing.

A WOVEN BOWL

When weaving clay, it is essential that it should be smooth, plastic and moist. In addition, ensure, if possible, that the clay you use has the lowest possible degree of shrinkage as it dries from its plastic state. When rolling out the clay to form the coils, try to roll it with a gentle, continuous outward motion, as otherwise the sections you make will be oval, not round and difficult to work with as a result.

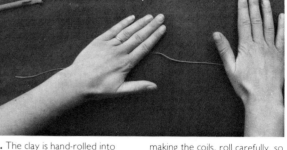

1. The clay is hand-rolled into long, thin coils. For the base of the dish, these coils are cut into pieces long enough to overlap the base of the mold by about ½in (1cm) on either side. When making the coils, roll carefully, so that they are true rounds and not ovals, as the latter are difficult to work. Keep the coils covered with a damp cloth until required for use.

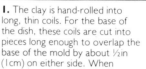

2. The coils are placed over the base of the mold, equidistantly spaced.

3. Starting from the center, the coils are interwoven. They can be sprayed with a little water to keep them moist as they will dry out very rapidly.

4. Continue to weave the coils until the base of the mold is covered. The strips can be woven closely together or loosely.

5. The woven base is sprayed with a little water from an atomizer to keep it moist prior to rolling.

6. The weaving is covered with a damp cloth and rolled gently with a rolling pin.

7. The coils are now flattened so that the pattern is compressed and consolidated.

8. The excess clay is trimmed from the base shape with a trimming tool to leave a circular piece for the base of the pot.

9. Two twisted coils of clay (colored with body stain) are prepared. One should be thin to encircle the base and the other should be thicker, for the rim.

10. The thin twisted coil is placed around the base and the two ends are joined. Any extra length can be cut away.

11. The larger twisted coil is put around the rim of the dish mold.

12. A half-inch gap is left between the coil and the edge of the mold and the ends of the coil are joined together.

13. Start laying coils for the sides of the bowl equidistant around the mold. Leave 4 in (10 cm) of coil spare at the top and bottom of the shape.

Points to remember
● The rim can easily split if it gets too dry, so try to keep it moist.
● Some shapes do not lend themselves to weaving. Try to stick to curved shapes.
● Keep the clay malleable at all times.
● When you begin to make weaveware do not be surprised if the failure rate is as high as 50%. As you learn the technique this will decrease.

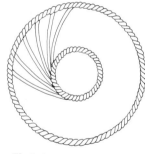

14. The weave is gradually built up to create the intricate criss-cross pattern shown here.

Weaving the coils (right)
Start weaving the coils, gradually working your way around the mold until it is complete. You should weave a third of the area at a time and work fairly fast as the clay will dry quickly, making it difficult to manipulate. You can either weave from top to bottom or from bottom to top.

First stage

Second stage

Third stage

WICKER WEAVING

Wicker weaving involves using the clay in the same way as a wickerworker would use wicker, working upwards from a round clay base. The clay is shaped in the same way as for the woven bowl, though the actual weaving technque is simpler in this instance.

1. Cut out the clay base and drill holes in it at regular intervals. Insert the clay uprights.

2. Having completed the basic framework, the actual weaving can start. Spray with water to keep the clay moist.

3. Weave from the base upwards, running the clay alternately behind and in front of the uprights.

HAND-MADE CERAMICS

Hand skills in ceramics have become increasingly diverse, particularly with the advent of a pottery generation weaned on hand-building techniques at school. Unlike most production pottery, hand-built ceramics lend themselves more to the variety reflected in individual gallery pieces.

Hand-built stoneware clock
Ann Clark, UK
Height: 10½ in (26 cm)

Off-white stoneware clay was used to construct this slab-built and hand-modelled clock. Pigment was added to the clay before firing with a transparent glaze to 1280°C (2340°F). The clock is decorated with biblical inscriptions, alluding to 'time' and 'peace', an olive branch and doves.

Hand-modelled Raku cats
Agalis Manessi, UK
Height: 3-4 in (8-10 cm)

These Raku fired cats are made from 'T' material, an excellent clay containing a percentage of molochite grog. It is also suitable for making mural panels and hand-building, and can be fired at both earthenware and stoneware temperatures. The cats are decorated with colored slips and oxides and then glazed with a clear bisilicate glaze.

Slab-built form
Jacqueline Poncelet
9 in x 14½ in x 12½ in
(24cm x 37 cm x 33 cm)

One of a series of slab-built and shaped forms, based on the theme of architectural structures. The thin lines are inlaid and the squares are sprayed on with underglaze color. This form is made with a stoneware body, and it is given a high bisque firing to 1180°C (2150°F), and a low glaze firing to about 1060°C (1940°F).

Burnished pot
Magdalene Odunda, UK
Height: 10 in (25 cm)

Hand-built from a Suffolk red clay, this pot has a coiled asymmetric form and features delicate relief linear modeling. Before burnishing, the leather-hard pot was dipped into red slip. Odunda fires her pots between 900-1060°C (1650-1940°F). Some are left red and unglazed while others are carbonized — a process where a red hot pot direct from the kiln is buried in sawdust or other combustible material and covered to prevent ignition. The carbon from the smoldering sawdust then permeates the pot — to a rich black.

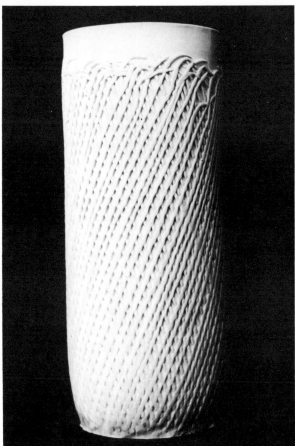

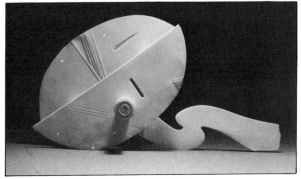

Slab vase
Wendy Patterson, UK
Height: 11 in (28 cm)

This slabbed vase is made by laying areas of thin colored coils at opposing angles on a rhomboid slab of clay. The coils are then rolled or pressed into the clay and the slab formed into a cylinder and fixed to a circular clay base. (For technique of making, see page 40).

'Germinating seed' (above)
Porcelain free-standing sculpture
Eileen Nisbet, UK
Height: 12 in (30 cm)

Extremely thin translucent porcelain made in sections and joined after firing. The recipe used is David Leach porcelain (page 19) and the body is given an oxidized firing to 1240 -1250°C (2260 - 2280°F). The surfaces are inlaid, pierced and painted with colored slips. The concept is metamorphic, symbolizing growth from seed to bud, or to flowering, as suggested by the colors.

Throwing and turning

THE TECHNIQUE OF THROWING CLAY has always fascinated man. It is a term used to describe how the rotating wheel 'throws' the clay outwards and the potter uses his hands to control and mold it against this force. To the observer it looks easy and effortless, but learning the process requires great patience and determination. For this reason it is important to understand the principles and mechanics involved in the technique. Personal instruction is always advisable, otherwise bad habits are acquired at an early stage and these prove difficult to correct. Once the technique of throwing has been mastered, the potter will be able to create a whole range of shapes with speed and ease.

In this, more than any other form of making, an even consistency of clay is essential. All clay should be wedged immediately before being thrown as even a slight drying of the outer surface of a ball can make centring difficult. Prepared clay should not be placed on a dry bat or board as they will absorb the essential moisture from the clay in contact. The clay should be placed on a plastic sheet and, if you are preparing several pieces at once, covered lightly with a moist cloth.

Start with a dry wheelhead and place the ball of clay firmly in the middle of it, ready for centring. In order to be able to control the clay for shaping it must be revolving evenly and smoothly in the center of the wheel. By applying gentle, but firm pressure to the clay you can 'center' it against the force of it being thrown outwards as the wheel turns.

While you are centring the clay, the wheel needs to revolve at speed, but as the clay is 'opened up' and the walls of the pot become thinner, the speed is proportionally reduced until in the final stages of shaping, it is turning very slowly.

Both hands are involved in shaping and manipulating the clay and this is essentially a squeezing process with the clay being allowed to expand evenly. Steady, firm pressure should therefore be applied to the sides and top of the clay with the flat palms of the hands, or the fingers. If points of pressure are applied, rather than flat areas, the clay quickly becomes ribbed or grooved and the points will meet, severing the pot in two. You will then have to start again.

Depending on their shape and size, pots can usually be thrown on the wheelhead and cut off it with a wire. A little water splashed on to the wheelhead and drawn underneath the pot for lubrication, will make it easier to slide the pot off as you cut. From the wheel it is transferred to the palm of your hand, held level with the wheelhead, and then put onto a bat or board and left to dry to a leather-hard state before being turned.

Turning

When a pot is at the leather-hard stage, it is turned on the wheel so that layers of uneven clay can be trimmed off with turning or trimming tools. Any turning to reduce the thickness of the walls or to form a footring (a raised base for the article to stand on) can be done by the various methods illustrated.

Bowls can be held in position for turning by placing them on a thin, firm layer of clay, previously thrown and then turned on the wheelhead. Other shapes, particularly narrow-necked forms and enclosed shapes, can be turned in a clay chuck — a thick, open-thrown shape of clay with a wide base which can be secured to the wheelhead with a thin coil of clay. The shape of the chuck will depend on the forms to be turned, but they are usually variations on a cylinder. If it is kept well wrapped in plastic and stored in a cool, damp place, a chuck can be kept for months.

Another technique of turning, used for tall pots, is to wet the base of the pot and center it on the wheelhead. It will soon stick firmly and, when turned, it can be removed with a swift firm movement. Knobs for lids can be turned from the surplus clay, left for this purpose when throwing.

Tools for throwing and turning Natural sponge (1) for mopping up surplus water and sometimes for applying pressure to the clay when shaping the inside of large bowl. Metal turning tool (2) for turning off leather-hard clay. This tool is also used for trimming surplus clay from the lower walls of a pot which is being thrown. Single strand or twisted wire (3) for cutting clay when wedging, or when cutting pots from the wheelhead. Flexible steel kidney (4) for scraping or smoothing the surface of the clay when turning. A rubber kidney is used for perfecting the inside shape of a bowl during throwing. Calipers (5) for measuring widths of apertures and dimensions of lids and other fitting forms. Large heavy needle (6) in wood or cork for cutting the top sections of a pot when throwing. It is also used for testing the thickness of the clay and for puncturing air bubbles.

Cleaning the wheel The tips of the fingers are locked together firmly and used as a scraper to clean surplus clay from the wheelhead after throwing a pot. The wheel should be revolving at speed while this is done.

Parts of the hands used in throwing In throwing, pressure is applied to the spinning clay with the hands in order to control and shape it against the outward thrust of the revolving wheel. Different parts of the hands are important at different stages of the process.

Fleshy pad is used for applying downward pressure during centring of the clay, and for flattening the clay to form the flat inside of a plate.

Fingertips are used for secondary thinning and then shaping with gentle, but firm pressure.

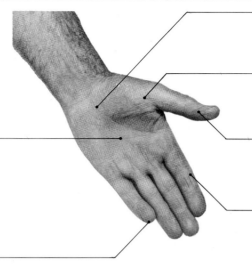

Base of the palm is used when direct pressure is applied to a lump of clay which is being centred.

Thumb joint is used for crooking over the top edge of a revolving thick circular form to keep the top even.

Thumbs are used for opening up, and later for keeping the tops of shapes level. The end of the thumb is used to shape a casserole gallery.

Knuckles are used when the fist is clenched to flatten large lumps of clay. Also for flattening the inside of large dishes, as in the picture (*bottom left*).

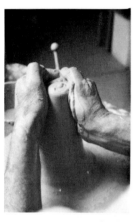

Hand positions The pressure applied by the hands in shaping and modelling the clay is essential to the control of the form. The positions shown here indicate the different purposes to which the hands are put in pottery making. The clay is coned with the palms of both hands, and the fingers overlapping (*above left*). The whole of the clay surface is controlled with pressure from both hands (*above centre*). A cylinder is collared at the top, ready for further knuckling or thinning (*above right*). The knuckle and edge of the first finger are used to level the inside base of a dish (*left*). Note the position of thumb and fingers for squeezing and shaping a bowl (*right*).

CENTERING AND OPENING UP

The clay must be evenly mixed before centring is commenced. Centring needs to be done quickly and firmly. It is a skill which requires good personal tuition to develop a sound technique. Once you have opened up the form, begin to thin the clay against the outward thrust of the revolving wheel.

Points to remember

● If the clay is too soft it will not expand and hold its shape, and if too stiff the pressure needed to thin the walls will strain the pot and it will become twisted.

● Success lies in judging the exact degree of pressure needed on both the inside and outside of the pot.

● If the clay is worked for too long it becomes tired and will not expand easily.

1. The wedged clay is placed firmly in the center of the wheelhead, ready for centring. There will be less strain on the wheel bearings if the wheel is not revolving when the clay is placed onto the wheelhead.

2. Steady pressure is applied with the palm of the left hand and the fleshy pad of the right hand. The hands are interlocked to give a steady firmness for controlling the clay.

3. When centring, the top is always slightly domed so that coning is easier from the sides, with the palms of both hands.

4. The clay is squeezed upwards to create a spiral movement within the clay particles. This will give added strength to the finished pot.

5. The cone is depressed, but with the correct amount of pressure so that the contours of the pot remain curved. Remember that downward pressure is slightly greater than inward pressure at this stage.

6. If the arm and wrist are kept straight you will fully utilize your energy to provide enough pressure against the clay as it is thrust outwards by the revolving wheel.

7. The top of the lump of the clay is hollowed out so that the thumb can be inserted for opening the clay out. Note that the hands work together whenever possible to give greater stability.

8. The thumb is held firm in the center and the fingers run along the outside of the clay to guide it. The pressure of the thumb on the clay is slowly increased until the required depth is reached. It is then opened out.

9. The pot is further opened by inserting a thumb.

10. The right hand is supported by the left as the thumb is pushed outwards from the center of the clay to form the inside base of the pot.

11. Gripping the lip of the pot between the fingers and thumb of one hand, with the outside fingers supported by the free hand, further widen and deepen the inside.

THROWING A TALL VASE

For this shape you must start with a tall, narrow cylinder before shaping and completing the final thinning of the clay. The skill in making the cylinder is to leave the clay thicker where it will have to stretch farthest when being shaped (alternatively the thickness can be distributed where necessary in the final thinning and shaping). As the pot gets tall and thinner, the wheel should be revolving slower and slower until it is only just turning in the final stage of shaping.

Points to remember
● Any excess thickness on the outside of the base can be trimmed carefully with a pointed turning tool or with the edge and corner of a metal or wooden rib.

1. When the clay has been opened up it is lifted up to form the walls of the pot, using inward and upward pressure from the left palm, and lifting and squeezing pressure from the right thumb and fingers. The hands are firmly locked together for support.

2. The neck of the pot is collared by the left and right hand while the crook of the right thumb applies downward pressure to keep the top level.

3. The hands guide the pot lightly for the final phase of lifting. The clay tends to expand outwards as it thins so that collaring will be necessary to control it after each thinning movement.

4. The cylinder is narrowed before it is made into a taller cylindrical form. The top of the pot should be kept level. The pot may expand when the hand is inserted so always collar in after each knuckling.

5. The pot is collared using the thumb and palms of both hands for complete control.

▷

6. The process where the clay is lifted and thinned into a cylinder needs to be done twice so that the clay is thinned sufficiently to commence shaping the pot.

7. The vase is thinned as it begins to take shape. Pressure is applied with the flat edge of the right hand's first finger while the fingertips of the left resist this pressure, lifting the clay upwards from the bottom of the vase.

8. This cross-section shows the position of the hands and the lifting action of the inner finger-tips. The surplus clay visible at the base of the vase is turned off when shaping is complete.

9. This cross-section illustrates the positional change-over of the hands, from outward to inward shaping.

10. The belly of the base is shaped as the fingers of both hands draw opposite each other on either side of the curve. By moving the inside fingers up the vase its inwards. The pressure applied to the outside is greater.

11. The outward flare at the top of the vase is shaped with the inside flat of the finger tips. Gentle thinning, as well as shaping, can continue up to this point.

12. The top of the vase is collared to increase the narrowness of the neck before further shaping with the fingertips.

13. The tips of the fingers are used to shape the neck of the vase with firm, but gentle pressure.

14. As the wheel revolves slowly, the final shaping and thinning of the top of the vase is done, using the tips of the fingers.

15. The base of the vase is turned and trimmed with a pointed, V-shaped tool. Once the wet slip has been turned away, the pot can be cut off the wheelhead.

16. The vase is cut from the wheelhead with a plain or twisted piece of cutting wire.

18. When a vase is made in this way very little turning is necessary, unless the footring is to be turned. If the pot should lose its shape a little when lifted, a gentle squeeze while it is on the bat will restore it to the correct shape.

17. The pot is lifted from the wheel with dry hands before placing it on a board or bat to dry.

STRAIGHT-SIDED VASE

Start with a reasonably wide base as this can be narrowed later with firm squeezing if desired. The vase is made thin by knuckling and lifting which slope its walls inward. A single steady and fairly slow shaping movement is used to make the walls of the vase vertical. Finally the finished vase is trimmed at the base and lifted off with dry hands.

THROWING A BOWL

First center the clay and insert a thumb inside the shape to determine the inside curve of the bowl. The thumb and fingers are used to squeeze the clay firmly into the required basic form of the bowl. Wide open bowls should be thrown slowly in order to control the movement of the clay.

1. The initial shaping of the bowl is done with the thumb and fingers while the left hand controls and supports the form.

2. The clay is squeezed and thinned to make a basic bowl shape.

3. This cross-section shows the position of the thumb inside the shape. Note also the thickness of the base, thinning out as the walls extend and then getting thicker again at the top.

4. The first squeezing and thinning action is completed, but the left hand still controls and supports the outside of the bowl.

5. Both hands are used to thin and extend the shape. The fingers of the right hand are both shaping and resisting the pressure from the fingers inside the bowl.

6. The top edge is thinned and shaped, using the fingertips.

7. The top edge is held firm with the fingers of the left hand, while the forefinger of the right hand shapes and finishes the edge of the bowl.

8. The flat of the thumb is used to give sharper definition to the inside curve of the bowl.

9. A sponge is used to give final thinning and shape to the form, while the right hand supports the outside of the bowl.

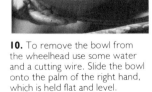

10. To remove the bowl from the wheelhead use some water and a cutting wire. Slide the bowl onto the palm of the right hand, which is held flat and level.

11. Once removed from the wheelhead, the bowl is lowered onto a dry bat.

12. Place a firm piece of tissue paper across the moist rim of the bowl to hold it steady until it is firm enough to remove from the wheelhead. When the bowl is firm reverse it into a flat surface and allow the base to dry to a leather-hard state before turning.

STACK THROWING

This technique of production is useful for throwing a number of small items such as cups, bowls or articles which are so small that they are difficult to center The size of the pot is limited to any shape which can be lifted off the stack without distortion.

Points to remember
● The technique requires skill to cut the clay off while it is still in motion with a thin blade or a large, strong needle.
● The clay must be firm.

1. The clay is centred into a tall cone and from this a large knob is formed to make the first bowl.

2. The basic shape is squeezed from the lump, while the left hand is used to contain and control the expanding clay (most of the work is done by the thumb and forefinger).

3. A side view of the bowl being shaped from the top section of the clay cone.

4. The left and right hand work together to complete the thinning and shaping of the bowl.

5. The bowl is extended and enlarged with pressure and firm support from the pads of the fingertips. Note the position of the hands.

6. The clay is cut at a slight upward angle with a pin. The left hand should be held ready to lift the clay as soon as the bowl is severed from the cone.

7. The bowl is cut and lifted from the wheel using both hands. It is then placed on a dry bat ready for turning.

MAKING AN OVAL DISH

To make an oval dish, you can use a shallow round dish which has been thrown on a plaster bat, and placed on a dry surface. When it has dried out a little and is soft, but no longer shiny, cut a leaf shape from the base and close up the gap by pressing the sides of the dish together.

1. The leaf shape is cut with a thin blade at a slightly outward, inclined angle.

2. The cut piece is lifted out of the dish with a knife. The 'ovalness' of the dish will be determined by the size of the piece cut from it.

3. The base is gently eased together by applying pressure to the sides of the dish. The two edges should be sufficiently soft to adhere together.

4. The two surfaces are joined in the middle as a result of the pressure applied to the sides of the dish by both hands.

5. A V-shaped wooden tool is used to compress the join in the center of the dish.

6. A coil of clay is placed into the compression in order to join the base firmly so that the dish withstands any strains during firing.

7. The inside surface is scraped and smoothed and then left to dry.

The use of a bat greatly facilitates throwing forms which are difficult to lift off the wheel. If plaster or another very absorbent material is used it also helps to dry the base of articles ready for turning. Circular bisque tiles also make excellent bats for throwing on. A centred, then flattened, ball of clay is grooved with the finger tips to make suction areas when the bat is pressed onto the clay (left). Wet the back of a dry plaster bat before placing it onto the grooved clay (right). If the bat is too dry it tends to lift away.

THROWING A PLATE

Plates need to be thrown on a bat because it is difficult to remove them from the wheelhead without distorting them.

Points to remember
● If the base of the article is too thin it may crack in the drying.
● Always leave sufficient thickness for firing the footring.

1. The clay is centred on the plaster bat.

2. Pressure is applied to the clay with the palm of the hand in order to spread the clay out as the wheel revolves.

3. The clay is flattened with pressure from both hands.

4. The inside dimension of the plate is flattened with the edge of the hand and a steadying grip from the right hand.

5. The final levelling of the plate is done with the edge of the thumb, leaving enough clay at the edge for forming the rim of the plate.

6. The rim is thrown and shaped from the surplus clay around the edge of the plate.

7. The edge of the plate is defined and then rounded. Do not make it too thin or too sharp as it has a tendency to chip with heavy ware.

8. After gauging the plate's thickness with a needle, lever the bat from the wheelhead with a metal tool or the end of a mild steel turning tool. The plate should shrink off the bat. If this fails the plate can be helped off by inserting a long thin-bladed knife between it and the bat.

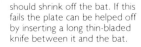

THROWING A CASSEROLE

Large casseroles can be thrown on a bat and the outside turned before removing from the wheel.

Points to remember

● When throwing a casserole leave plenty of clay at the top for forming the gallery for the lid, and a sufficient flange.

● Always retain enough clay from the initial wedging for either throwing, pulling or forming the handles or lugs.

1. Start by opening up the large center lump of clay. Note that pressure is applied with both thumbs.

2. The flat base is opened up from the center and formed with firm pressure from both thumbs. The fingers hold the clay steady on the outer surface.

3. The inside base is levelled with the crooked edge of the first finger.

4. The full width of the inside base is defined, prior to throwing the main body of the pot.

5. The clay is pulled up and thinned to form the pot walls. Pressure is applied from the wrist section of the left palm, with the squeezing action of the right hand.

6. Both hands work closely together as they reach the top of the pot.

7. The top of the shape is collared and the thickness of the walls is evened out with pressing and squeezing actions. The right hand keeps the top level.

8. The walls are thinned, and shape is given to the casserole by knuckling the outside of the pot as it revolves.

9. The top of the form is shaped, making sure that enough clay is left to make the flange and gallery for the lid.

10. The flange and gallery of the casserole are defined using the thick clay from the top edge. The right hand supports the left as it smooths the surface of the flange.

11. The gallery is shaped and the index finger applies pressure to stop it from becoming too thin.

12. The final shaping of the casserole. A few small adjustments to the profile are made with the edge of the little finger. When turning the casserole it is wise to have an inner and an outer footring to support the wide level area of the base.

LIDS

Shown here are some of the basic shapes for lids, although each one is open to individual interpretation. In very few cases is it possible to complete the making of a lid on the wheel without some turning, and this is particularly necessary for casserole lids (2) and some versions of the ginger jar lid (1) which takes its name from the Chinese ginger jar. In some instances the knobs are thrown as part of the lid shape (2, 6) while for others (3, 4, 5) the knob is turned from surplus clay left for the purpose, or it is thrown on after turning. A flat lid can be made with a lid flange (3) or a very simple cover made which fits into the gallery (4). For easy stacking, particularly with wide containers, the knobs are made so that the top is not above the level of the top of the container (2, 6). These recess knobs would both be suitable for casseroles. The teapot lid (5) has deep flange on the lid to lock it so that it does not fall out when the teapot is fully tilted.

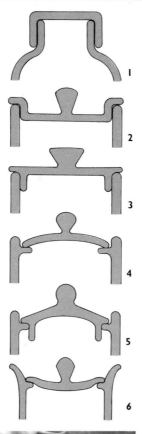

Using calipers 1. A pair of calipers is used to check outside diameter of the rim to ensure that the lid smugly fits the aperture of the pot.

2. The same technique is used to measure the inside diameter of the rim.

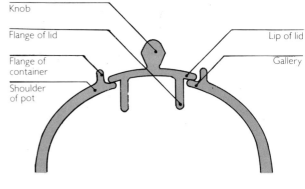

Knob

Flange of lid

Flange of container

Shoulder of pot

Lip of lid

Gallery

Teapot lid 1. From a cone of clay squeeze a large knob-like shape into the palm of the left hand and insert the right-hand thumb into the center of it.

2. The initial shaping is done with both hands working closely together. The form should be thick at the edges for making a flange.

3. The edge of the clay is supported and pressure is exerted with the first finger of the left hand to form the flat edge of the lid.

4. Check the dimensions of the lid with calipers to make sure it fits the aperture of the teapot. Ideally, bodies and lids should be made at the same time.

5. The angle and height of the flange is determined and carefully thinned.

6. The final shaping of the flange is done by gently holding and supporting the wall with the left hand, while the forefinger of the right smoothes the top rim.

7. Use the thumb and index finger of each hand to squeeze and narrow the lid to a point at which it can be severed from the cone. Leave enough clay for the knob.

8. The lid is lifted from the cone of clay. Sometimes a knob is thrown after the lid has been turned.

Throwing a knob 1. The area of the turned lid, to which the knob will be attached, is wet with a little water prior to throwing the knob.

2. The clay ball for the knob is fixed on top of the lid, ready for throwing.

3. The knob is centred and thrown, using the minimum of water, and shaping is done with the ends of the fingers.

4. The final shaping of the knob is done with the little finger, while the fingers of the other hand support it as it revolves on the wheel.

LUGS

Lugs, or handles and knobs, are made in many forms by several techniques. Their form generally depends on personal judgement of which type of lug most suits the character of the ware in question. Techniques include thrown and pulled lugs besides those shaped from a single piece of clay. Practical considerations also play a large part in deciding which type of lug to adopt. With pots designed for oven use, such as casseroles, lugs must facilitate easy gripping and lifting with oven gloves whilst being compact enough to preserve oven space. Lugs are applied when the pot is finished and at the leather hard stage and have to be dried slowly to prevent them being too soft and lifting away from the pot in drying.

The examples (right) show various types of lug. The lugs **(1)** and **(3)** were made from a piece of clay which was roughly pre-formed on the bench and then applied to and shaped on the pot with water. The lugs **(2)** and **(4)** were pulled, shaped and formed from the section of a pulled strip

A curved lug 1. A piece of clay is shaped to make a curved lug for the casserole.

2. The lug is wet with a little slip before it is fixed to the side of the casserole. This will make it adhere more firmly to the pot.

3. The top side of the lug is luted to the side of the casserole with the thumb, while the rest of the hand supports it underneath.

4. The underside of the lug is joined to the pot with one finger while the other hand supports it at the top.

5. The curve and angle of the lug are defined to give satisfactory grip for lifting the casserole.

Pulled lug 1. Moisten the surface of the pot with a sponge at the point where you are applying the lug.

2. One end of the pulled section of the lug is luted to the side of the pot.

3. The other end of the lug is fixed to the pot and luted to the side, using your thumb.

Horizontal lug 1. This can be made and attached to the sides of the pot. One finger is used to support one end while it is luted.

2. The ends of the lug are shaped and luted to the pot.

ROUND LUGS

Both of these articles can be thrown, and when firm, attached as a knob to a turned lid or applied to the side of a casserole or jar as a type of lug. Both pot and knob should be at the same state of dryness to prevent variable shrinking and the risk of cracking at the join.

1. The knob is shaped from the top section of a cone of clay, using mainly the thumb and forefinger of each hand.

2. The top of the knob is shaped with the little finger, while pressure is exerted on the sides with the fingers of the left hand.

3. The top of the knob is indented to both reduce the height and give variation to the shape.

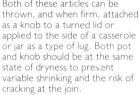

4. When finished the knob is cut from the cone, (while the clay is revolving) with a long needle held at an upward sloping angle.

5. When it has been severed the knob is lifted from the cone with a swift movement. It is placed on a dry surface until it is ready to apply to the lid.

HANDLES

Although handles may be made in several ways, basically they are either bent to the desired shape from a prepared strip of clay or pulled into shape from a lump of clay. Pulled handles are usually stronger and their individual shape gives them aesthetic appeal.

Points to remember
●Pulled handles are strongest when made from well-wedged clay with a regular consistency.
●Always prepare more clay than necessary when making pulled handles.

Pulling on the pot 1. A circular strip is pulled and then pinched into sections to be applied and pulled on the pot as a handle.

2. A section of the strip is pinched off with the thumb and forefinger, performing a scissor action.

3. The pinching or severing of the section for the handle, showing the flat end which will be attached to the jug.

4. The section of clay in the palm of the hand is held gently between the thumb and forefinger so that pressure can be applied for fixing to the body of the jug.

5. The short clay section is pressed onto the jug, while the fingers of the right hand take the pressure inside the neck.

6. Overhead view of the section being applied before shaping is commenced.

7. The jug is held horizontally while the handle is pulled. The strip must be very moist for pulling.

8. The handle is shaped and pulled between thumb and forefinger.

9. An oval cross-section of the handle before final grooving or shaping with the end of the thumb.

10. Support the shaped handle at the top before attaching the lower end to the belly of the jug.

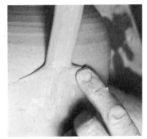

11. The base of the handle is fixed firmly to the pot with a few deft strokes.

Pulling separately 1. A circular strip is pulled from a thick oblong lump of clay.

2. It is shaped into an oval section by pulling it between thumb and forefinger.

3. This picture shows the position of the thumb and forefinger for pulling the handle.

4. The strip is cut off at the base, ready to shape into the curved handle. Leave the handle to harden before applying it to the jug.

Above: Handle made by attaching a round section of plastic clay to the jug and pulling the handle on it. This is a quick satisfactory method of application, but it requires skill and practice.

TURNING THE BASE OF ARTICLES

Many domestic stoneware pots are thrown and trimmed on the wheel while the clay is plastic. They are then cut off neatly with a twisted wire and left without a footring. This is to save labour and handling costs because sometimes turning a footring can take as long as throwing a pot. A footring is used to give greater definition to a shape (particularly a bowl), a more precise finish and to reduce to the minimum the area in contact with the table surface. It also means that glazed articles for firing can stand on their footring on the kiln shelf and so reduce the amount of glaze which will run onto it. Articles without footrings have to be balanced on a stilt during firing and this may leave unattractive marks on the base of the pot, which will have to be ground down after firing. If a footring is turned it should be in the correct position on the article so that it can take the weight of the pot. It is often the practice to make more than one footring for a large stoneware form, dish or plate. When throwing the footring, leave the base of the article as free of surplus clay as possible by turning off the excess clay with a rib or turning tool before removing it from the wheel. This will mean less work later on, and the base will dry more evenly before it is turned at the leather-hard stage.

Turning is a personal technique and every potter uses his own selection of tools (or makes his own). Turning can be done with the edge of a scraper, the edge of a steel six-inch rule, or with a bent and shaped metal strip from a packing case.

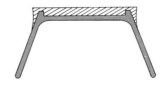

Straight-side deep dish incorporationg footring

Standard footring which sits on rounded profile

Bold internal footrings

Shallow dish with single footring

Flat wide plate with two footrings

Methods of attaching pots to the wheelhead for turning
The pot can be secured, upside down, with a thick coil of clay which is pressed around the rim of the pot (**1**). A pot with a narrow neck, or a weak lip, can be held firmly in place in a clay chuck (**2**). The chuck must be centred on the wheelhead first. Alternatively the pot can be attached to the wheelhead, right-side up (**3**), or placed onto a thin layer of stiff, turned clay which is damp enough to grip the top edge of the bowl firmly (**4**).

TURNING A FOOTRING

When throwing any shape, but particularly a bowl, the eye must be trained to remember the exact profile of the inside of the shape so that when turning the outside, and the footring, the outer profile will exactly match the inner. The pot should be of an even thickness throughout. It is also useful to check the thickness of the base and walls of a large pot with a thin pin before turning to gauge the amount to be turned.

I. The fingertips are held still while the pot is slowly revolved on the wheel, As the concentric revolutions touch the fingers, gently and swiftly tap the pot into position.

2. The surplus clay is trimmed from the base with a hoop-like turning tool, in preparation for shaping the foot. The tool is useful for cutting small curves.

3. A straight-sided turning tool is more commonly used for turning, prior to shaping the footring. This tool can also be used for trimming surplus clay and making the base of the pot flat.

4. A pointed turning tool is used for cutting away excess clay at an angle before making the footring.

5. The overall width of the foot is marked out after measuring the diameter, if a set of them is to be made.

6. The clay is turned to determine the height of the foot.

7. The sides are turned, above the foot of the bowl, to complement the inside curve of the form.

8. The base inside the rim of the foot is cut away. Note the position of the hands, supporting and steadying the tool.

9. The width of the footring is marked and the inner side is cut vertically so that it relates to the outer side of the foot.

10. Any excess clay is turned from the base to keep the sides and base of an even thickness throughout.

11. Now a flat base is cut. Start from the centre of the base and work gradually to the outer edge.

12. Any imperfections should now be removed but make sure 'chattering' does not occur. This is a series of small corrugations, caused by a blunt or badly sharpened tool, or clay which is not properly mixed or is too soft or too dry.

TURNING IN A CHUCK

A tall chuck is very useful for holding a large inverted bowl when turning the footring. This will prevent it from becoming dented or damaged. A selection of thick clay chucks can be thrown and left until leather-hard. If they are stored in a cool place, wrapped in plastic, they will keep for months or years. If they do begin to dry out, dowse them under a tap and rewrap them. To hold the chuck in position, center it and secure it with a coil of clay.

1. A vase is held in a clay chuck and the excess clay is turned from the base of the pot, working from the top downwards.

2. A hoop tool is used to turn the body of the pot. The chuck has been left to stiffen after throwing so that it is firm enough to support the pot.

3. A curved tool is used to turn out the base, after the sides have been turned. The base must be the correct thickness to support the walls of the pot.

TURNING RIGHT WAY UP

The pot for turning must not be too damp. Make sure that tools are sharp and, where possible, use an oval turning tool. A firm, sharp twist will detach the pot from the wheelhead when you have finished turning.

1. The pot for turning is fixed to the dampened wheelhead. A V-shaped tool is used to secure the edge of the pot to the wheelhead.

2. The surplus clay is turned from the lower wall of the pot. Do not turn right down to the wheelhead, but leave ½ in (1 cm) at the bottom to give stability.

3. When shaving off surplus clay move the tool slowly and be careful not to dig into the pot. Tilt the tool to follow the curve of the pot.

TURNING A KNOB

The clay for the knob should be leather-hard as it will distort under the pressure of turning if too soft. Damp the wheelhead first to assist adhesion and use very stiff clay for the domed profile. If there is space, attach the lower flange of the lid to the wheelhead with a thin coil of clay for added stability.

1. The clay is centred and trimmed to form a chum for holding the lid. When it has stiffened to firm, the thrown lid will be placed on it.

2. The diameter of the chum is checked with calipers to make sure it fits inside the lid snugly. If it is slightly too small, press the center firmly with the thumb.

3. Calipers are also used to measure the internal diameter of the flange of the lid.

4. The lid to be turned is placed firmly onto the chum, with the rim resting on the wheelhead. If there is sufficient space use a thin coil to hold the lid in place.

5. The surplus clay is turned to form the knob. The left hand lightly supports the right and stablizes the top of the lid.

6. The profile of the lid is shaped. It is turned when leather-hard, as a soft lid will distort too easily.

Points to remember
● The pot's shape is determined during throwing and turning is really a corrective procedure so that only a minimum amount of clay should need shaving.
● As the pot is leather-hard at this point the utmost care should be taken to avoid holing or damaging it.

THROWN CERAMICS

Throwing has always been a quick method of producing utilitarian pottery in quantity. Although technology has taken over many of the basic production techniques, throwing is still used for more functional ware. Individually made pots have a subtle quality unobtainable by reproduction. It is now possible to buy well-designed and made thrown articles which are cheaper than the industrial equivalent. This is because a small workshop or one-man studio does not have the extra overheads for advertising, marketing, and pension contribution which most factories need to stay in business.

Lidded wood-fired jar
Michael Casson, UK
Height: 26 in (66 cm)

This is an example of lively and vigorous throwing, expressed in the form and the direct manner in which the lugs have been applied. The jar is salt glazed.

Hand-thrown luster goblets
Alan Caiger-Smith, UK
Height: 5 in (13 cm)

These are hand-thrown in red earthenware and glazed with a low melting alkaline-based white glaze. The gloss firing is to 1060°C (1940°F). The individually prepared lusters are painted on and the decorated goblets are given a reduction firing to a temperature of 660°C (1220°F). The lusters are a mixture of ocher or kaolin mixed with compounds of silver or copper, used singly or together. Both the firings are with willow wood or poplar, which give long, gentle flames.

Hand-thrown Egyptian paste
Dick Studley, USA
Height: 14 in x 15 in
(36 cm x 43 cm)

These are record-sized pieces for thrown Egyptian paste, made by a potter who has thoroughly researched and developed the technique. The body contains various forms of soda which migrate to the surface during drying to leave a layer of flux which, when fired, gives a glaze on the surface. During firing this combines with the oxides in the body to give very rich colors. A large part of the throwing is done in sections with considerable trimming on the inside and the outside.

THROWN CERAMICS WITH ADDITIONS

Thrown ceramics, as the examples here demonstrate, can be treated in a variety of ways. Cut and joined pieces can be applied to a basic form, or the smooth surface can be incised and inlaid, or pierced, to give a different texture. Whatever the treatment, they all retain their functional quality.

Thrown and painted porcelain bowl
Nicholas Homoky, UK
5 in × 8 in (13 cm × 20 cm)

Nicholas Homoky's pieces are in the English tradition of humorous ceramic decoration. The wit is in using a familiar object, such as the symbolic teapot, to form the decoration of the tea bowl. The bowl is thrown and the teapot inlaid and painted with black slip, using a body stain. The illustration is superbly placed on the tea bowl to give the maximum effect to the design. The bowl is fired to 1260°C (2300°F) and, when cool, the pieces are polished with carborundum paper to remove the rough clay crystal formations. At this temperature the body has vitrified to glass.

Krater porcelain pot
Robin Hopper, Canada
Height: 9½ in (24 cm)

This simple, basic thrown shape has been given character by the addition of thrown and cut forms. The porcelain clay used for the body was chosen not for its translucent quality, but for its whiteness and ability to show through the glaze, giving a vibrancy of color. The pot was once-fired with a metallic luster glaze.

Thrown and fluted porcelain celadon bowl
David Leach, UK
Diameter: 8 in (20 cm)

Fluting can be done with either a metal or a wooden tool when the clay is at the leather-hard stage. For this bowl a broken-off hacksaw blade, ground to a chisel end, was used. The bowl was glazed with a Y'Ching celadon glaze and fired to a temperature of 1280°C (2340°F).

Recipe for glaze
Cornwall stone	25%
Kaolin	25%
Whiting	25%
Quartz	25%
(with 0.5% red iron oxide)	

Thrown and pierced earthenware
Tony Clark, UK
Width: 4 in (10 cm)

A pot pourri dish, thrown with fine white earthenware and pierced at the leather-hard state with a metal pastry cutter. After bisquing, a clear transparent glaze is applied and the dish is fired to 1140°C (2080°F).

Faceted stoneware jars
Bruce Martin, New Zealand
Height: 8 in (20 cm) and 6 in (15 cm)

There is a long tradition of faceted ware, both hand-built and thrown. These jars were slab-built, although the footring, gallery and knob were thrown. Both jars are glazed with a papa rock glaze and fired to a temperature of 1280 -1300°C (2340 - 2370°F).

Making and using molds

MAKING AND USING MOLDS Molding has been used as a pottery technique since earliest times. This section tells you first how to make up plaster — the most commonly used molding material — and then how to make the commonest forms of moldd.

Plaster

Plaster of paris is of great value to the potter because it is the basic material for mold-making in pottery. It is a specially prepared form of calcium sulphate, in powder form, which sets to form a hardened mass when it is mixed with a given quantity of clean water. When the plaster has completely dried out, it is very porous and can absorb moisture from clays or from liquid casting slip. There are several types of plaster and those used in pottery vary in porosity, speed of setting and hardness when set. Once the chemical reaction of setting has taken place, the process cannot be reversed; if the plaster is subsequently heated above a certain temperature it becomes soft and crumbly and is called 'dead' because it is no longer suitable for molding. In the process of setting all plasters expand slightly.

The following is a list of plasters used in ceramics. **Hebor alphor** is a fairly slow-setting plaster — finer and harder than potters plaster. It is used for models, sledging and making working molds.

Potters plaster has more texture than Hebor, but it does not wear so well and will deteriorate with use. It is slow setting and is mainly used for making working molds.

Kaffir 'P' is a hard plaster, used for making casings. In casting, it takes 12 to 15 minutes to blend before being poured. It will provide the maximum hardness with the minimum expansion.

Kaffir 'D' is a very fine dental plaster which needs a dense mix.

Crystacal is a fine, smooth plaster, employed in the making of plaster models and for giving strength to handles in model-making. It takes a long time to blend and sets extremely hard. When a percentage is added to a softer plaster, such as potters plaster, it gives added strength and is good for use in mold-making for jolleying techniques.

Superfine plaster is another fine quality plaster, used in model-making.

Mixing the plaster

Start by placing enough clean, cold water in a bowl or bucket. The amount should represent the volume of the

MIXING PLASTER

Always use more plaster than necessary when mixing up for molds. Excess plaster can be poured into a standby round bat mold and used as a base for throwing or for drying small amounts of clay. The plaster should aways be added to the water, distributed in large handfuls over the surface until the water is completely saturated. Leave the mixture to soak for 5 minutes before blending.

Points to remember
●Air must be kept out of the mixture during blending and any air bubbles in the plaster released by tapping the bowl firmly on the bench before pouring.
●Plaster sets fairly quickly, so it is better to pour too soon, rather than too late.

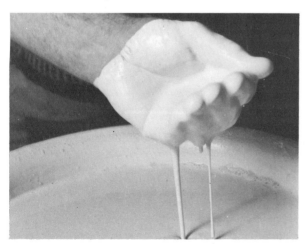

ONE-PIECE PRESS MOLD

One of the easiest ways of making shallow dishes is with a one-piece press mold. This can be used several times providing that it is stored away between use where it cannot become chipped or damaged in any way. Take great care to make sure that the original clay mold is the shape you want the dishes to be before you pour over the plaster.

Clay model

Plaster mold

Finished dish

1. The clay model is made up of little pieces of clay, which are shaped with a rectangular flexible blue steel scraper, or a flexible steel kidney.

2. Rolling out a wall to retain the plaster during pouring. The wall is formed by a thick slab of clay, which is cut into strips and joined.

3. A 2in (5cm) gap is left between the model's base and the slightly higher wall. An extra edge of clay is placed around the base of the wall to prevent plaster seepage.

4. To avoid trapping air bubbles, pour the plaster at the edge and allow it to slowly cover the model.

5. The top of the model should be evenly covered with plaster.

6. While the mold is still wet, trim the back with a steel scraper, duplicating the inside shape. This makes the mold lighter and of even thickness.

mold to be cast. Add liberal handfuls of plaster evenly over the surface of the water until it is absorbed and the plaster is level with the water. Alternatively you can mix a given weight of plaster with a specific volume of water, usually in the proportions of 2 pints (1 litre) water to 3 lbs (1.5 kg) plaster.

Mix the plaster thoroughly with one, or both hands, making sure that there are no lumps in the mixture. When it is blended and begins to thicken it is ready for pouring. Never pour the plaster directly on top of your models because air bubbles will get trapped in the edges or grooves of the mold. Always pour to the side, so that the plaster flows around the model and the level rises slowly to cover it. Depending on the article being cast, the plaster can be scraped or shaped while setting. When set it can only be trimmed with a sharp tool or a surform blade.

Molds and mold making

Many potters make use of plaster molds in their work for making forms which are not hand-shaped by building or throwing. These molds are primarily employed for the reproduction of specific shapes by casting or pressing clay slip into either a hollow concave or convex mold. The most simple is a one-piece concave mold for pressing dishes, or a one piece drop-out mold of two or more pieces can be made and very intricate models, such as a figure, may need up to six pieces to reproduce the original — this would be done in a six-piece mold. The clay or plaster master model is shaped by hand or turned on a wheel or lathe. A plaster mold of one or more pieces is then cast from the original mold so that the interior surface of the mold will form the exterior surface of the article.

One-piece press molds

These are generally used for making shallow dishes. The best method is to draw out the planned shape of the dish on a piece of level marble slate or wood, allowing for approximately 10 per cent shrinkage. Add small pieces of clay (about the size of a walnut), working inwards from the edge of the drawn shape and building the convex form so that it closely resembles the contour of the proposed dish. Once you are satisfied with the shape, fill in all the uneven bits of the surface and use a steel strip or kidney to smooth it. Remember, as in all clay techniques, to use only very well mixed and smooth clay for preparing the model. When you have completed the model, encircle it with a wall of clay, measuring 1½ to 2 in (4 to 5 cm) from the edge of the model and high enough to stand above the base. Pour the plaster over the clay shape to produce a working dish mold. When the mold is dry, the rolled slab of clay is pressed into it and trimmed to fit.

A convex hump (or mushroom) mold can be cast from a one-piece dish mold. The dish mold is first soaped and sealed to prevent the fresh plaster from sticking to the plaster mold. This is done by applying several coats of liquid soap (available from most ceramic suppliers), which is worked into the surface with a natural sponge. When the surface is sealed fresh plaster can be poured into the hollow

PRESS MOLDING A DISH

Pressed dishes are more suitable for firing to earthenware than stoneware temperatures as they tend to retain their shape less well as the temperature rises. The clay for the dish should be well wedged and should be rolled on heavy absorbent medium weave canvas. Lift the clay from the cloth between each rolling and always roll from the centre, working towards and then away from you. When the dish has been made do not remove it from the mold until it is firm. Reverse the clay dish onto a dry, clean board so that it retains its shape while it is drying. It should be dried in an even atmosphere, free from draughts, and fettled while leather-hard to prevent dust from forming.

Points to remember
● The shape of the dish should not be too shallow if you are firing to high temperatures.
● Use a plastic clay which is not too soft.

I. The clay slab is laid on a flat, dry working surface and rolled out with a roling pin to the desired thickness. This should be even.

2. The rolled slab of clay is laid over one arm for carrying to the mould. It is then placed carefully into the concave dish mold so that it overlaps the edges.

3. One hand is used to support the clay and gently ease it into the mold. Make sure you have positioned it so that it is centred.

4. A rubber kidney is used to smooth the clay in the mold, to an even thickness all over. The edge is defined by running the kidney around the mold.

5. A piece of cutting wire is used to cut the surplus clay from around the edge of the mold, as with pastry. Hold the wire flat so that you are cutting evenly.

6. The edge of the clay dish is smoothed with a rubber kidney.

A more decorative method of making a dish in a dish mold is to use pieces of colored clay to build up a pattern. Small lumps of clay are taken from large lumps of different colored clays and rolled into balls. Each ball is pressed into the mold, one on top of the other, in layers. The layers are built up until you have covered the inside of the mold to the rim. The clay is then cut round with a cutting tool to level the edges. The clays you use for this technique should be of similar viscosity so that they shrink at the same rate.

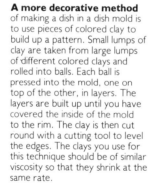

PRESSING A NUMBER

This simple technique can be used to create decorative letters as well as numbers. The basic casting of the one-piece mold is the first task; the clay is then simply pushed and shaped to fit the plaster mold. The same mold could also be used for slip casting.

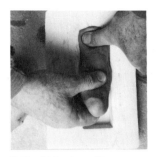

1. The equipment needed is a one-piece mold, clay in the form of a ball, strip steel scraper and a wooden batten for flattening the clay.

2. The thicker top of the sausage is pressed into the top of the number with the fingers.

3. Press the bottom end of the sausage — the thinner end — into the base of the mold.

4. Smooth and press the clay down evenly into the mold, using the wooden batten.

5. Trim away any surplus clay with the strip steel scraper.

6. Take a small clay ball and use it to lift the number carefully out of the mold, working from the top end.

7. Another way of releasing the clay from the mold is to tap the mold gently on one side so that it falls out.

dish mold until it just overflows onto the flat edge. The next stage is to place a clay collar onto the firm plaster surface and fill it with plaster. This produces a stem or stalk for the mushroom mold to stand on. Working on this type of raised, convex mold makes it possible to obtain a more defined edge on the dish. The dish is made by laying the clay over the mold and trimming it. Decoration can be applied in the raw clay state or after bisque firing.

Making a mold of two or more pieces
As well as a one-piece press mold, you can make a mold of two or more pieces for pressing or slip casting. Firstly, a block mold is made from a master model. The surface of the negative block mold is then soaped and sealed and a positive case mold is cast with freshly made plaster. From each piece of the case mold another section is cast and this becomes the working mold. This will be identical to the original mold, but will be used for casting or press molding the article. A series of working molds can be cast from the pieces of the block molds, and these are then dried and stored until they are needed.

Press molding in a two-piece mold
This is a technique used mainly for making simple forms to which further clay details can be added. Alternatively any embellishment, in the form of decoration, can be added to the article after bisque firing or glazing in order to give it greater definition.

Articles are made in a two-piece mold. Each piece is

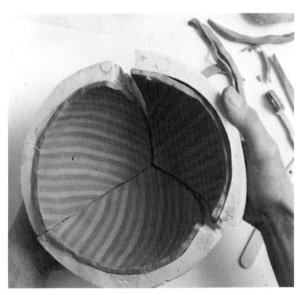

Three-piece press mold Clay can be pressed into a mold of two or more pieces, which can then be fitted together to make a whole.

MAKING A HUMP MOLD

A hump mold, so-called because of its mushroom shape, is an ideal vehicle for the molding of dishes, particularly when it is intended to apply clay pieces or slip to the surface as part of the decorative process. The actual shape is created by simply pressing a sheet of clay onto the finished mold.

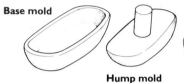

Base mold   **Finished dish**

Hump mold

1. The inside of the base mold is sponged with soft-soap size. This stops the plaster sticking to plaster.

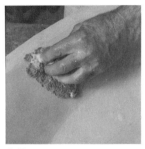

2. The sides of mold are also coated with soft-soap, using a sponge held as shown so as not to mark the surface. Remember it is important that this is even.

3. Mix the plaster and then pour it into the hollow of the mold slowly and carefully.

4. The plaster should fill the mold until it is just level with the top edges. Leave it for a few minutes until it has a cheese-like consistency.

5. Smooth out the surface of the plaster to the edges of the mold, using a rubber or steel kidney.

6. The central area, which will form the foundation for the stalk, is roughened up with a metal scraper.

7. Roll out a slab of clay to form a collar, joining the ends carefully and sealing them with a clay and water mixture.

8. Place the clay collar over the roughened central area to form the mold for the stalk.

9. Pour fresh plaster into the collar to fill it to the top.

10. Allow the plaster to dry, then carefully remove the collar.

11. Using a metal scraper, smooth down the top of the stalk.

12. Next, smooth the sides of the stalk. It is important that, as well as the surface, all edges should be clean and smooth.

13. To ensure the edges are smooth, trim them with a surform, if necessary.

14. The completed mould is now ready for use.

MAKING A DISH ON THE MOLD

Having completed the hump mold, use it for press molding dishes in the manner shown here. The easiest way to build up the form is to press the clay directly onto the mold. Remember to keep the hump mold in the hollow base when not in use, so that its edges will not be damaged. Once the clay has dried and been removed from the mold, the dish can be decorated *(below right)*.

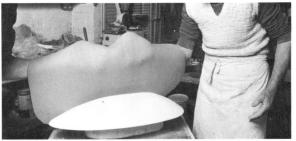

1. Having rolled out the clay with wooden battens to an even thickness, position it carefully and centrally over the mold. If a large amount of clay is being used, you may need help carrying it. The shape is created by pressing the clay firmly onto the mold, starting at the middle and working towards the outside edges.

2. Use a damp cloth to avoid indenting the clay. Make sure the clay fits the mold tightly.

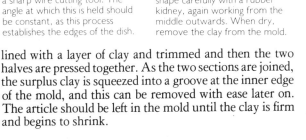

3. Trim away the excess clay with a sharp wire cutting tool. The angle at which this is held should be constant, as this process establishes the edges of the dish.

4. Smooth down the overall shape carefully with a rubber kidney, again working from the middle outwards. When dry, remove the clay from the mold.

lined with a layer of clay and trimmed and then the two halves are pressed together. As the two sections are joined, the surplus clay is squeezed into a groove at the inner edge of the mold, and this can be removed with ease later on. The article should be left in the mold until the clay is firm and begins to shrink.

Slip casting

This method of pottery making is used extensively in industry for semi-automatic and automatic producton, but it is now also used by many small potteries and studio potters. It is a process by which an article is cast in a mold and removed when the clay is firm. Shapes are made in open and hollow molds of two or more pieces to give a complete article, or several components are made in separte molds and joined together with casting slip. A teapot body, spout and handle can be made in this way. The idea of slip casting is to reproduce shapes of a standard size and thickness.

The greatest expenditure is in the making of the original model, the block and case molds and a set of some 10 to 20 working molds. These will need replacing when the surface becomes worn after constant use, which can vary from 30 to 100 castings. The molds are filled with liquid casting slip — plastic clay in which fluidity has been induced by the addition of chemicals and a smaller percentage of water than that used to make ordinary slip.

The composition of casting slip

Casting slip contains 40-45 per cent water, while ordinary slip contains 60 per cent and plastic clay only 22 per cent. The addition of sodium silicate or soda ash acts as a deflocculant to separate the clay particles and keeps them in suspension so that the slip is fluid.

Start with the principle that you will add to your plastic clay or dry clay ingredients approximately 0.3 and 0.6 per cent of sodium silicate and sodium carbonate (soda ash) respectively. Sometimes sodium silicate is used on its own.

Sodium silicate is a mixture of finely ground sodium oxide and silica. It is available in various degrees of concentration, defined as degrees of twaddell ($^\circ$T). 140°T is a thick starchy liquid, which contains 45 per cent water, while 100°T is a thinner liquid containing 60 per cent water. Both these solutions are used for plastic clay bodies.

MAKING SLIP-CASTING MOLDS

The use of molds is an integral part of slip casting, especially when an object is to be reproduced more than once. In such cases, a series of identical molds should be made to simplify the process. Called working molds by potters, these can consist of two pieces or more; for a complicated model, as many as six pieces may be required. In most instances, however, a two-piece press mold is adequate.

A solid clay model of a seal, ready for setting up for molding (right). The model has been skilfully designed so that the number of pieces needed for casting is reduced to the minimum. Apart from the base, only three pieces of mold are needed. Objects such as animals are best modelled in clay and kept in the leather-hard state until ready for molding. Symmetrical models, on the other hand, are best made of plaster, since this makes them easier to turn on a lathe.

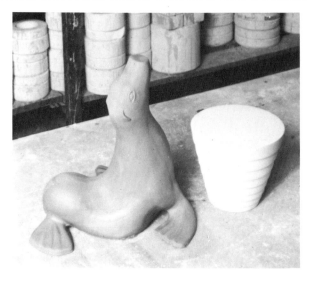

Setting up and casting a plaster model The plaster model (below left) is soft-soaped and then embedded in clay to half its depth and walls built up around it to contain the plaster. Check the model first (left) for the exact position of the halfway point and mark it in pencil. A thin plaster template, cut to the shape of the model's profile, is then placed in position as shown; alternatively a thin, stiff slab of clay can be used. Cover the section to a depth of about 1 in (2.5 cm) with heavy, wet plaster, having first wound strong string around the walls to hold the plaster in place after it has been poured. Allow the plaster to set. Remove the template, take out the model, clean it, replace it in the mold as shown (below right) and repeat the process to create the second half of the mold. Having completed this, proceed to cast the base.

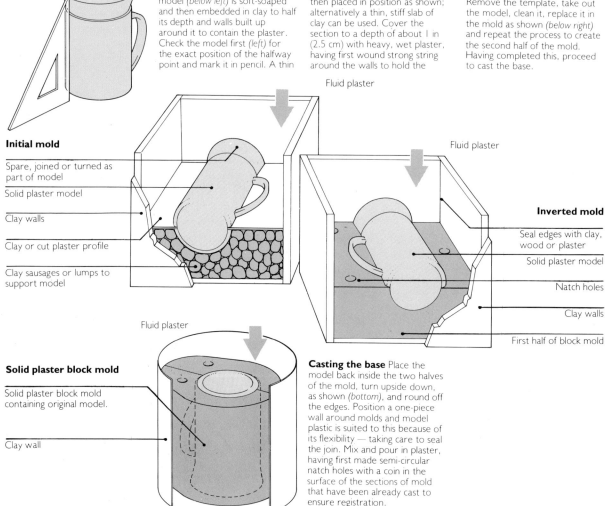

Fluid plaster

Initial mold

Spare, joined or turned as part of model

Solid plaster model

Clay walls

Clay or cut plaster profile

Clay sausages or lumps to support model

Fluid plaster

Inverted mold

Seal edges with clay, wood or plaster

Solid plaster model

Natch holes

Clay walls

First half of block mold

Fluid plaster

Solid plaster block mold

Solid plaster block mold containing original model.

Clay wall

Casting the base Place the model back inside the two halves of the mold, turn upside down, as shown (bottom), and round off the edges. Position a one-piece wall around molds and model — plastic is suited to this because of its flexibility — taking care to seal the join. Mix and pour in plaster, having first made semi-circular natch holes with a coin in the surface of the sections of mold that have been already cast to ensure registration.

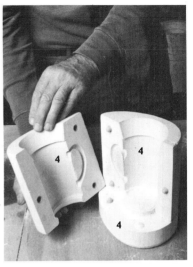

A solid plaster model (**1**) and its three-section block mold (**2**), consisting of a base and a two-section body mold. This block mold can become a working mold for further reproductions, the model being redundant.

Each section of a block mold (**2**) is used to cast a case mold (**3**). Such molds are made by sealing the surface of the block molds with soft-soap solution, first thoroughly dampening the plaster. What was reversed in the block now becomes a solid relief. The two end pieces — the outer case — make it easier to pour the plaster onto the sealed case molds. The end result is a series of working molds.

Each of the three pieces of the working mold (**4**) were made from a solid piece of case mould and are identical to the original three pieces of block mold cast from the original plaster model. Each time such a working mold is made, the case mold should be gently treated with two or three coats of liquid soft-soap, which is worked gently over the surface and then wiped off with a sponge and clean water.

The grouped illustrations here show all the stages from plaster model to block mold, case mold and working mold. The spare on top of the plaster mold is turned as part of the mug model.

Plaster model with spare for top. Here, the spare is a separate piece, attached to the main body of the model by two nails cast into the spare and fitting into two corresponding holes in the model. The original spare was made of clay and removed when the two side pieces of block were made. At this stage, the nails were nailed into the top of the mold and the plaster cast around them, the spare lifting out with the nails when the plaster had set.

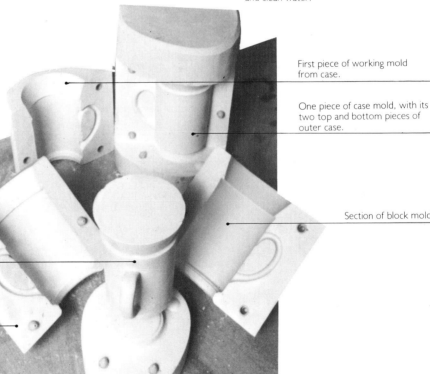

First piece of working mold from case.

One piece of case mold, with its two top and bottom pieces of outer case.

Section of block mold

Section of block mold

Base of block mold

USING A TWO-PIECE PRESS MOLD

This mold is used to construct simple symmetric or asymmetric forms, such as handles for jugs and mugs. Different colored clays may be used for each pressing. Alternatively small pieces of contrasting colored clays may be inserted into the mold underneath the main body of the clay.

1. The V-shaped groove in both halves of the mold allows surplus clay to escape during pressing. Natch holes are also cut as registration marks. Enough soft clay should be pressed into each half of the mold to leave a slight overlap at the edges.

2. The clay overlap prevents holes appearing in the finished form, while creases are avoided by filling the mold with a soft clay sausage.

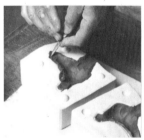

3. Trim the surplus clay at the edge of both halves, leaving slightly raised sections in the center that will fuse.

4. Prior to pressing both halves of the mold together increase their plasticity by moistening them with a thin layer of slip or water.

5. Press the halves firmly together and leave for 10 to 15 minutes before separating.

6. After separation it is apparent that the surplus clay has been forced out of the mold and into the groove. Gently remove the finished model *(right)*.

75°T is a thinnish solution better suited to less plastic porcelain and china clay casting slips. If used alone, sodium silicate gives more fluidity than soda ash and produces a broken, stringy effect in the slip when it is drained from the mould. It gives a harder cast than soda ash as it tends to make the clay adhere to the mold and, when it dries, it becomes brittle.

Sodium carbonate (or soda ash) comes in a white powder form. It must be kept in an air-tight container as it quickly absorbs moisture from the atmosphere to become sodium bicarbonate. If this happens it will act as a flocculent rather than a deflocculent. When used alone, its presence in a slip aids drainage of the mold, but may give a soft cast which tends to sag away from the mold and make drying difficult.

With more plastic clays, soda ash gives a rapid cast, but the slip will be less fluid. It also gives a high surface tension which breaks the flow of the slip when filling the mold and traps small air bubbles in the clay. These bubbles later come to the surface causing pin holes in the clay which are more obvious when the ware is bisque fired or glazed.

Preparation the slip for casting

Slip can be made from dry raw materials plus water and deflocculents, or by the addition of water and defloccluents to an already prepared plastic clay. If this is a standard bought clay, the manufacturer will readily supply a recipe for casting slip.

Weigh out the sodium silicate on a piece of clear plastic

SLIP CASTING

Used to manufacture objects that are difficult to throw or make by other means and where reproduction or detail must be constant, this technique is suitable for most forms and colors of clay except for clay containing medium to heavy grog.

Points to remember

●Clean all dry clay from the inside the mold to ensure that both halves fit snugly.

1. Make a clay sphere by pouring casting slip into a two-piece slip casting mold, using a heavy rubber bar d or string to hold the mold together.

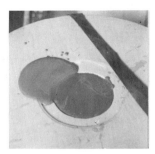

2. The clay slip is topped up as its water is absorbed by the plaster.

3. Pour the surplus clay from the mold. The time taken to fill the mold depends on whether it is bone dry or has recently been used and on the plaster.

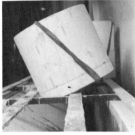

4. Up end the mold and allow the surplus clay to thoroughly drain until the clay lining the mould is matt rather than shiny.

5. The cast object's base may be given a sharp edge by cleaning the pouring hole with a sharp knife to remove spare clay before it hardens.

6. Alternatively, if a rounded edge is sought, remove any surplus clay by pressing your thumbs against the bottom of the pouring hole.

7. Any spare clay may then be lifted away with a fettling knife.

8. Lift the mold's top section to reveal the plaster model (*left*). Then tap the edge of the model to loosen it from the clay and gently remove it from the mold.

9. Place the freed mold on a plaster bat to dry before fettling and sponging.

When casting flat objects it is easier to open the mold in the same way as opening a book. The spare clay in the pouring hole is removed after the mould has been opened.

JOLLEYING

Jolleying is the name given to the pressing of clay shapes between a revolving plaster mold and a template, which is brought into contact with the mold to create the missing side. The clay used can be red or white, but must be smooth and not contain coarse grog; templates can be made of hard wood, metal or perspex. The equipment required is shown (below). It consists of a deep cuphead for use with mug and mug molds (**1**) a working mold (**2**) and a detachable jolley arm, which lifts the wheel (**3**). Here, the template is attached, together with a backing plate to increase the firmness and weight of the profile. The wide cuphead (**4**) is used for making plates, saucers or shallow dishes. The photograph (*right*) shows a bowl mold being placed in the cuphead ready for insertion of the clay lump for jolleying the shape. The plastic clay is placed in the middle of the mold and pulled up the form with the fingers before the template is used to create the inner profile. Surplus clay should be regularly cleaned off the profile with the thumb.

and put it, together with the soda ash, in a small jug with enough warm water to dissolve it. When the mixture is dissolved, place it with the rest of the water, into a blunger bucket or a barrel, according to the quantity being prepared. Add the ingredients, in small quantities, stirring all the time until they are dissolved. If you are using plastic clay and a mechanical mixer, do not add too much clay at a time . The clay should be blunged for several hours.

Slip should not be used immediately after preparation, but left for at least 24 hours to allow complete combination and chemical action to take place. It should then be mixed again before use. If small quantities of slip are being made by hand-mixing or stirring, make sure you do not beat any air into it. Keep the mixture covered so that the water does not evaporate, and to prevent a skin forming on the surface. If the skin is stirred into the slip it can form brownish patches on the sides of the ware when cast. Sometimes it is necessary to add extra deflocculents to the slip to compensate for the percentage absorbed into the mold when casting. When making a coarse slip the grog or sand must be added last, after the slip has been sieved. Grogged slip is used for casting large or relief tiles.

When a casting slip is stored after preparation, it tends to gel or flocculate if it only contains enough electrolyte to bring it to the maximum state of deflocculation. However if sodium silicate is present, this will be prevented.

Casting

If you are using a mold of two pieces or more, make sure it is well tied so that the weight of slip when full does not force the pieces apart and allow the solution to flow out. Pour the slip in such a way that it runs down the inside edge of the mold and does not strike the base or side directly. If this happens you will get a concentration of alkali or flux which will fuse or vitrify the clay in the firing at the point of impact, causing balding when glazed and fired due to reduced porosity. This is called flashing.

Once the slip is poured into the mold, making contact with the plaster surface, the water in the slip is absorbed into the plaster and leaves a layer of hardening clay on the inside of the mold. This causes the level of slip in the mold to drop so that it will need regular topping up. For earthenware, casting in a dry mold should take between 20 and 40 minutes, but it could be longer if the clay is very plastic. If the molds are not dried out between castings, the casting time gets progressively longer. Non-plastic porcelain or china slips can be cast in a matter of seconds.

When the slip has been in the mold for the required amount of time, tilt the mold to see how thick it is at the top edge of the cast. When it looks ready, pour the slip out of the mold gradually so that you do not create a vacuum which may bring the layer of clay away from the mold surface. When the slip has stopped dripping, return the mold to an upright position and leave it until the surface of the clay is no longer shiny, but matt. Remove the 'spare' (piece of clay) at the top of the cast by pressing it out with your thumbs or trimming it with a suitable knife. Care must be taken not to cut or pare the plaster or the thickness of the top edge will be reduced in future castings. Take the mold apart very carefully and place the article on a clean

1. Dampen the surface of the mold before adding the clay and adjust the template angle to make shapes of the correct cross-section.

2. Put the ball of clay into the mold. The jolley arm is lowered and the mould rotated for the template to force the clay outwards.

3. Jolleying in progress. Keep the template dampened during use.

4. On completion, lift the jolley arm. Note how the clay has built up on the profile.

5. Trim off surplus clay at the edges with a thin wire cutting tool.

6. Take the mold out of the cuphead. Leave the finished article in the mold to dry before firing.

board or plaster bat to dry. When it is still leather hard, trim away any seams and sponge it to get a clean, smooth surface. Never leave a cast for too long in a very dry mold as it can crack if it shrinks too rapidly.

Jolleying

This particular type of ware is made using a metal template to shape a layer of clay onto or into a revolving plaster mold. The plaster mold is put into a metal cuphead which is attached to an electric wheel and a layer of clay is slapped over the top, before the wheel is set in motion. A hinged, metal arm, to which a template is attached, is lowered slowly and firmly onto the spinning clay. The templates can be made from hardwood, perspex, brass, mild steel or any hard, but workable material. As the profile wears it can be refiled and shaped and used again.

The clay used for jolleying should be reasonably plastic for strength and ease of handling and can be white, buff, chocolate, black or red in color. If more than one color is used in a small workshop great care should be taken so that they do not contaminate each other.

For making a concave shape such as a cup or deep dish, a lump of clay is placed in the bottom of the spinning hollow mould and roughly shaped and drawn up with the fingers of one or both hands. The profile is then introduced into the mold and the final shaping carried out, keeping the surface moist with a sponge. The slab for a shallow shape can be made with a spreader (a straight metal template, set just off the horizontal) which flattens the clay lump onto a spinning plaster bat. The angle of the spreader allows the clay to become thicker towards the center so that when it is placed on the mold and the template applied, there is sufficient thickness to form the footring of the article. In mass-production industry this is now done with highly sophisticated automatic machinery.

When the article has been jolleyed, the mold is left in the atmosphere until the clay shrinks sufficiently for the article to be removed. It can then be placed in a hot cupboard to speed up the drying process. This process of production allows the manufacture of simple, uniform shapes which can be decorated with a wide range of techniques, either individually or by reproductive methods. Patterns or designs can be incised into the mold and these give an extra dimension to the clay surface and a special effect when the article is glazed with a colored transparent glaze. A famous example of jigger and jolley ware is the Wedgwood green cabbage leaf plates.

Lamination and agateware

Lamination and agateware are produced from a variety of techniques, but they are basically decorative ideas which use the cross section layers of clay of contrasting colors. Colored clays which contain a high percentage of certain oxides can bubble and blister during firing. This is the result of the high fluxing properties of these oxides. For some techniques this may be a desirable quality, but for those which require clear definition in the pattern and a smooth surface, it is essential that the clays are mixed very carefully to prevent bubbling. Color tests should therefore always be done first. When staining the clay it is best to add

TILE MAKING

Most industrial tiles are extruded or made from clay dust, using automatic machinery *(right)*. Less sophisticated machinery is used for paving tiles and roofing tiles, which are made form extruded clay *(below left)*. Hand-made roofing tiles are made from sections of extruded slabs, which are wide enough for many different sizes and shapes of tile to be cut from them. A wooden template is placed on the slab and the tile cut out using a stiff sharp knife *(below left)*; then, other smaller square tiles are cut to fill the spaces between the main tiles.

Other tiles can be impressed or inlaid with a contrasting colored clay, or slip. Raised patterns are applied to a wooden template, which is then pressed into the soft clay surface. This should be allowed to dry a little before the clay, or slip, is inlaid *(below right)*. When leather hard, the surface is scraped evenly to give a sharp definition to the design.

Another traditional method is to press-mold tiles, using a plaster mold. Thin mild metal strips are cast into the plaster to prevent wear, after the surface has been scrapped level with a wooden batten. Special over-sized tiles, or large slabs can be made by slip casting them into two-piece plaster molds, using a heavily grogged slip *(bottom left)*.

Points to remember
● The most important factor in the making of tiles by hand is to use a sufficiently grogged or sanded body. This reduces warping.
● Always make sure that tiles dry slowly and evenly.

I. A large tile is slip cast, using grogged slip. The mold is tiled as the slip is poured on to allow it to flow to the extremities. Use both pouring holes.

2. The two pieces of the mold are separated after casting. It is now ready for trimming and smoothing at the pouring points.

3. The edge of the mold is tapped with the fist to loosen the tile. It is then tipped forward to release the tile, which should be supported when demoulded.

4. The released sun tile is placed on the lid of the mold so that it dries flat.

the stains to powdered clay, make it into a slip, sieve it and then dry to a plastic state. If color is added to plastic clay the color could be streaky and uneven. Dark colors may need up to eight per cent of stain added, but blues seldom more than two per cent.

The clay can be mixed in different ways, but it is usually produced in molds by cutting sheets from the block of agate clay. It can also be thrown to produce spiral markings rather than evenly divided layers of color.

The technique of agateware can be random and free or it can be a slow, exacting operation which requires great precision in the construction of the layers, as in Marion Gaunce's work. Here the layers are laboriously built up, strip by strip, with a thin layer of slip brushed on the surface of each join. Even with great care, the failure or 'seconds' rate is high during handling, drying and firing.

The most difficult, but important factor is to ensure an even shrinkage of the different colored clays. The article must be dried as slowly as possible in a container, or wrapped in plastic. Some potters keep the pot in a moist damp atmosphere in order to even out the dampness before beginning the slow drying. When the clay is dry, the surfaces will need careful scraping with a metal kidney and finishing with steel or wire wool. Wet and dry fine abrasive paper may be used at the biscuit firing state.

Many potters leave their agateware unglazed when firing while others use a transparent glaze to brighten the colors and accentuate the pattern.

A similar type of ware to agate is called inlay or marquetry. In this technique the specially shaped pieces of colored clay are rolled or pressed into the surface of a very thin white clay. When it is leather-hard the surface is scraped to leave a sharp outline between the two colored clays. This technique will be described in Chapter 5.

Tile making

Most potters attempt at some time to make tiles, assuming it to be a simple operation, but often they are unsuccessful. The main complaint is that the tiles tend to buckle and do not stay flat. If these difficulties are dealt with, tile making has great possibilities, plus the additional advantage of requiring the minimum of equipment for making.

The two essential ingredients for success are the composition of the clay body and the technique of drying. The clay must contain a fair percentage of sand or grog which will reduce the rapid shrinkage rate of the body, caused by the high plastic content of most clays. The higher the grog content, the higher the firing will need to be to obtain reasonable strength for the ware. If you require a tough tile body to fire at earthenware temperatures then it may be necessary to add some flux as well as grog to the body to aid fusion. The inclusion of frit as a flux lowers the vitrifying temperature to compensate for the high grog content.

There are several different methods of making tiles.

Slab making This preparation of clay for tile making is similar to preparing a slab for slab-building. A sheet of clay is rolled using battens to determine the thickness, and the tiles are cut from the whole. The thickness will depend on the size and use of the tiles, but usually between ½ in (1 cm) and ¼ in (0.5 cm) will be sufficient for hand-made tiles.

Casting tiles can be slip cast with grogged slip in a plaster mold.

Extruding The tiles can be cut from an extruded clay strip, but you need a large extruder to produce flat slabs of clay, which are wide enough.

Hand-pressing The tiles can be hand-pressed in a plaster mold, using a coarse body clay.

For all these methods, with the exception of press-molding, you will need to calculate the clay shrinkage and decide whether to cut your tiles from the damp slab or leave the clay until it is leather-hard. It is often a good idea to mark the surface of the clay lightly with the outline of the tile when it is still soft and leave the cutting until it has dried to the leather-hard state. Cutting should be done with a stiff, thin-bladed knife and you can use a metal, wood or card template (or a wood, plastic or metal set square) to ensure that you have a square tile when making large tiles.

Drying If a standard clay is used, very careful drying is essential. The tiles must be dried as slowly as possible on rigid, slatted trays which allow the air to reach both surfaces. Three or four trays should be ample, unless you are making large quantities of tiles. The trays can be made quickly and easily using standard battens of 1 in x ½ in (2.5 cm x 1 cm), nailed to 1 in x 1in (2.5 cm x 2.5 cm) cross pieces and allowing ¾ in (2 cm) between the slats. The most manageable length is 3 ft (1 m) long with cross supports in the middle and at both ends. For maximum rigidity use slats on both sides.

If well grogged, tiles can be dried in a warm atmosphere, but you must at all costs avoid draughts to prevent uneven drying. Depending on the thickness, they can be dried singly, by stacking or by standing them on edge. Large tiles of 12 in x 12 in (30 cm x 30 cm), or larger, should be dried as slowly as possible in a cool, draught-free atmosphere and they can be wrapped loosely in a sheet of plastic and left until hard.

Relief modelling can be added to a tile in the leather-hard state or, if you are using the press molding method, it can form part of the tile. In this case the relief is applied to the clay model before it is cast.

Firing This should be slow in the early stages because of the density of the tile pack. They can be fired in stacks of four to six tiles, or on their sides. Large tiles of 12 in (30 cm) in diameter or more need to be fired on an extremely flat kiln shelf with a thin layer of sand to aid movement, as they contract during firing.

MAKING AN AGATEWARE BOWL

The techniques shown here have been developed by the British potter Marion Gaunce. She makes her bowls from carefully prepared and stained porcelain clay, though the same techniques can be used with earthenware or stoneware bodies.

The first point to remember is shrinkage. By adding oxides to the clay, this is cut down, so keeping a good balance between the white, dark and light colors. Before adding the various strips of clay to create these, great care must be taken to keep the different ones as evenly moist as possible to reduce the problem of variable shrinkage.

There is, however, still a need for extremely slow drying. When made, the bowl is first placed in a bucket, supported by a saturated plaster slab, and the top of the bucket sealed with plastic. This allows the moist atmosphere to permeate the entire shape, though regular checks should be made to ensure that excessive condensation does not build up. For the actual drying, the bowl is wrapped lightly in polythene.

The rim is an extremely important design element, the aim being to contrast the main shape as much as possible. The contrast can be established either in the depth of the rim, or the way in which its decorative pattern is related to the patterns on the main body of the bowl. Gaunce uses an extremely interesting decorative technique here. Pieces of fabric are sewn together to make a hollow form into which the mold for the rim is cast.

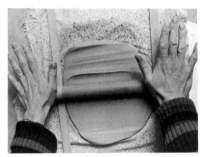

1. Roll a slab of single colored porcelain clay onto a cloth prior to cutting it into strips. The clay should be lifted off the cloth between each rolling. Wooden battens determine the thickness of the clay although cardboard ones may be used if thinner layers are desired.

2. Using a thin stiff-bladed palette knife cut strips off the slab. The wooden batten acts as a straight edge for cutting while the width between battens serves as the width of the clay strip.

3. After roughing the strip's surface, apply slip with a toothbrush to the colored strips. Repeat the process with different colored clays.

4. Join the different colored strips of clay into a roughly shaped slab and place it in a polythene bag. This assists the spread of moisture evenly throughout the clay, making it more plastic and preventing the strips separating during firing.

5. A paper template is used as a pattern for cutting a section of the bowl's shape from the slab. Fit the shape into the appropriate plaster section of the mold leaving a little spare clay strip all round for trimming.

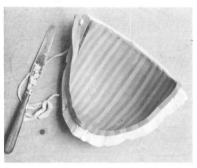

6. This illustrates the section of the bowl which has been cut using a template. It has been prepared into a section of the mold and the surplus clay has yet to be removed.

7. Cut the surplus clay from the edge of the mould with a sharp knife, leaving enough to fuse with the other sections when all three are pressed together. Thin strips of polythene can be tucked under the edges of the clay to prevent its moisture from being absorbed.

8. Rough up the edges of the three sections before applying slip to them to help them stick together.

9. Press the three sections of the mold together before the slip dries.

10. When the joined sections are almost leather-hard and the bowl is able to hold its shape, the pot is removed from its mold and a rim of patterned clay attached to the bowl's outside. Carefully scrape the bowl's edge with a metal kidney to smooth the surface.

11. Finally, before firing, scrape the bowl's inside with a steel, flexible kidney to make the colors crisp. The bowl is left to dry slowly in a plastic bucket sealed with a plastic bag. This creates a humid atmosphere so it is important to remove any condensation before it drips back onto the pot.

Striped pot with checked rim
Marion Gaunce, UK
Height: 7½ in (19 cm)

This pot, which was oxidized to 1240°C (2260°F) in an electric kiln, shows the asymmetric quality of Gaunce's work and the importance of the design and proportion of the bowl's edge to its overall shape. The pattern reflects her interest in fabrics. Her method involves sewing pieces of fabric together to make a container for the plaster to create the model for the eventual mold. She has deliberately avoided running the strips together to make the design more interesting.

CERAMICS MADE IN MOLDS

Molds can take many forms. They can be simple, as in the case of the shallow or deep plaster mold, both of which can be used as a support for hand-building and shaping. James Tower used the equally simple idea of an open, shallow plaster dish to mold the two halves of his large sculputural form. The bowl by Penny Fowler and the Sandra Black vases and dish all utilized slip case drop-out molds, while Malcolm Gooding used more intricate slip casting molds for his spaghetti jar.

Porcelain bowl
David Brokenshire, New Zealand
Diameter: 8½ in (22 cm)

Pressing and shaping porcelain clay into lightly bisque clay molds allows the creation of a very thin section. The clay used was the David Leach porcelain recipe (p19), which, after biscuiting, was fired to 1305°C (2380°F) in a reducing atmosphere. The colouring was created with solutions of copper, iron and cobalt sulphate salts, applied before glazing.

Large sculptural form (left)
James Tower, UK
Height: 21 in (53 cm)

This composite piece consists of two pressed dish shapes, which were glazed with a dark manganese glaze and then fired to 1100°C (2010°F). After this, it was glazed again with a white bisilicate tin glaze. When this had dried, the potter scratched through this top layer. A further firing created the final texture, with the black and white glazes beginning to merge. Tower's main interests lie in the qualities of English landscape, sea and weather, which are intuitively expressed through his handling of clay and glaze.

Cast semi-porcelain bowl
Penny Fowler, UK
Height: 4 in (10 cm)

This slip cast bowl is made from partially mixed colored slips, several coats of which were poured and twisted separately into the mold to give a varying pattern to the surface. After discarding the surplus, plain slip was added to enable the bowl to be cast to normal thickness. The bowl is unglazed. After firing to 1200°C (2190°F), it was given its final texture by wetting the clay and polishing it with carborundum paper.

Pierced porcelain and bone china vases and dish
Sandra Black, Australia
Height: 4-5 in (10-13 cm)

The dish is porcelain, the remaining examples being of bone china. All of them were cast in one-piece molds, being carved and pierced when they were leather-hard. The next step was to bisque them at 800°C (1470°F) and then polish them with carborundum paper after a soaking in water. They were then fired in a gas fiber kiln to 1280-1290°C (2340-2350°F), the firing cycle lasting eight hours with a very light reduction for 30 minutes at the end.

Agateware jars
Paul Philp, UK
Height: 4 in (10 cm)

These agateware jars are press molded, using a selection of richly colored clays. When leather-hard, the surface was cleanly turned to sharpen the contrast between the colors, it was then coated with a transparent glaze.

Earthenware spaghetti jar
Malcolm Gooding, UK
Height: 18 in (48 cm)

This striking jar is a fine example of the intricacies of slip casting. The fine white earthenware molds were made in separate sections. The pieces are joined with slip at the leather-hard stage. Colors were then created carefully and, after bisque firing, were glazed with a transparent glaze before the final firing.

Jolleyed bowls
Kenneth and Ann Clark, UK
Diameter: 5 in (13 cm)

Once the bowls are made, they can be used as blanks for decorating with an infinite variety of techniques and colors. An increasing number of small potteries are producing blanks by jolleying or casting, but continue to decorate them individually; as there is at present a move towards more decorative ceramics. The bowl *(centre)* has been glazed with a turquoise glaze and fired to 1060°C (1940°F) after a 1120°C (2048°F) bisque firing. The other bowls were glazed with a lead-frit-based tin glaze and decorated with basic oxides of manganese, iron, cobalt and copper.

Recipe for turquoise glaze:

Frit (potterycraft 2955)	80
Nephyline syenite	10
Flint	10
Copper oxide	2.5

Jolleyed earthenware dish
Wedgwood, UK
Diameter: 10in (25cm)

This is an example of a shallow relief molding on a jolleyed plate. The technique was commonly used for dust-pressed Victorian tiles and can be applied to slip cast ware also. The plate is given a coat of transparent green glaze to accentuate the design.

Deep bone china bowl
Angela Verdon, UK
Height: 10 in (25 cm)

A cast bone china bowl with pierced and semi-pierced sections. The article is cast in one piece and the mold is filled and quickly emptied. It is then allowed to dry for several hours so that the slip shrinks away from the mold. After bisque firing to 1080°C (1970°F), the bowl is fettled with wet and dry abrasive paper and then pierced. The final firing is to 1220°C (2230°F) with a two-hour soak. On cooling, it is burnished to a semi-matt sheen. Bone china is very fragile in the raw state, but extremely strong after final firing.

Deep and shallow agateware bowls

Marion Gaunce, UK
Height approx: 8 in (20 cm)

Most of Marian Gaunce's bowls and dishes have been made in three-piece molds, so that each section is supported before they are joined together. Great skill is needed in making and joining in order to retain the balance and continuity of the design. The potter's interest in fabric and patchwork is evident in the decoration of the bowls, and particularly in the rhythm and asymmetry of the shallow bowl. This influence is also apparent in the way in which the edges are finished — an essential factor of all her ceramic designs (see page 80).

3
RAW MATERIALS, PIGMENTS AND GLAZES

Color is an integral part of the appeal of pottery. Clay, of course, possesses its own attractive colors; as far as the natural clays are concerned, the color range varies widely from pure white through to carbon black, though the earth colors naturally predominate. In addition, it is not only possible, but sometimes desirable, for a potter to alter the color of a clay body. This can be done by a variety of processes, all of which are essential elements of any potter's technical skill.

The simplest method involves adding the appropriate coloring oxide — or compound of the oxide — to the clay. Such oxides come in powder form and can be mixed with the dry body formula before water is added. Similarly, clay bodies can be stained before they are fired. As with the oxides, there is a wide range of staining formulae available; they can be either mixed and used directly on clay bodies — though some stains are more complex to prepare than others — or mixed in with clay and then applied. The final color is governed by the particular oxide — or combination of oxides — being used, the nature of the stain compound itself, the firing technique selected — this can be either oxidaton or reduction — and the type of glaze used, assuming that the potter decides to apply one.

A typical black stain, for instance, consists of 54 per cent chrome oxide, 26 per cent red iron oxide, 15 per cent

manganese dioxide and 5 per cent cobalt oxide. The ingredients should be mixed, calcined and then finely ground for as long as necessary. This last point is vital, since most stains will not produce true colors unless they are ground finely. After mixing with water to the consistency of milk and straining, the stain is ready for application, either by spraying or brushing.

These procedures are fairly simple to accomplish with a little practice. Glazing, however, is the ultimate decorative technique and so can be one of the most complex procedures in the whole pottery process. Not only does the preparation of the glaze have to be more accurate, if results are to be predictable; the eventual quality of the final glaze depends as much on a clear understanding of the effects of firing as on the care of preparation.

Nevertheless, the subject is not as problematic as many beginners believe. Fundamentally, any glaze is a thin glass coating, fused to the clay's surface by the process of firing the body at high temperature. Silica is used as the glass-forming compound, to which flux and a refractory element are added. The former lowers the silica's melting point; the latter stabilizes the glaze, reduing its fluidity and making it more durable. This whole process is covered in more detail in this section. A wide range of commercially prepared glazes is available, but it can be both interesting and challenging to try to prepare your own.

Stoneware fired crackle glaze
Julia Colman, UK
Height approx: 12 in (30 cm)

Whenever the shrinkage of a glaze is greater than that of the body a crackle glaze will result. This is seen to advantage when the glaze is opaque or semi-opaque. After cooling, the surface of the pot is brushed with an oxide or stain to accentuate the pattern of the crazing. If a basic oxide is used the pot may be refired so that the oxide combines with the glaze and gives a softer pattern. This particular pot was fired to 1275°C (2330°F).

Recipe for crackle glaze

Soda felspar	80
(Kaolin)	10
Whiting	10

Raw materials

MOST RAW MATERIALS for use in glazes, clay bodies and stains for clay bodies come to the potter in the form of finely ground powders, some of which are indentifiable by their color. They originate from rocks or earth deposits, but the form in which they are mined varies greatly. There are still some areas of the world in which potters find their own deposits of raw materials and prepare them for use themselves. Depending on the cost of labor and machinery, this may prove to be cheaper or more expensive than importing or buying from an indigenous supplier.

CERAMIC CHEMISTRY DEFINITIONS

The following list of chemical definitions is designed to provide a basic understanding of the chemistry of ceramics in relation to raw materials and glazes. Even a limited understanding will prove useful when experimenting with glazes and pigments for coloring and decorating pottery.

Element: This is a substance which, as far as it is known, cannot be chemically broken down into simpler substances. There are few pure elements; most are combined with other elements or compounds.

Atom: The smallest particle of an element which can take part in a chemical change. It cannot exist on its own, but combines immediately to form molecules.

Molecule: The smallest part of an element which can exist in a free state. It is rarely found in its pure form, but diamond, being carbon, is the nearest to a pure element.

Chemical compound: The result of the chemical union of two or more elements.

Mixture: A mixture of elements, rather than a new compound. In a mixture a physical change occurs in the mixture and it may take on different properties, but it does not form a new substance or change weight. This may often be reversed, such as the freezing or melting of water.

Chemical change: This occurs when substances combine to make a new substance with new properties, appearance and weight.

Atomic weight: This represents the relative weight of one atom of hydrogen (being the lightest) compared with one atom of an element.

Bases and acids: In pottery the term basic means something which is not an acid. However, although all alkalis are bases, not all bases are alkalis. Bases in glazes are often referred to as fluxes.

Salts: Compounds formed by the combination of an acid oxide and a basic oxide (eg silica and lead).

Oxides: Elements combined with oxygen. Most ceramic raw materials consist of them — the basic oxides are metals and the acid oxides are non-metals.

A formula: The chemical composition of a glaze.

Recipe: The raw materials used in a glaze, and their quantities.

THE COMPOUNDS USED IN CERAMICS

Compounds	Formulae	Molecular Weight
Lead bisilicate	$PbO\ 2SiO_2$	343
Lead sesquisilicate	$2PbO\ 3SiO_2$	626
China clay (kaolin) or plastic clay	$Al_2O_3\ 2SiO_2\ 2H_2O$	258
Felspar (soda)	$Na_2O\ Al_2O_3\ 6SiO_2$	524
Felspar (potash)	$K_2O_2\ Al_2O_3\ 6SiO_2$	556
Felspar (lime)	$CaO\ Al_2O_3\ 2SiO_2$	278
Nepheline syenite	$2(Na_2OK_2O)\ 4Al_2O_3\ 9SiO_2$	1130 1220
China stone (purple) (variable)	$0.012\ MgO$ $0.157\ CaO\ Al_2O_3\ 6.82SiO_2$ $0.340\ K_2O$ $0.244\ Na_2O$	569
China stone (white) (variable)	$0.048\ MgO$ $0.204\ CaO\ Al_2O_3\ 7.5\ SiO_2$ $0.280\ K_2O$ $0.040\ Na_2O$	594
Bentonite	$Al_2O_3\ 4SiO_2\ 9H_2O$	364.4
Petalite	$Li_2O\ Al_2O_3\ 8SiO_2$	612.6

Grogs are usually categorized according to the grain size or the sieve mesh they will pass through. The smaller the number of the mesh, the larger the aperture size. Therefore grogs described as 40s to 60s are those which will pass through a 40 mesh sieve, but not a 60 mesh. The addition of grog to a clay body will reduce its shrinkage. This is because grog has already been fired and the shrinkage has therefore already occurred. It also reduces warping in the making of tiles and is useful for helping a clay body to dry evenly. When making large modelled, sculptured or hand-built forms, grog is nearly always added to the clay. The practice is to add a grog which is more refractory, or has already been fired to a higher temperature, than the clay it is being mixed with. The quantities added will range from 10-30 per cent to d: clay weight, depending on the clay body and its physical properties, as well as what it is being used for. Clays will need thorough testing when the grog has been added, in particular to discover their firing qualities.

1. 30s to dust molochite
2. Silversand (silica sand)
3. 85s to dust molochite
4. Waterground molochite
5. 20s - 30s grog
6. 20s - 30s molochite
7. 30s to dust grog
8. 30s - 85s molochite
9. ⅜ in - ⅛ in (0.4 cm - 0.1 cm) grog
10. ⅜ in - ⅛ in (0.4 cm - 0.1 cm) white grog
11. 12s to 20s molochite
12. 10s - 20s grog

Lithium carbonate	Li_2CO_3	73.8
Borax	$Na_2B_4O_7\ 10H_2O$	381.2
Boracite	$6MgO\ MgCl_2\ 8B_2O_3$	893.9
Colemanite	$2CaO\ 3B_2O_3\ 5H_2O$	411.0
Talc	$3MgO\ 4SiO_2\ H_2O$	304
Magnesium carbonate	$MgCO_3$	84.3
Magnesium sulphate	$MgSO_4\ 7H_2O$	138.4
Plaster of paris	$2CaSO_4\ H_2O$	290.4
Wollastonite	$CaOSiO_3$	116.2
Calcium carbonate (whiting)	$CaCO_3$	100
Bone ash (Calcium phosphate)	$Ca_3(PO_4)_2$	310.3
Calcium sulphate	$CaSO_4$	136.2
Fluorspar (Calcium flouride)	CaF_2	78.1
Barium carbonate	$BaCO_3$	197.3
Dolomite	$CaMg(CO_3)_2$	184.4
Cryolite	Na_3AlF_6	210.0
Alumina	Al_2O_3	102.0
Bauxite	$Al_2O_3\ 2H_2O$	138.0
Flint	SiO_2	60.1
Antimony oxide	Sb_2O_3	291.6
Potassium carbonate (pearl ash)	K_2CO_3	138.2
Sillimanite	$Al_2O_3\ SiO_2$	162.1
Sodium carbonate (soda ash)	Na_2CO_3	106.0
Sodium silicate (waterglass)	Na_2SiO_3	122.2
Sodium bicarbonate	$Na_2CO_3\ 10H_2O$	286.0

THE ELEMENTS USED IN CERAMICS

Element	Symbol	Atomic Wt. approx. H = 1	Melting Point, °C	Melting Point, °F
Aluminium	Al	27	660	1220
Antimony	Sb	120	630	1166
Barium	Ba	137.4	704	1299
Bismuth	Bi	208	269	516
Boron	B	11	2250	4082
Cadmium	Cd	112.4	321	609
Calcium	Ca	40	852	1566
Carbon	C	12	volatilizes above 3000	volatilizes above 5432
Chlorine	Cl	35.5	−103	−217
Chromium	Cr	52	1831	3328
Cobalt	Co	59	1492	2718
Copper	Cu	63.6	1084	1983
Fluorine	F	19	−224	−435
Gold	Au	197	1063	1945
Hydrogen	H	1	−257	−495
Iron	Fe	56	1526	2779
Lead	Pb	207	327	621
Lithium	Li	6.9	186	367
Magnesium	Mg	24.3	649	1200
Manganese	Mn	55	1242	2268
Nickel	Ni	58.7	1455	2651
Nitrogen	N	14	−210	−410
Oxygen	O	16	−219	−426
Phosphorous	P	31	44	111
Potassium	K	39	64	147
Silicon	Si	28.3	1415	2579
Silver	Ag	108	960	1760
Sodium	Na	23	98	208
Strontium	Sr	87.6	772	1422
Sulphur	S	32	116	241
Tin	Sn	119	232	450
Titanium	Ti	48	1798	3268
Zinc	Zn	65.4	419	786
Zirconium	Zr	90.6	1856	3373
Vanadium	V	51	690	1270
Selenium	Se	79	217	423

RAW MATERIALS IN COMMON USE

The following list of raw materials is for easy reference and only includes the ones in common use.

Plastic and ball clays

These contain mainly silica and alumina, together with trace elements of other minerals and a proportion of a flux or fluxes to give adhesion when firing . The following is an analysis of a plastic pink firing clay (a mixture of red and white) and a ball clay.

Pink clay

Silica	64.92
Alumina	22.66
Iron oxide	2.92
Lime	0.21
Potash	1.33
Soda	0.15
Loss on ignition	8.89

Ball clay

Silica	48.8
Alumina	33.6
Ferric oxide	2.5
Lime	1.2
Potash	1.7
Soda	0.8
Magnesium oxide	0.6
Titanium oxide	1.4
Loss on ignition	9.4

The lime, potash, soda and iron oxide all act as fluxes to the clay body and combine with an applied glaze. The ball clays generally have a lower silica content (average 55 per cent) than the pink clay.

Plastic clay is used for glazes in which the pot is glazed in the unfired clay state without the intervening bisque firing. Ts is called raw glazing. The plastic clay in the glaze allows it to shrink at the same rate as the unfired clay, be it tile, vessel or figure. Depending on the color, plastic clays can also be used for making slips for slip trailing (using 50 per cent ball clay and 50 per cent china clay). They can also be used in stoneware glazes where they make up at least 40 per cent of the total glaze and give varying effects, according to the composition and the minerals present. Although they are plastic clays, this does not exclude their use on bisque fired pots, when used as a percentage of a glaze.

China clay or kaolin

This primary clay is pure, white and has little plasticity. It is composed of 46 per cent silica, 40 per cent alumina and 14 per cent water.

China clay is used in the composition of prepared bodies to give whiteness to earthenware, stoneware, porcelain and bone china and to control vitrification. It is also used in earthenware bodies to reduce their drying shrinkage. This is due to the fact that they contain ball clays, which in themselves have a high shrinkage — the china clay therefore counteracts the ball clay. In a glaze, it provides the alumina and silica and, when used in excess, it acts as a matting agent

Cornwall stone

This is crushed rock which is not a single mineral like china clay or quartz, but is composed of felspar, quartz kaolinite, mica and fluospar. It is sometimes used as a substitute for felspar as it contains several fluxes, such as soda, potash, magnesia and calcium. It is also used to give whiteness to bodies as it is almost free of iron, and it is used in both high and low-firing glazes.

Cornwall stone can be used as a hardening agent when mixed with basic oxides, such as manganese or cobalt, for painting or silk screen underglaze printing. Because it varies so much it does not have a standard chemical formula, but a generalized formula for Cornwall stone might have the following analysis:

Silica	72.00
Titanium oxide	0.02
Alumina	14.95
Iron oxide	0.05
Soda	4.13
Potash	3.83
Calcium	2.08
Magnesium	0.09
Calcium floride	1.07
Loss on ignition	0.86

Felspar

The felspars are a group of minerals which come from crushed rocks and they can supply upto 25 per cent of the fluxes in a body, and varying proportions in a glaze. There are at least twelve types — the three most common being: potash felspar (or orthoclase), soda felspar (albite) and the lime felspar (anorthite). Each of these contains alumina, silica and a flux, but in varying proportions. These form the main constituents of many stoneware glazes.

A felspar has all the necessary ingredients for forming glaze at a high temperature, but to be satisfactory it needs the addition of further flint, and whiting or kaolin. Felspar glazes tend to have a milky quality, due to very fine bubbles in the body of the glaze.

When experimenting with glaze it is a good idea to test the different qualities of each of the above felspars when they are used separately. A potash felspar may have the following composition:

Potash	16.9 or 14.02
Alumina	18.3 or 18.57
Silica	64.8 or 64.24
Soda	1.25
Calcium	.34

Nepheline syenite

This mineral is similar to felspar, being part of the felspar family. The most widely used is a Norwegian or American product.

The advantage of using it in glazes is that it contains more of the alkaline flux and less silica than the felspars or china stone. It can be used in both earthenware and stoneware glazes, working well with an alkaline frit. The Norwegian nepheline syenite has the following analysis:

Silica	56.5
Alumina	24.8
Iron	0.08
Calcium	0.80
Magnesium (trace)	
Potash	9.2
Soda	7.9
Loss on ignition	0.7

Because of its flux content and lack of impurities it is considered a good constituent for vitreous earthenware bodies.

Petalite (Lithium felspar)

This is the most commonly used of the alkaline lithia compounds. It is used in both glazes and bodies. Its increasing use has been for domestic and flame-proof ware because of its low expansion.

Other members of the petalite family, spodumene and lepidolite, are not used for their flux contribution either because they are scarce or too expensive to prepare economically.

Silica (flint or quartz)

Silica, the glass-forming material of glaze, occurs naturally as sand and flint. The flint form is a source of silica favored by potters and it is prepared from calcined flint stones which are ground to a fine powder. Silica is also available from silica sands, which can have up to 99.5 per cent silica content, the rest being made up of calcium carbonate or chrome. This supplies the acid ingredient to all glazes which, in combination with the flux, is balanced by the alumina. It is used in clay bodies to give whiteness, hardness and resistance to crazing. Flint adjustments to the glaze may be necessary to reduce crazing.

In earthenware bodies flint is used in preference to silica sand or quartz because of its easier cristobalite conversion at certain temperatures. However for stoneware a coarser grained sand or quartz is used.

Quartz is another form of silica rock which is 100 per cent pure. It is also found in the form of sand which can be used as a grog. It sometimes combines with other oxides and these are termed silicates. They include kaolin, China stone, felspar nepheline syenite, bentonite, lepidolite, petalite, spodumene and other less well- known minerals.

Alumina

Alumina or oxide of aluminium is not found in a pure state, but in chemical combination with other minerals. One of its purest forms is bauxite from which it is separated out by heating and is then processed with cryolite, one of the chief compounds used in the operation. The method employed is electrolysis, which requires a plentiful supply of water and electricty.

Its reaction in body and glaze is complex but it gives stability to the base and acid oxides present. By itself it will not melt until it reaches a temperature of 2000°C (Silica alone melts at 1700°C/3090°F). However, if 5 per cent alumina is added as an impurity to pure silica the fusing temperature drops to 1545°C/2800°F.

Besides being a refractory material, alumina increases the fusing point of a clay and makes the ceramic less likely to melt. When used alone, as a matting agent, it works well but does not stop the glaze flowing in its matt and mature state. It is also used as a fine sand in high firings and as a bed or support for bone china articles.

Dolomite (Magnesium carbonate)

This is a double carbonate of magnesium which is prepared from dolomitic limestone rocks. It can vary considerably in composition. The natural rock often contains impurities such as iron, felspar, clay, mica and quartz, giving it a range of color from off-white to red, and bluish-grey to black.

When added to stoneware glazes in small quantities it acts as a flux but when between 10 per cent and 25 per cent is added it gives a silky matt quality not unlike sugared almonds.

Whiting

Whiting is prepared by grinding chalk very finely then levigating the sand impurities out in the water. It originates from the shells of minute organisms. As an ingredient in earthenware bodies it has the advantage of giving whiteness and preventing warping.

Whiting is the source of calcium in glazes. By itself it is fairly refractory, but in combination with other ceramic materials such as felspar, it acts as a common flux for stoneware glazes which can contain up|to|23 per cent. Its fluxing qualities begin above a temperature of 1100°C (2012°F) and therefore it is unsuitable for adding to stoneware bodies because it would melt too quickly and produce the wrong reaction. Because of its high rate of contraction, whiting is also good for reducing crazes in glazes.

Whiting is added to earthenware glazes in small quantities, although it is only marginally a flux and is used when more than one base is required. It has a hardening effect on glazes and also increases their acid resistance. Combined with zinc in an earthenware lead bisilicate glaze it will form what is called a lime zinc matt surface, which could be due to crystallization.

Bentonite

Bentonite is a highly plastic mineral which is not strictly a clay although it has the same formula. It originated from decomposed volcanic rock and is notable for its ability to give greatly increased plasticity to a clay when up to 2 per cent is added. It will absorb a great deal of water, swelling up into a jelly-like substance. Another quality is its ability to

keep materials in suspension. This can be seen when 1 per cent is added to glazes, with the addition of a little calcium chloride in solution.

Colemanite

This is a mineral with very advantageous fluxes. However it must be used in small quantities due to the 27 per cent of water it contains in combination. This is rapidly released at the appropriate temperature and you may find that if too much is present in the glaze, most of it will end up on the kiln shelf rather than the pot, causing sudden shrinkage when the water is released.

Bone ash (Calcium phosphate)

Bone ash is prepared from calcined and ground cattle bones giving calcium and phosphorous pentoxide. The fluxing quality comes from the calcium; the phosphorous pentoxide is the glass-forming element which, at the same time, checks any rapid tendency to fuse. Its main use in England is in the preparation of bone china which contains some 50 per cent of bone ash. It is fused with china clay and china stone, forming one of the toughest and thinnest ceramic bodies. Its strength was illustrated admirably some years ago when a London bus was jacked up and lowered so that each wheel was resting on an inverted bone china teacup. The teacup took the strain!

It can also be used to assist opacity in certain glazes and reduce the amount of tin needed.

Talc

A mineral high in magnesium and therefore used both in glazes and bodies. In stoneware glazes it has a rather complex action which sometimes causes it to revert to a matt, opaque glaze on cooling, due to the formation of crystals.

It is also used to make stoneware bodies which are resistant to thermal shock, but they must contain as little free silica as possible. It should not be used arbitrarily, but only after careful research and testing has been done.

Borax

Borax is the name given to a crystalline mineral found in specific parts of the world which

contains boric oxide and soda. By itself it is soluble in water so that in order to introduce the boric oxide as a flux into glazes it is fritted with silica.

The boric oxide is seldom found alone but in combination with water, soda, calcium and magnesium. When heated borax decomposes into boric oxide, sodium metaborate and water.

Lead sesquisilicate

This is a low-solubility, coated lead frit, containing a higher proportion of lead to silica than lead bisilicate. This is achieved in the manufacturing by coating the finely ground frit grains with a very thin layer of silica in an impervious and insoluble form. Should any of the lead frit be ingested, the coating will protect it from the solvent action of the acidic liquids in the stomach, such as saliva and gastric juices, and so leave the lead frit non-toxic.

Lead sesquisilicate contains some 68.9 per cent lead, while lead bisilicate contains 63 per cent. Silica makes up the bulk of the rest. Lead sesquisilicate is the best lead frit to use when a rich lead reaction is wanted in a glaze. It is also good for combining with other bases, as shown in the section on glaze formulae.

Lead bisilicate

This is another low-solubility, coated lead frit, containing less lead than the sesquisilicate and more silica (34 per cent against 26 per cent in the sesqui). It also contains smaller quantities of other fluxes and alumina, which together make up the remaining 3 per cent of the frit. It makes a good stable lead glaze with the addition of some 10 per cent kaolin, felspar or nepheline syenite and it works well for an earthenware glaze firing between a temperature of 1080°C (1980°F) - 1150°C (2100°F), or lower.

Magnesium carbonate

This mineral is found in two forms — as magnesite, and in combination with calcium carbonate in the mineral dolomite. When it is used in a glaze as magnesite it decomposes at a temperature of around 350°C (660°F), forming magnesia and giving off carbon dioxide. The magnesia is a highly refractory mineral, acting as an opacifier up to a temperature of

1170°C (2140°F), after which it becomes an active flux. On cooling it may crystallize out to give an opaque matt glaze (see crystalline glazes, page 151).

In dolomite, both magnesia and calcium act as matting or fluxing agents, depending on the temperature of firing. They are also affected by the glaze composition and the type of dolomite. It is used extensively in stoneware glazes and in reduction firing reacts with different minerals in the body as well as reducing the small iron content of most stoneware bodies. It gives an attractive color and texture when used thickly in reduced stoneware glazes.

Wollastonite

This mineral contains both calcium and silica, although using it is more expensive than using calcium carbonate and silica separately. When used in glazes it forms crystals during cooling to give opacity and a matt quality to the glaze.

Frits

When certain forms of lead, soda or potash have a low melting point or are soluble in water, they are made stable by melting with silica and small quantities of other minerals to form what is called a frit. In the molten state it is run off into water when it shatters and is then more easily ground to a fine powder for using as the main source of flux in glazes.

Frits are seldom used in their pure state, as they need the addition of alumina. This can be supplied, along with silica, in the form of china clay or a similar compound, to strike a balance in the glaze. There are many excellent frits produced by manufacturers based on lead, soda and borax, and these are the basis of the glazes used by most production potteries concentrating on earthenware. Calcium borax frits are also used in stoneware recipes (see list of suppliers).

SAFETY

Many chemicals contain toxins or form poisons when mixed so an awareness of their composition and properties is important. When mixing glazes wear a mask and gloves in case poisons are absorbed through your skin.

Pigments and stains

THE COLORING PIGMENTS for use in ceramics are all derived from metals, and are the same as those which colour our natural rocks and stones. Most metals are first mined in the form of ores, but they are not suitable for use in ceramics in this state. They are seldom pure and are usually physically or chemically combined with other metals. They are therefore separated by the industrial methods of smelting, grinding, precipitation and electrolysis. The metal used in ceramics for coloring is not always the pure oxide of the metal, but a dioxide, carbonate or sulphate, which can affect the intensity of the final result. The color produced by a pigment is governed by the temperature of firing, the other materials present and the quantity of pigment used.

When used for coloring glazes or bodies, oxides need to be extremely finely ground to give even color and good dispersion. Some oxides melt and disperse more easily in glazes than others —a factor affected by the chemical composition of the glaze. Almost all metal oxides are stable up to 1040°C-1060°C (1900-1940°F) when used in an earthenware glaze or body, but from a temperature of 1100°C

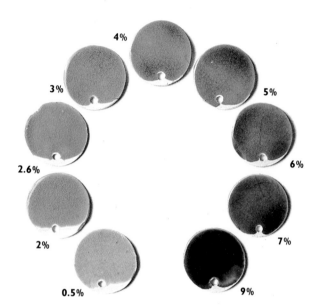

	4%	
3%		5%
2.6%		6%
2%		7%
0.5%		9%

Alkaline glaze	Lead-based glaze

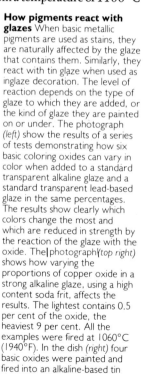

1
2
3
4
5
6

How pigments react with glazes When basic metallic pigments are used as stains, they are naturally affected by the glaze that contains them. Similarly, they react with tin glaze when used as inglaze decoration. The level of reaction depends on the type of glaze to which they are added, or the kind of glaze they are painted on or under. The photograph (left) show the results of a series of tests demonstrating how six basic coloring oxides can vary in color when added to a standard transparent alkaline glaze and a standard transparent lead-based glaze in the same percentages. The results show clearly which colors change the most and which are reduced in strength by the reaction of the glaze with the oxide. The photograph (top right) shows how varying the proportions of copper oxide in a strong alkaline glaze, using a high content soda frit, affects the results. The lightest contains 0.5 per cent of the oxide, the heaviest 9 per cent. All the examples were fired at 1060°C (1940°F). In the dish (right) four basic oxides were painted and fired into an alkaline-based tin glaze. The choice of glaze gives the copper a brighter blue-green quality and the manganese a deeper purple hue. The tin content stabilized the color.

1. Copper
2. Cobalt
3. Manganese
4. Yellow stain
5. Chrome
6. Iron

Iron oxide gives a reddish brown reaction in a strong lead based glaze

Manganese oxide gives a purple reaction in an alkaline based glaze.

Copper oxide will give a sharper green when used in a lead based glaze.

Cobalt oxide is little affected by the type of glaze.

Underglaze colors and crayons The photograph *(right)* shows the range of some of the underglaze colors available for painting onto bisqueware. The colors have been stabilized, so that they will not soften and fuse with the glaze when fired. They can be used for inglaze painting on transparent or tin glaze, but they should be mixed with a little flux (frit) or base glaze. They are not suitable for use under an opaque tin glaze, since many contain chrome oxide. This can react with the tin oxide to produce unwanted pink areas. The tiles *(near right)* show how under-glazed crayons and pencils can be used, their subtle colours being ideally suited to delicate design work.

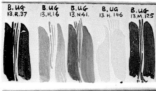
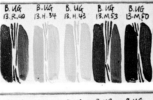

Samples of stained porcelain *(above)* These samples can be used as a reference library when making up bodies for agateware. Color and clay are mixed together dry, made into a slip and dried until they are plastic. The stain content ranges from one to 10 per cent.

In the illustration *(right)*, the stripes were printed by silk screen directly onto the surface of the tile. When dry, they were spray-glazed with transparent colored glazes For screening, an oil-based medium was mixed with the powder pigment. Here, stablized colors were used, but basic metallic oxides, dry-mixed with about 10 to 20 per cent of china stone and sieved through a 100 mesh, are also satisfactory. They give an attractive, but variable, result when glazed and fired.

Blue stripes. Pigment made from 80 % cobalt oxide and 20% China stone finely ball milled.

Printed with a bought yellow inglaze pigment. All are mixed with silk screen printing oil.

Printed with a green inglaze bought color and, as with others, printed onto the bisque surface before glazing.

Using a pink inglaze pigment. All the inglaze pigments are stabilized for remaining inert.

Printed with a grey inglaze pigment.

Printed with a brown inglaze pigment.

Brown green glaze   **Burnt Sienna glaze**   **Pale brown glaze**

(2010°F) some begin to volatalize and fire away.

As coloring oxides vary in intensity, limited tests should be carried out before using them on a finished article. The percentage of oxide to a body or glaze will vary from 0.5 per cent to 10 per cent; it will seldom be higher. With cobalt you can achieve a positive blue in a glaze with an addition of 0.1 per cent or less. With most oxides, (which vary in color in their raw state) the color does not become apparent in the firing until they react with the fluxes and silicates in the clay body or the glaze.

The metal oxides you choose to give color in the decoration, body-staining or glaze coloring of pots will depend on several factors — the function of the article, the desired effect of the design and possibly health restrictions governing the use of certain metallic compounds. Coloring pigments can therefore be divided into two categories — those prepared for a specific use or technique and those which can fulfill more than one function, being both decorative and utilitarian.

There are many less common coloring pigments which can be tried, but few give the positive color results of those listed below.

Various form of the listed colors are available but if the dioxide, chloride or sulphate of the metal is used, more will be needed in the mix than if the pure oxide is used as it is not as intense.

Basic coloring oxides

These are commonly used in their prepared or processed form in ceramics for coloring glazes, and occasionally for staining clay bodies. They are seldom available in their pure state, but for anyone who has time to acquire and prepare them, the natural basic oxides can produce some interesting effects. Experimenting can be done using the ore, or rock, with such minerals as cobalite, manganese, iron deposits and other natural minerals. The easily available coloring oxides or their salts are: iron, manganese dioxide, zirconium, cobalt, copper, tin, vanadium pentoxide, nickel, chrome and titanium dioxide. However, of these, only iron, manganese and cobalt are suitable for body staining. Those oxides needing special preparation and firing are: gold, silver, platinum, selenium/cadmium, chrome/tin. These are used as decorative and onglaze colors.

The list of coloring pigments shown below gives the range of percentages of stain added to a glaze or body to produce a particular coloring.

Clay body stains

There are times when the potter may wish to alter the color of the clay body or slip and this can be done with the addition of coloring oxides. As stability, permanance and consistency are required when coloring bodies, the stains must be specially prepared. It is best to buy them ready-prepared from a manufacturer who will supply you with a list of the body stains available.

The process of preparation is called stabilizing, or modifying. The coloring oxide (or oxides) is mixed with a stabilizer, such as zinc oxide, tin oxide, zirconium silicate or titanium dioxide. Lead oxide, lead basilicate or a combination of fritted lead and boron compounds with silica can be added to act as a flux. These components are all fired to a specific temperature which is governed by the color required. This is called calcining and results in the stabilization of the mixture before it is water-ground to a fine powder. In some circumstances the color is calcined more than once.

When preparing a stained body, the ingredients should

BASIC COLORING OXIDES

The following list of coloring pigments shows the range of percentages of stain added to a glaze or body to produce a particular coloring.

Iron oxide (0.5 - 10 per cent) When added to certain earthenware glazes, this will give a pale straw yellow to a rich rust red color. In stoneware glazes it produces colors ranging from pale celadon green to intense black, depending on whether it has undergone an oxidized or reduced firing. It can also be used for clay bodies and slips, giving a color range from pale cane to red.

Manganese dioxide (0.5 - 8 per cent) As an addition to eartherware or stoneware glazes it will give effects ranging from pink to bright purple, brown and black.

Copper oxide (0.5 - 5 per cent) An addition of copper produces greens, turquoise, blue and copper reds in a stoneware glaze but the color is very dependent on the composition of the glaze. When added to low lead solubility glazes, copper becomes unstable and unsuitable for use in domestic ware.

Nickel oxide (1 - 3 per cent) This produces a color range from grey to greenish black, depending on the type of glaze. It is best used in small quantities to modify or darken colors obtained from other oxides.

Chromium oxide (0.1 - 5 per cent) This oxide will give a range from sharp acid green to dark green or pink, depending on the type of glaze and the other materials present. If the smallest trace of tin is added, it will produce a pink flush and will become unstable, so use it with caution.

Cobalt (0.1 - 2 per cent) This produces a range of blues when added to most glazes. An increase in temperature will intensify the color.

Vanadium (2 - 10 per cent) Gives a yellow or orange coloring to most glazes, but in a hard glaze it tends to become dry and opaque.

Antimony (2 - 8 per cent) When lead is present it produces a range of yellows, but handle with care as it is a toxic color and can be dangerous to use.

first be mixed in a dry state, and a mask must be worn for protection against dust. Water is then added and the mixture stirred well and sieved through a 100-mesh sieve. Small quantities can be mixed in a ball mill.

Underglaze colors
These are also stabilized colors which are mixed with a medium or gum and painted or printed onto a bisque surface. The medium gives cohesion to the color and prevents smudging when handling. The ware is then hardened by firing to burn away the medium, so that it does not rupture the glaze in the subsequent glaze firing.

Underglaze pencils and crayons are now widely used, and, if not purchased from a manufacturer, can be made from plaster of paris, water and pigment and cast into soft clay in the shape of crayons. Another method is to mix the colors with kaolin and water and extrude as a pencil, then fire to the desired hardness for drawing on the biscuit. The color is applied as with a normal crayon, on to the bisque ware before glazing and firing.

Most stabilized colors contain just sufficient flux to adhere to the ware at the correct temperature of the glaze firing. More flux can be added to an underglaze color if you wish, so that it can be used as in inglaze pigment. Inglazing is when liquid colors are painted onto the glazed pot before firing. If color is applied by hand or printing to a once-fired glaze surface, and is then refired until it sinks in and combines with the glaze, it is called inglaze decorating (see page 151).

Enamel colors
These are the lowest firing colors, applied by painting, printing, stippling, ground-laying or spraying on to a once-fired glaze surface. The process may be repeated several times with decreasing temperatures to suit the lower firing colors, which will include the lusters or precious metal preparations, bought from a manufacturer. So that they will adhere to the glaze they contain a proportionately high percentage of flux and are fired at a temperature between 700°C (1290°F) and 850°C (1560°F).

If the colors are to be painted onto the ware they are first ground on a tile, glass palette or glazed porcelain slab and mixed with fat, oil of turps and pure liquid turps. A little lavender oil and aniseed or poppy oil is often used to give the desired quality of fluidity to the color and to control the rate of drying. The color fuses onto the surface of the glaze, but does not penetrate.

Silk screen colors
Silk screening may be carried out either on the bisque article, or on a once-fired glaze. Depending on the result required you can use basic oxides, underglaze colors or enamel colors. For screening, a special medium is needed and coarseness, or fineness, of screen mesh will greatly affect the result (see silk screen printing, page 162).

Opacifiers
The inclusion of oxides, such as tin or zirconium, in a transparent glaze will make it opaque and white when fired, and will sometimes modify the surface texture of the glaze. Opacifiers combined with stains produce a wide range of glaze colors. The degree of opacity depends on the type and amount used, as well as the type of glaze. Commercial opacifiers are available, but the following are the most common metallic oxides which act as opacifiers.

OPACIFIERS

Tin oxide (2 - 10 per cent) This oxide produces the best quality white. When chrome is present it can give areas of pink to a tin glaze.

Zirconium oxide (6 - 15 per cent) This gives a milkier white which is not as intense as the tin colourant and therefore needs more additions. It is supplied under various trade names and comes in varying degrees of intensity.

Titanium dioxide (5-15 per cent) In its pure state, titanium produces a creamy white color, but if the impure form (called Rutile) is used, it gives a pale brown to fawn color. It is widely used in crystalline glazes.

SAFETY

Before making glazes and mixing stains it is essential that you familiarize yourself with any possible toxic ingredients. Always use a mask and wear gloves when mixing alkaline ingredients. Make sure that the area in which you are working is adequately ventilated.

OXIDES

Mined metallic oxides and scientifically prepared stains or enamels can be used to give color to ceramics. They will vary in strength and stability depending on whether they are an oxide or a salt of a metal.

Thrown porcelain vase
Lucy Rie, UK
Height: 10 in (2.5 cm)

Practically all basic coloring oxides are fluxes, which explains why they melt and disperse into glazes to resemble colored glass. If basic oxides are applied thinly, either mixed or singly, to a clay surface and fired, they will combine and react with the silica and alumina and form silicates and aluminates. If cobalt, which is a black metal when raw, is brushed onto a white porcelain body and fired to 1300°C (2370°F) it will give an intense blue although there is no glaze present. This is because of its reaction with the glass-forming silica and the presence of alumina in the body. If, however, an oxide or oxides are applied very thickly a proportion will react with the body but the rest will, in time, begin to melt and flow down the surface of the pot. For this vase a mixture of two oxides, copper and manganese, together with some gum arabic, was painted onto the unfired porcelain. Lines have been scratched through the clay and the pot was then fired to 1250 -1260°C (2280-2300°F). At this temperature the thick areas of pigment begin to flow, the surface being oversaturated with oxides. The use of oxides in the clay body, on the surface and in the glaze is a feature of much of Lucy Rie's pottery.

Underglaze pencil and crayon decoration (below)
Ann Clark, UK
Height: mug 4 in (10 cm)
beaker 5½ in (14 cm)

Ceramic pencils and crayons make it possible to draw illustrations and lettering on bisque ware with freedom and precision. These are being used increasingly in ceramic sculpture for adding areas of textured colour. The pieces show the use of line, area and detail with both pencils and crayons. The prepared stains are mixed with a vehicle or stiffener until they will stand the pressure of use.

Egyptian paste bottle (above)
Dick Studley, USA
Height: 16 in (41 cm)

Stabilized stains are used to color clay. If the basic oxides of copper manganese and cobalt are used the effect is much softer. It is only in recent years that manufacturers have been able to increase the firing temperatures of reds to as high as a stoneware firing.

Raku dish
David Miller, UK
Diameter: 12 in (30 cm)

A spontaneously thrown shallow dish with freely incised lines and a dented edge. The clay was highly grogged with the addition of talc to improve its tensile strength. After bisque firing to 980°C (1795°F) it was given a thin coating of copper slip and rapidly fired to 1000°C (1830°F). When removed from the kiln it was subjected to reducing and smoking in a metal container with combustible materials. This example of a pink copper metallic surface illustrates just how diverse the colors from a metal such as copper can be, depending upon the materials it is fired with or the techniques of firing.

Glazes

A GLAZE is a special kind of glass which is chemically formulated to adhere to the surface of the clay, or fuse into the body, when fired. Most functional pots are glazed to make them water-resistant, durable and easy to clean. Glaze can be highly colored or opaque and when used for decoration it is very effective.

The three essential ingredients of a glaze are silica, the glass-forming element, flux,which aids the melting of the glaze, and alumina which gives stability. The other ceramic compounds commonly used in glazes and bodies are a mixture of minerals, oxides, and chemical compounds. Most of them come in the form of finely ground powder, identifiable by color. These raw materials originate from rocks or earth deposits, but their composition varies greatly. There are still areas of the world where potters find their own deposits of raw materials and prepare them for use in glaze or clays. Because of the cost of labor and machinery the economics of this will vary from country to country, so check what it costs to import, or buy from an indigenous supplier.

Once you have understood how raw materials behave in glazes and in combination when firing, it is easier to formulate and develop glazes yourself. Many potters become complete absorbed in the chemistry of the subject and pursue specific and particular aspects, producing glazes of individuality and giving their products added character.

For beginners and those not contemplating ceramics as a full or part-time career, there is no immediate need to get deeply involved with the business of glaze chemistry and experiment. For such potters, the main interest will be in making, and then plenty of variety can be achieved by using a few good glaze fits or standard glazes to which coloring oxides or opacifiers can be added. With most earthenware frits the addition of between 10-20 per cent of china clay gives a good transparent glaze and 8 per cent of tin oxide or 12 - 15 per cent zircon opacifier gives a good white to fire at 1060°C (1940°F).

Ceramic materials which are poisonous or injurious to health are listed on page 198. These should be treated with great care at all times, especially if they are being used by those beginning to experiment with glazes. Most glazes are supplied in powder form and as the dust can be injurious to health, always wear a mask when handling powdered glaze. You should also make sure that working areas are vacuumed and wiped down regularly to reduce the presence of fine dust.

The composition of glaze

In the composition of glazes, differences can be brought about by using different raw materials. By knowing what different raw materials contribute to a glaze, roughly how much of each oxide they contain and approximately how much of each is needed to give a satisfactory glaze, you can

Flux	Source	
Lead oxide	Litharge Galena (lead sulphide) Red lead White lead (lead carbonate) Lead monosilicate	Poisonous state
	Lead bisilicate Lead sesquisilicate	Safe fritted leads
	and lead frits from various manufacturers called low solubility frits	
Sodium oxide	Felspars China stone Nepheline syenite Borax Cryolite	Found in combination
	Sodium carbonate Sodium bicarbonate	
	Also in wood ash	
Potassium oxide	Felspar China stone Nepheline syenite	Found in chemical combination
	Potassium carbonate (pearl ash) Potassium nitrate	
Calcium oxide	Felspar Dolomite China stone Nepheline syenite Colemanite Calcium sulphate Wollastonite Bone ash (calcium phosphate) Fluorspar	Found in combination
	Calcium carbonate (marble, chalk, limestone)	
Magnesium oxide	Dolomite Talc Boracite China stone	Found in combination
	Magnesium carbonate	
Barium oxide	Barium sulphate (barytes) Barium carbonate	
Boric oxide	Colemanite Borax Boracite	Found in combination
	Boric acid	
Lithium oxide	Lithium carbonate Petalite	Found in combination
Zinc oxide	Zinc oxide	

The chart here gives a list of fluxes and the various forms of raw materials that contain them. In most cases, they are just one of several elements making up a particular compound. Because lead, in the forms of litharge, galena, lead carbonate and lead monosilicate can be poisonous if ingested, low solubility lead frits should be used instead.

in time see at a glance if a glaze is likely to work by looking at the formula and the recipe.

A formula is a method of showing the mineral or chemical composition of a glaze, using chemical symbols for each mineral. This is then translated into specific ceramic minerals which will be used in the composition of the glaze.

Glaze is a combination of one or more basic oxides (fluxes), an acid oxide, and a neutral oxide (alumina) to balance them. The basic ingredients of any glaze are: silica, fluxes (basic oxides), substances which give body to the glaze, such as felspar and clay, refractory components which give strength and hardness, and frits for fluxing and coloring. In addition, opacifiers will give opacity to a transparent glaze and stains and metallic oxides will provide color.

The flux, or base, of the glaze is the essential ingredient and it influences the color and texture as well as the temperature at which the glaze melts. It also acts as a solvent for the silica when the various components become chemically active in the heat of the kiln. When looking at any formula, the flux is the first component to be mentioned. Alumina, which is present in all glazes, is theoretically a base oxide, but in glazes it is termed neutral, because it has a balancing effect between the acid and base. In a glaze it can be stated as the amount of clay used. It is also called an amphoteric, meaning that it can act as acid and base. In a glaze formula bases are always shown as a total of one, how ever many are used, as in the following formula:

Base or flux	Neutral	Acid
0.6 PbO	0.3 Al_2O_3	2.5 SiO_2
Total I 0.2 K_2O		
0.2 K_2O		

The common basic oxides used in the composition of glazes are: lead, sodium, potassium, calcium, zinc, lithium, barium, magnesium, but there are other less important ones.

The acid oxides are: silica, introduced into the glaze as flint, sand, quartz, felspar, kaolin or china stone, and boric oxide, introduced as borax (fritted soda and oxide) or crystal boric acid.

It is important to realize, when making up a glaze, that the proportion of acid to base and acid to neutral must be correct and within a certain limit. This is stated as a ratio of one to the other, for example one equivalent of base to two to four equivalents of acid (eg 1 to 2-4).

For soft glazes From 1 of base to between 2 - 3 of acid.
For hard glazes From 1 of base to between 3 - 4 of acid. Proportion between neutral (alumina) and acid (silica) is alumina 1/5th - 1/10th of acid. The acid must still remain in correct proportion with the base.

The reaction of the glaze will depend on several factors — the number of bases used, the type of base, the amount of alumina, the presence of boric oxide in addition to silica, the proportion of base to acid and the temperature and atmosphere of the firing. The amount, as well as the type, of base used will effect the fusing point (the point at which the glaze matures). The choice of base is also important and, while some glazes have only one, it is more satisfactory to use several. A simple glaze formula, and how it is translated into actual weights and percentages of raw materials, is shown in the earthenware glaze below, which uses three bases. It is called a lead, lime and potash glaze.

Bases	Neutral	Acid
0.6 PbO		
Total I 0.2 CaO	0.3 Al_2O_3	2.5 SiO_2
0.2 K_2O		

This glaze should be fired at a temperature between 1060 - 1100°C (1940 - 2010°F).

The same principle applies to stoneware glazes, while observing the limits of proportions between bases and acid, and acid and neutral.

Care must be taken to select the best raw material for a formula or you may have an excess of a particular oxide. This is why it is important to know your raw materials and be familiar with the list at the beginning. Should you wish to discover more about the chemistry of raw materials there are several good books listed in the index which would be of assitance, particularly Frank Hamer's *Dictionary of Materials and Techniques*.

Testing glazes

Although all glaze is glass, it does vary greatly according to its composition, and the results obtained may range from high gloss to opaque and from a clear, bright color to dense black. In order to understand these qualities you

The table here shows you how to calculate the percentage of raw materials needed for lead lime and potash glaze. Multiply the molecular parts by the molecular weight to obtain the number of parts by weight. Converting these to percentages gives the required amount of each ingredient.	PbO	CaO	K_2O	Al_2O_3	SiO_2	Raw Material	Mol. Pts.	Mol. Wt.	Pts. by Wt.	%
	.6				.9	Lead sesquisilicate	.6 x	313 =	187	52.6
		.2				Whiting	.2 x	100 =	20	31.1
			.2	.2	1.2	Felspar	.2 x	556 =	111.2	5.6
				.1	.2	China clay (kaolin)	.1 x	258 =	25.8	7.2
					.2	Flint	.2 x	60 =	12	3.3
	.6	.2	.2	.3	2.5	Total			356.0	99.8

GLAZED CERAMICS

The examples show how successfully glazes can be used to heighten the effect of the ware.

Thrown bone china and coloured glazes (above)
Kenneth Clark, UK
Diameter: 2.½ - 3 in (6 - 8 cm)

In one instance here, a clear earthenware glaze has been applied to accentuate the whiteness of the bone china. Other clear and semi-opaque colored earthenware glazes have taken on added luminosity during the firing process. All the pots were bisqued to 1240°C (2260°F) and the glazes were fired to 1060°C (1940°F). The bowls were heated in a kiln in order to hold and dry the glazes before they could run off the vitrified surface.

Blue stoneware form (right)
Alan Peascod, Australia
Height: 16 in (40 cm)

The rich blues of this pot were achieved by using a variety of slips which were based on the alkaline earths — barium, sodium and potassium. A number of coloring oxides were applied, often in soluble form, including iron cobalt and copper. The pot was thrown in stoneware clay and then force dried. The decoration is sgraffito, drawn though the layers of slip to reveal colors lying underneath. The pot was fired to 1240°C (2260°F) with a rapid two and a half hour cycle in a gas-fired kiln with a carefully controlled oxidized and reduced atmospheres. Like this pot, pieces are often force dried by electrolysis methods in which the clay is exposed to an alternating electric field. If the clay is dried quickly, it makes it much easier to apply slips by dipping. Before the stoneware firing, pots should be bisque fired to 1060 - 1100°C (1940 - 2010°F) in a reducing atmosphere.

Decorated tin glaze bowl (left)
Alan Caiger-Smith, UK
Diameter: 9 in (23 cm)

This example shows tin glazed painting at its best, the qualities having been improved because it has been wood fired. The body is a red North Devon clay from Fremington, England bisqued at 900°C (1652°F) and glaze fired at 1040°C - 1060°C (1904 -1940°F). The glaze is mainly lead frit based with a little borax, china stone, calcium and kaolin incorporated to aid suspension. Approximately 10 -11 per cent of tin has been added.

Decorated white glaze jar
(above)
Daphne Carnegie, UK
Height: 10 in (25 cm)

This jar has been glazed with an opaque white glaze. Basic oxides were used for decorating, but were mixed with a little of the basic glaze together with a red stain, and some extra glaze for the red spots. As with most decorated white glazed ware, an off-white body through to the red gives more life and depth to the glaze. In this instance, a buff, red mixture was used and the glaze firing temperature was to 1060°C (1940°F) after a 970°C (1780°F) bisque firing.

Earthenware pillow pitcher
(left)
Betty Woodman, USA
Length: 16 in (41 cm)

This pieces shows a vitality and exuberance in both the way the clay has been handled and in the glazing and decorating techniques. Similar methods were used in early Chinese ceramics, as well as by medieval potters. Green glaze or copper oxide has been freely applied to the yellow glaze. The darker accents are provided by manganese. The temperature of firing and the hardness of each glaze are vital factors when applying glazes in such a way.

MIXING A GLAZE

Purchased glazes usually come in powder form and merely require weighing out and mixing with water, before passing the mixture through a sieve.

Points to remember
● Wear a mask when mixing glazes as dust rises from the powder and this can be harmful.
● Once mixed, glazes can be stored in plastic containers with well-fitting lids.

1. The dry powder is weighed out, according to the recipe, and placed in a mixing bowl.

2. Water is added to the powder, just enough to cover it. The mixture is stirred and left to soak for 30 minutes. The surplus water is then poured off and the solution stirred again.

3. The mixture is sieved through a 100-mesh sieve.

4. You will have to help the glaze mixture through the sieve with a stiff rubber kidney or bristle brush, as it will not all flow through.

5. The final consistency of the glaze should be that of thick or thin cream, according to the thickness of glaze required and the method of applying it to the ware.

should carry out a series of tests along the following lines. The glazes are classified according to their firing temperature. If glazing bone china the practice is to use a clear earthenware glaze and fire between 1040 and 1060°C (1900 and 1940°F).

Tests for earthenware glazes

These six tests are for earthenware firing between 1060°C and 1080°C (1940°F - 1980°F).

1. Conduct a series of tests using a different main flux for each one (such as lead, soda and borax). Test the glaze on a piece of red biscuited ware, as well as on a white body. Observe the quality and appearance of the glaze, how it reacts with each clay and whether it fits or crazes.

2. Repeat each test in no. 1, adding increasing units of 10 (or 5 per cent) of kaolin or another matting agent. Observe the behavior of the glaze and the way in which the mattness increases.

3. Using the same glazes again, add higher percentages of an opacifier in units of two, starting with 2 per cent and going up to 10 per cent in the case of tin oxide. When using a zircon opacifier you can add up to 15 per cent.

4. In order to discover the effects of different basic oxides in a glaze, add as little as 0.5 per cent to each type of glaze and observe the intensity as you increase the amount in units of 0.5 per cent. Try using the oxides of cobalt, iron, manganese, copper, chrome, nickel, and vanadium.

When testing, always apply the glaze thinly first, and then thickly, onto each test piece. The results vary greatly, particularly when you get to the stoneware tests.

5. If time and cost permit, tests 3 and 4 can be combined, giving the result of lighter tones and opaque colors.

6. Using the same glazes as in 1 and 3, brush different strengths of basic oxides onto or under the glaze to show the variations, and to gauge the strength of application necessary to achieve the correct intensity of color.

Results

You will discover serveral important points when conducting these tests. For example, certain oxides, in particular quantities, tend to have an opacifying effect on the glaze. Some oxides cause bubbling in a glaze, due to the escape of gases at a crucial stage of the firing (this is particularly common with manganese) and on cooling will often leave small, sharp craters. If a colored glaze is subsequently refired at a lower enamel transfer firing, the color can change out of all recognition, but sometimes with attractive results. The turquoise blue of a copper alkaline mixture will become green as the amount of alumina is increased in the glaze.

Some glaze colors cannot be achieved with the use of basic oxides, so that prepared glaze stains must be used instead. Because of their composition, these tend to produce less transparent colors in a glaze and this applies to purples, yellows, pinks, grays and certain blues. Some colors are affected or contaminated by other minerals (two of these are chrome and copper) or salts which have been volatilized in previous firings and absorbed into the kiln walls or the kiln furniture and revaporized in subsequent firings.

If you require red to orange glazes, it is more satisfactory to buy these ready-prepared, and then by intermixing you can increase the color range as well as the reaction of the basic oxides applied as decoration.

You must accept that crazing or cracking may be the characteristic of a particular glaze and that to eliminate it may mean losing the quality of color in a glaze. However, remember that crazing is not good on eating and drinking vessels as it is unhygienic. For this reason many colored glazes will be used purely to create a decorative effect and cannot be used for utilitarian domestic ware.

Stoneware glazes

Because of the composition of stoneware glazes and the higher temperature at which they are fired, they have a very different character to earthenware glazes. They are seldom glossy, but tend to be slightly shiny, silky or matt. Their richest qualities are produced in the dark rusts to black range, achieved by reduction firing, which gives distinctive qualities not achieved by other methods.

A reduction firing is when the intake of air into the kiln is restricted so that the atmosphere around the pots has insufficient oxygen for full fuel combustion, as it would in an oxidize firing. Oxygen is then taken from the metallic oxides in the glaze and body, affecting the color of both. Those oxides most affected are copper and iron and, at earthenware temperatures, the salts of metals used in a luster firing. (For a fuller explanation of reduction firing, see page 183.)

The following tests should be carried out for stoneware glazes with a firing temperature between 1200-1300°C (2190°-2370°F).
1. In order to develop stoneware glazes, first test various transparent glazes, using a variety of bases for coloring, opacifying and mattness. These should be tested on a white body and an iron-bearing body. This procedure will also apply to any stoneware glazes being tested.
2. Using a felspathic-based glaze, make two sets of tests, starting with 0.5 per cent of iron oxide and adding units of 2 per cent, until 12 per cent is reached. Fire one set in an oxidizing atmosphere and the other in a reducing atmosphere. The results should show a marked contrast in the glaze and the body.
3. Repeat the second test, using dolomite, and observe the matt and crystalline effect as the quantities are increased.

There is much subtle variation between the stoneware glazes and, if you do not have facilities for reduction firings, you will have to exercise great care in selecting the particular ingredients for your glaze. A variety of texture, color and decorative effect can be achieved by using any one of the following raw materials in differing proportions. Try using wood ash, ball clay, red clay, tin, rutile, nickel, or ilmenite (as well as the basic oxides), in combination or singly. If a very glossy stoneware glaze is required it may be necessary to add up to 20 per cent of a soda or borax frit.

Porcelain glazes

The particular quality of a porcelain glaze is that both the body and the glaze mature and fuse together to give a tough translucent body. Translucency depends on the composition of the body and, while it is possible to obtain a wide range of colors and effects on porcelain, the desired effect is often to enhance the particular quality of the body by using a transparent glaze. The beauty and subtlety of incising the raw clay for decorative purposes is emphasized when the article is clear glazed.

The glaze for porcelain should reflect the fine quality of the ware and therefore it is usually thinner than a stoneware glaze which suits a more robust body. Delicate, pale, transparent colours are more suitable for a porcelain body, with its white translucency.

Glazes to test for porcelain could include those with small additions of coloring oxides, as well as matt and shiny glazes.

Opaque glazes

Certain oxides such as tin, titanium or zircon act as opacifiers when added to glazes. Some degree of opacity is also produced when very fine bubbles are trapped or given off in the glaze. This can happen when it is underfired or at the maturing temperature of the glaze.

Some other oxides will tend to cloud a glaze and reduce its transparency. For example bone ash in an earthenware glaze can assist opacity. The addition of at least 8 per cent opacifier is needed to make a glaze fully opaque.

Functional or decorative glazes

For utilitarian domestic ware, glazes need to be hard and craze-free, otherwise they stain easily as the surface wears and are not hygienic to use.

As a general rule, glossy glazes are softer than matt glazes, provided that the mattness is not due to under firing. Hardness can be achieved by the addition of lime, china stone, kaolin or dolomite to the glaze and by

Blossom jar — 'Shipley winter blue mountains'
Peter Rushforth, Australia
Height: 12 in (30 cm)

The jar is made with a natural clay body fired to stoneware temperature (1280°C/2340°F). The glaze is a heavily reduced chun glaze over a basalt glaze with wax-resist decoration. The extremely attractive quality of blue is unusual for stoneware; it is produced by the chemical reactions of the glaze in the firing process, rather than by the addition of a color oxide or stain.

Stoneware and porcelain bowls
Lucy Rie, UK
Diameter: 5 - 7 in (13 - 18 cm)

The bowl (left) is thrown porcelain with a transparent uranium yellow glaze. A porcelain body (right) with a transparent yellow glaze of a darker hue is used for another bowl, and a yellow-stained barium matt glaze is used on a stoneware body (center). All the bowls were fired between 1250-1260°C (2280-2300°F) and they show a range of possible high-temperature yellows. Most glazes are brushed on in the raw clay state and the pots are fired once. The oxides brushed onto the surface are mainly a mixture of copper and manganese.

Decorated stoneware bowl
Janice Tchalenko, UK
Diameter: 14 in (36 cm)

This is another example of a
richly colored stoneware pot in
which the color comes from the
decorative overglaze rather than
the main glaze. It is necessary to
have a harder glaze for the
background and a magnesia semi-
shiny white glaze is used for this.
The glaze used for decorating the
bowl is a copper red glaze. When
decorated the bowl is fired in a
reduction stoneware kiln to
1260°C (2300°F).
Recipe for decorative glaze

Potash felspar	301
Borax frit	35
Whiting	74
Copper oxide	1.5
Tin oxide	3.8

Recipe for background glaze

Potash felspar	55
China clay (kaolin)	15
Quartz	15
Whiting	10
Talc	5

Stoneware platter
Bryan Truman, Australia
Diameter: 6½ in (47.5 cm)

This is one of a series of platters
depicting trees, birds or
landscapes which express well the
character of the Australian
countryside. A combination of
pigments and glazes are used to
decorate this platter, together
with wax resist for the imagery.
The glazes used are chun and
copper red with the pigments
iron, titanium and rutile. The
platter is made of porcelaneous
stoneware and fired to a
temperature of 1305°C
(2380°F).

APPLYING GLAZE

A glaze can be applied to an article by brushing, pouring, or spraying, or the pottery can be dipped into the glaze. Achieving consistency of glaze is difficult, but it will become easier with practice and experience.

Points to remember

● The glaze should be stirred before use as the solid ingredients will settle at the bottom, even if the mixture is left for a short period.

● When spraying glaze, it must always be done in a spray booth, and a fume extractor mask should be worn.

Brushing 1. Place the pot on a banding wheel. Always brush the outside first. Use a wide, soft mop brush to lay on the glaze and work from top to bottom.

2. When using a brush it is difficult to apply the glaze evenly. Several coats of glaze should be applied.

Pouring 1. A small jug is used for pouring the glaze and a larger vessel for catching the drips. Pour into the inside first, holding the article at an angle, so the glaze does not fill the footring.

2. The glaze is poured over the pot until the surface is completely covered. Any finger marks can be touched up later.

To glaze the inside of a pot, some glaze is poured in, swilled around and any excess poured away. A pot to be dipped in glaze should be glazed on the inside first.

using multi-based rather than single based glazes.

If the purpose of the glaze is purely decorative, then softness or crazing may be quite acceptable. In fact in some instances the texture of crazing, especially in alkaline turquoise glazes, is attractive to many people.

When you are not restricted by the use of the article an infinite range of treatments, colors and qualities of glaze and surface is possible. Some potters have made their reputation from wares which have a surface texture of volcanic, pitted or thick flowing glaze or slip glaze mixture.

Domestic earthenware, fired at 1100°C (2010°F) and above tends to be more functional and less likely to craze than the lower fired earthenware. However stoneware, with a well-fitting glaze, is considered to be more satisfactory and harder wearing. The health hazard caused by glaze solubility obviously does not apply to a glaze used on a wall plaque or mural so that for this area of ceramics you have a wider scope for using certain color treatments.

Raw glazing

Throughout the history of ceramics, raw glazing has been the rule rather than the exception. It is the process of glazing the ceramic ware in its unfired clay state, prior to a combined (bisque and glaze) firing. With the increase in the cost of materials and the process of firing, efforts are being made by potters to shorten the firing cycle, to fire at lower temperatures and to reduce the time spent in handling the ware. It therefore follows that a great saving in time and cost is made if only one firing is necessary.

The article can be raw glazed at various stages of dryness, but the essential factors are that the glaze should fit the clay body without flaking off, (both body and glaze shrink in the firing) and that the inside of the hollow ware should be glazed before the outside. Some articles will need the addition of plastic clay to assist the fit and shrinkage, while others will be perfectly satisfactory without these additions. The glazing should be done quickly; **great care**

Dipping glaze 1. A large container is filled with glaze. The pot can be held steady with glazing tongs or by bracing the fingers inside the neck of the pot to hold it firm.

2. The article is dipped for a few seconds only. It should be completely immersed in the glaze.

3. The article is removed and any surplus glaze allowed to run off. Any finger marks on the inside of the pot can be touched up.

Spraying 1. The tile for spraying is placed at an angle of about 90 degrees, 12 - 18 inches away from the spray gun and parallel to it. Start at the top and work down.

2. The inside of a bowl is spray-glazed, taking care not to concentrate for too long on one spot. A banding wheel can be used to revolve the bowl slowly and evenly.

3. The bowl is turned upside down on the banding wheel for spraying the outside. Be careful not to spray too much on or the glaze will start to run.

should be taken when handling the raw glazed ware. As a general rule the glaze should be applied more thickly than to a bisqued article. Sometimes the clay body may blister as the glaze is applied because the water in the glaze penetrates the raw clay, but it will usually remain smooth in the firing.

The glaze may be applied by dipping, pouring, spraying or even brushing onto the ware. It will cover the pot more evenly than it does on a bisqued article, as you tend to get variations of porosity in the bisque firing.

Raw glazing depends very much on the physical characteristics of the clay. Sometimes there is cracking immediately after glazing and occasionally the pot will collapse. Only by experimenting will you develop the correct technique.

Slip glazing
These are glazes which contain a high percentage of plastic clay (ball clay, red clay or body clay). It is essential that the body and glaze mature together because if the clay matures before the body the gases released from the body could impair the glaze. Slip glazes are used to obtain a smooth, matt surface and they are generally applied to stoneware rather than to lower firing wares, such as earthenware.

Biscuit firing
The advantage of giving the ware a bisque firing (the first firing before the glaze firing) are, firstly, that it can then be stored indefinitely. Secondly, it makes handling easier for glazing, particularly with large pieces, and when several processes of glazing or decorating are anticipated. When the ware is in a bisque state (and if not vitrified) it has greater porosity than raw clay and is therefore easier to glaze without fear of breakage.

The actual process of bisque firing will be dealt with in **Chapter 5.**

4
TECHNIQUES OF DECORATION

Throughout history man has produced articles for use as well as to express beliefs and feelings. In some cases these are purely functional, in others religious, and sometimes a combination of both. The functional includes articles for the preparation and storage of food, components in building, and ceramic tablets for written communication. For religious and ritualistic purposes these included clay figures as votive offerings and vessels for ceremonies, decorated with symbolic significance. Much of this decoration represents a wealth of cultural traditional and religious belief. In Mycenaean, early Greek and Islamic wares it is interesting to see how the graphic element is portraying scenes of daily life and religion.

Today religion and tradition, play a diminishing part in the graphic content of ceramics, so that this element is more often supplied by the vision or symbolism portrayed by the individual. The ceramic work of artists such as Picasso, Miro, Leurcat Autio, James Tower and many others very often owes little to native traditions. Particularly in the developed world, technology has largely replaced the craftsman in producing articles for everyday use with the result that increasingly, ceramics has become an expressive medium moving into the area of fine art. Whatever the future holds it is important that man retains and practises his skills and uses his knowledge in the light of diminishing resources. There may come a time when technology can no longer be sustained at the present level and man is once more forced to use his personal skills and resources for survival. This preservation of practical skills may be viewed by many as a leisure activity, but it is important nevertheless for us to retain a sense of balance between the functional and the purely decorative. The other important element which unites work and living could be called design. This has many definitions, but in the

context of pottery design it might best be summed up by Professor Papenck who said, 'Education for designers is based on the learning of skills and the acquisition of a philosophy. Design is the conscious effort to impart meaningful order.'

The ceramicist relies on drawing to explore and communicate ideas. Drawing should be an aid to creative thinking and a natural support to both concept and execution. At a fundamental level it can be used for the communication of facts, or for giving instructions that can be understood and carried out. For designers and craftsmen particularly, it can be used to explain in visual terms how an idea will be transformed into a finished article. This may be important when clients are involved so that they are aware of the implications before execution of a commission commences or an agreement is reached. Another form of drawing — a mechanical drawing — is used for giving exact instructions as to the making of an article (the designer and maker may not even meet).

Sometimes drawing is used as a method of recording and exploring direct visual experiences of forms or surfaces, but for many artists it is a purely expressive medium for recording feelings or ideas ranging from the descriptive to subconscious imagery. Whatever the purpose of the drawing, it is an essential technique for developing and exploring an idea and it gives the artist confidence to execute the design.

Few people have the ability to transpose unrecorded visual experience direct to working materials, although in past cultures this was probably a natural way of working. Drawing a rough design of the article before execution will save a great deal of time in the making and it is interesting to note the sequence of idea, drawing, design and the finished work which many craftsman employ.

Visual knowledge, recorded through drawing, is the

Laminated vessel
Dorothy Feibleman, UK
Height: 6½ in (16.5 cm)

This particular vessel was constructed in a mold and decorated with laminations and lines which were inlaid into a black slab. It was then wire-wool sanded, bisqued and the surface texture was refined with wet and dry paper before the final firing. The firing temperature was to 1220°C (2230°F). Some of the laminations were done separately, and then applied, while others were done in the mold. It takes much longer to plan and construct a non-repetitive laminated design, than a repetitive one; the success rate is also more limited due to the stresses set up by the non-uniform laminations.

INSPIRATION AND DESIGN

Nature, as experienced through our senses, and particularly our vision, is a source from which many of our ideas are realized. The process of executing these ideas will vary greatly from person to person. Some potters work closely to their original drawing, but still give considerable thought to developing the design qualities of movement, tone, interval, placing, color, techniques and surface relationships. With others the visual experience and knowledge retains a strong literal element from which certain qualities and feelings are expressed through the material, without it being immediately indentifiable. This is particularly true of Ewan Henderson who spends a great deal of time painting landscapes and keenly observing natural objects. It is an amalgam of his observation and subsequent feelings that he endeavours to express in the way he uses and treats his materials, and which finally gives authenticity and conviction to his work.

Sketches and dishes
Mary Wondrausch, UK

The decoration and design is strongly inspired by country pottery traditions. They include topical subjects, decorative patterns and a spontaneity of technique. In this instance Hungarian embroidery designs were the inspiration, as well as the hens in the potter's garden. Both bowls were made with red clay slipped with white and decorated with sgraffito design when cheese-hard. Washes of oxide were applied at the dry clay state, and after bisquing, the dishes were glazed with a lead sesquisilicate glaze and fired to 1040°C (19   °F).

basis of the artist and designer's vocabulary; factual knowledge is the root from which all visual and design elements can be selected and developed for both form and image. Nickolas Pevsner, writing about art training in the Coldstream Report, said: 'It is clarity of thought and expression, it is unbiased recognition of problems, it is the capability for discussion, and it is ultimately understanding one must achieve. But to understand one must know facts, to know facts, one must learn the facts and to choose relevant facts, one must command a surplus of facts'.

Decoration should be seen as a part of a whole, and should grow out of personal feelings relating to developing ideas and visual experiences. The design may be very simple, as in Siddig Nigoumi's dish with arrows, or follow the more intricate constructions of Eileen Nisbet, some of which are based on a fascination and study of early aeroplanes.

Continual practice is needed to select and arrange the desired elements of a design and relate them to a particular surface or form. This can be done on paper or on the dry clay article with a water color stain that can be sponged off before the exercise is finally executed and any small additions can be made.

If an article is purely decorative then there is practically

The Great Royal Wedding 1981
Siddig El Nigoumi, UK
Diameter 14 in (36 cm)

A red burnished and scratched plate celebrating, in Arabic, the royal wedding of Prince Charles and Princess Diana. It was made with Fremington clay and coated with a prepared red slip, (page 128). It was then burnished and scratched in the bone dry state. Firing was to 800°C (1472°F). The pages shown below are from his sketch book with ideas for a border and possible designs for an oval dish. The other illustration is of an Arabic brass plate which gives a fascinating comparison and contrast to the royal wedding plate where the central inscription is less calligraphic. The outer band of decoration on the wedding plate is treated with much more variation and asymmetry in the balance of the decorative units than the purely repetitive pattern arranged on the Arabic dish.

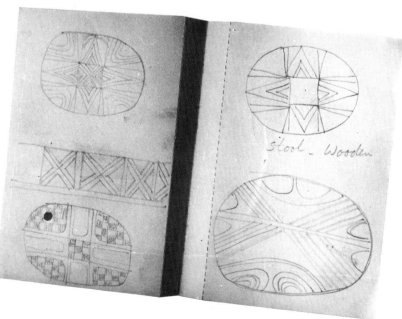

no limit to the techniques which can be used. If, however, the ware is to be utilitarian the suitability of material and technique must be the prime consideration. When choosing a clay body and method of production for a domestic item it is important to consider its function, the durability of the materials and any hygiene and health regulations governing their use.

Before we are aware of the detail or color of an object, visual recognition is by shape. Therefore it is essential to develop a highly practised awareness of two and three dimensional shapes. Observe and study shapes of different color, size and quality. While all shapes have a surface area, details will suggest texture, and their variety and contrast should be explored. The use and choice of color is personal, but the success of its use in ceramics is dependent on a considerable degree of experience and practice, combined with a basic knowledge of color chemistry and an understanding of glazing and staining techniques.

The qualities of contrast in direction, tone, area, color and texture, all contribute to the interest and richness of a design. Alternatively, repetition of line or texture may be equally effective, as shown in Sarah Walton's line work on a series of different shapes, and Fiona Salazar's effective use of an overall texture.

Decoration can be applied at any time in the making of ceramics. It can be the simple impression of fingers on a wet clay surface or an intricate enamel painting on a glazed article.

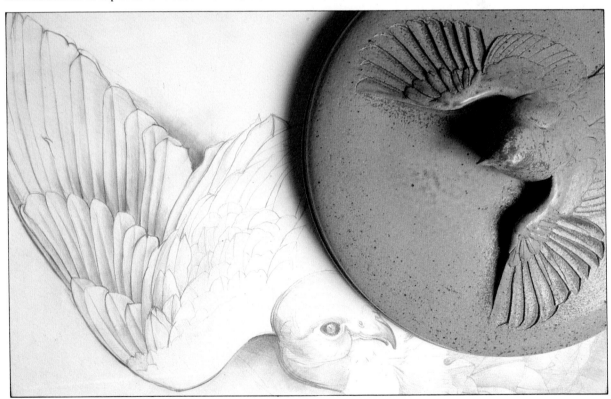

Stoneware lid with modelled bird
Kenneth Bright, UK
Diameter: 14 in (36 cm)

In this example the relationship between the relief modelling of the bird and the surface of the lid is crucial. This is a subtle relationship which connects the two and three dimensional qualities of the ceramic. The modelling is based on a series of drawings of birds in every aspect of flight, the glaze used is ocher ash and china clay which reacts with the iron in the body. It is then fired to 1280°C (2340°F) in an oxidizing atmosphere.

Watercolors and stoneware pot
Ewan Henderson, UK
Height: 18 in (46 cm)

There is a strong correlation between the watercolor landscapes and the quality of texture of the pot. The pot was made with a mixture of two stoneware clays. This body is pressed into wide strips or slabs which act as a central core to which other clays, slips and materials are added. This may include red clay, white earthenware, bone china or porcelain slips, grogs or other ceramic raw materials. When dry a raw nephyline syenite glaze is applied, together with pigments, to all or selected areas of the surface. It is then given a combined glaze and bisque firing in an electric kiln to a temperature of 1260°C (2300°F). Ewan Henderson is interested in testing his materials by taking the pots to the point of collapse in the firing.

Collection of stones, shells and agateware samples
Marion Gaunce, UK

The infinite variety in the shape and texture of shells, and other found objects, is a constant source of inspiration for Marion Gaunce's designs and forms. She continually makes notes in a sketchbook for reference and for working from. She is also influenced by fabric design and the way in which sections of cloth are sewn together to juxtapose the patterns. The pattern illustration samples (right) which are made into earrings, show the many ways in which colored strips can be arranged to give a variety of richness to the overall design.

As well as sketching various ideas, the New Zealand potter Brian Gartside uses reference photography extensively to provide ideas for decoration (*above*). He keeps such prints on file, ready to use with particular materials and decorative techniques, his aim being to create results that are alive with good ceramic qualities and have a spontaneous richness of their own (*right, below, below right*). As can be seen from the examples here, Gartside's use of reference tends to be implied, rather than being directly literal, with several themes often being combined. They also demonstrate why photographs can be invaluable aids in building up a personal sense of awareness and style. The importance of evolving an individual visual vocabulary goes hand in hand with increasing your knowledge of ceramic materials, how best to handle them and how to fire them.

Porcelain aeroplane
Eileen Nisbet, UK

This piece was slab-built, using David Leach porcelain (page 19), and painted and inlaid with colored slips. Each piece was fired separately and assembled together with extruded spacers. between each slab. Small drawing or notes are made on the subject until an idea is strong enough to be designed in clay. The inspiration for this particular piece came from the idea of a heavy object which has the ability to fly, can land delicately in the right place and can stand on three or four points. The result is an aeroplane sculpture, rather than a realistic reproduction of the machine. It gives an impression or suggestion of movement. The main pieces are made by rolling out thin slabs of porcelain, cutting them into the desired shapes and tapering them towards the edges. When dry they are painted and inlaid with several colors. The form is gradually built up to make each piece work against another and form a striking silhouette. Hollow cylinders of ⅝ in (1.6 cm) wide, of many different lengths, are extruded and used to space each slab. All the pieces are fired flat, to a temperature of 1240° -1250°C (2260 - 2280°F) in an electric kiln. Later they are assembled together and adjusted to fit.

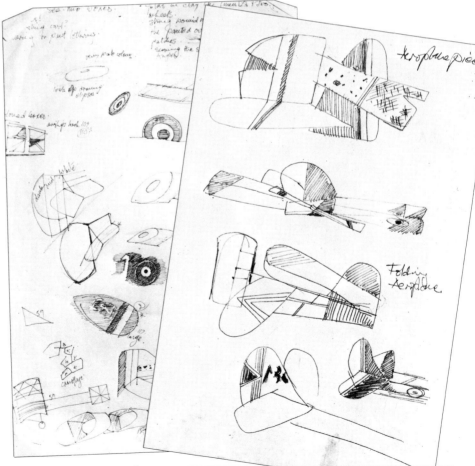

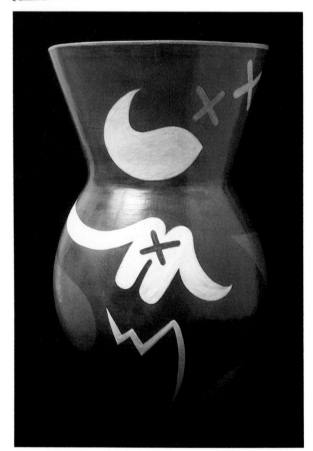

Decorated pots in terra sigillata
Fiona Salazar, UK
Height: 22 in (56 cm)*(left)*;
20 in (50 cm)*(right)*

Keeping a sketch book is a good idea for any potter, as this selection of pages from Fiona Salazar's sketch book *(above)* shows. She sketches subjects that interest her, together with drawings of ideas in the process of development. Her interests are diverse; they include Origami and Pueblo pottery, with its positive profiles and sharp dilineations. Since her ideas come from any sources — notably other artefacts, art and design forms of both past and present — they combine and fuse into an amalgam of symbols, many of which take shape as unconscious intuitive statements in her work. She tends to become absorbed in the juxtaposition and quality of colors and is constantly working out color combinations in her sketches that may eventually take shape on a form. Certain symbols reappear, the subtle variations between them being influenced by the color in use and the contours of the particular shape to which it is being applied.

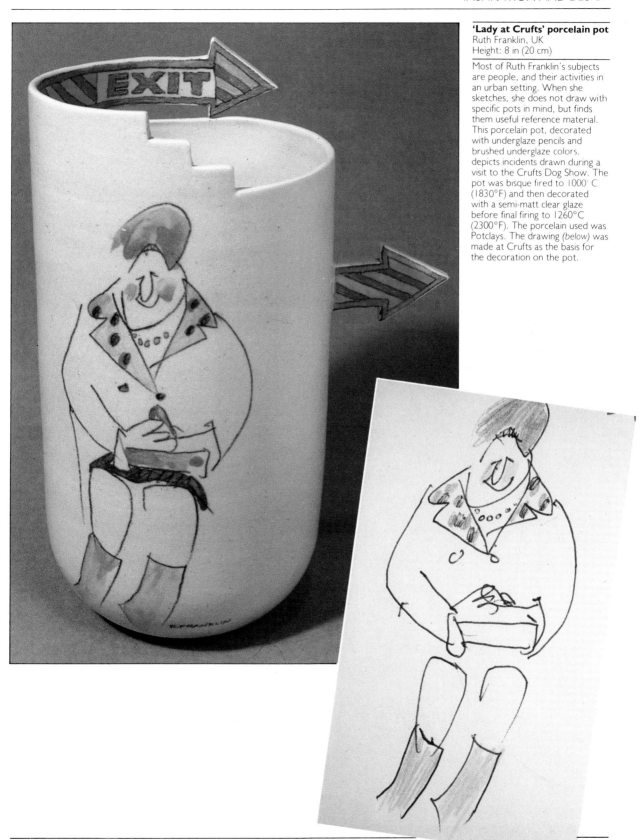

'Lady at Crufts' porcelain pot
Ruth Franklin, UK
Height: 8 in (20 cm)

Most of Ruth Franklin's subjects are people, and their activities in an urban setting. When she sketches, she does not draw with specific pots in mind, but finds them useful reference material. This porcelain pot, decorated with underglaze pencils and brushed underglaze colors, depicts incidents drawn during a visit to the Crufts Dog Show. The pot was bisque fired to 1000°C (1830°F) and then decorated with a semi-matt clear glaze before final firing to 1260°C (2300°F). The porcelain used was Potclays. The drawing (below) was made at Crufts as the basis for the decoration on the pot.

Decorative use of clay

CLAY ITSELF can provide its own decoration, as this section shows. Techniques range from using colored bodies and slips to creating something as simple as an incised pattern.

Sprigging

This technique has been used in one form or another throughout the history of ceramics — the most famous example being blue and white English Wedgwood. It is the applying of relief-molded, decorative forms onto a clay object, using slip as an adhesive. The method consists of carving the design into a hard or soft material and taking a clay impression, from which the relief image is produced (see photograph, page 118). This is then applied to the surface of the leather-hard ceramic article with a thin adhesion of slip (if too much is used the sprig will lift off). In many instances the sprig is first modelled in relief and cast. A master mold is then made and several working molds from it (molds can be cast from modelled clay or carved wood). Another method is to cut the design into a slab of plaster, allowing for the reversal of the design.

Incising

Incising is not unlike carving and is done using a bevelled tool (preferably hard wood or shaped bamboo) to scratch into the wet or leather-hard clay. When the article is glazed, the depth of the incision gives a subtle quality and variation of color as well as design.

Impressed and rolled designs

Any object or tool will make an impression in soft clay. This impression can then be filled with a contrasting colored slip or it can be pigmented for later glazing with clear, transparent-colored or semi-opaque, white glaze. Carved wooden, plaster or metal cylinders will roll a pattern into soft clay, or a plaited or woven cylinder of cane or fibre rolled across the surface can produce good results. Pigmenting is carried out when the clay is bone dry and any surplus color is scraped or wiped off with a dry cloth.

Designing with colored clay

Apart from the use of slip trailing already described, there are several ways in which stained clays may be used as a component of both making and decorating. When making pressed or slabbed shapes or dishes, pieces of clay may be laid onto and rolled into the surface of the moist clay. The clay is then placed over or into a mold, trimmed in the

Sprigging, inlaying and piercing Samples of sprigged inlaid and scratched black and white and blue clays by Ann Clark. The basic shapes were hand-shaped or modelled using a black basalt, a white and a pale blue clay. They were fired to 1150°C (2100°F) and left unglazed in an almost vitrified state.

Pierced stoneware dish
Jan Godfrey, UK
Diameter: 8 in (20 cm)

This is a good example of the decorative effect of a colored body breaking through the semi-opaque stoneware glaze at the edges. The piercing exposed the maximum number of edges as well as giving a richly patterned border to the dish.

DESIGNING WITH COLORED CLAY

Colored clay, in the form of slip or plastic clay, can be used in a great many different ways. As slip it can be brushed and burnished, trailed or sprayed onto the ware and, if plastic, can be thrown, rolled, coiled, modelled or slip cast when used as an aspect of decoration. The main restriction is the high cost of the stains for coloring the clay, so it is more economical to use the unstained clay forms with a large surface area.

Points to remember

● The percentage of stain in a body should never need to exceed 10 per cent, though more is needed to stain clays than glazes.

● The same clay should be used to make both the slip and the articles in order to retain consistent shrinkage.

● The stain is always mixed with dry powdered clay and then made into a slip and sieved.

1. Thinly modelled or pinched motifs in colored clay ready for applying to a dampened mold. The thinner the motifs the easier they will be integrated with the slab.

2. Finely shaped, rolled coils are applied to the shrimp motif before flattening. More than one color clay may be used per motif. They are prepared on a moist cloth to avoid excess drying.

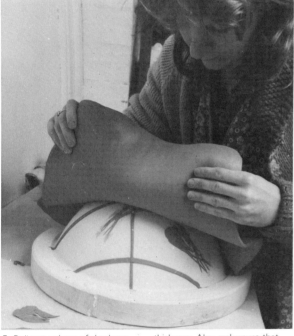

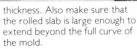

5. Roll out a sheet of clay large enough to cover the motifs and the mold, and carefully place it in position, having made sure that the clay is rolled to an even thickness. Also make sure that the rolled slab is large enough to extend beyond the full curve of the mold.

3. The small pieces are placed on a previously dampened hump mold. A wet brush is used to moisten the edges of the clay if pieces begin to lift off.

4. The flattened coils of colored clay are placed onto the dish design before applying the rolled out slab which will form the main body of the dish.

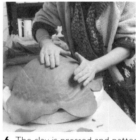

6. The clay is pressed and patted down firmly with the hands to integrate the motifs into the surface. Press particularly firmly around the rim.

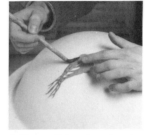

7. Trim off the excess clay at the rim which, if not removed, will tend to stretch the dish and pull the rim away from the mold.

8. The flat part of the metal kidney is used to smooth and level the surface of the dish. This will press the colored parts further into the slab.

9. The dish is lifted from the mold. When the clay is a little firmer, it can be placed on its base for shaping the rim.

10. The rim is squeezed to eliminate any unevenness and the curve is defined.

11. A surform blade is used to trim and straighten the top edge. This can be sponged over, or burnished to produce a smoother finish.

CLAYS AS DECORATION

The examples on these pages demonstrate that clay itself can provide its own decoration. Its range of natural colors lend itself to many subjects, without the need for further embellishment.

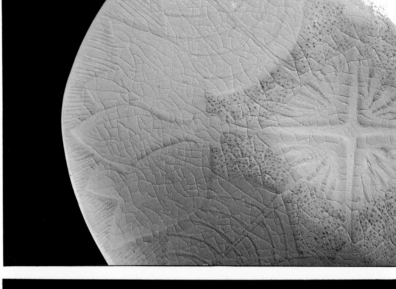

Porcelain incised dish (right).
Ann Clark, UK
Diameter: 8 in (20 cm)

The design was incised into the clay body at the leather-hard stage. When bisqued it was glazed with a transparent glaze and fired to 1280°C (2340°F). As the glaze is thicker in the incised areas, a subtle and delicate color is achieved in the glaze, and the quality of the porcelain body can be fully appreciated. The body used was David Leach porcelain (page 19).

Fragmented pot
Pamela Green, UK

This pot, made up from fragments of pottery, was produced by pressing very small pieces of porcelain clay into a plaster, bowl-shaped mold. When bone dry the surface was brushed with oxide mixed with water so that the solution entered all the spaces left between the small particles. When dry the whole surface is gently wiped with a soft dry cloth to remove the pigment from the surface but to leave it in the recesses. It is then fired, unglazed, to porcelain temperature. The edge is left untrimmed but still possesses a decorative quality.

Stoneware bread crock
Kenneth Bright, UK

In this well conceived design, the sprigged ears of corn on the pot are given movement by placing them across the pot at an angle and onto the lid to link the two pieces. Character is given to the pot by using the figure of a small fieldmouse as a knob for the lid. The crock was thrown in 'T' material and glazed with a dry-ochre wood ash and china clay glaze before firing.

Pressed inlaid dish
Indonia Van der Bilj, UK
Diameter: 16 in (40 cm)

The dish was made by placing flat-shaped pieces of colored clay onto a clay slab and gently rolling them into the surface. The slab is then laid into a shallow dish mold and trimmed. A hollow striped coil, made by rolling the clay round a piece of wooden dowelling, is then added to the rim. When bisqued it is glazed with a transparent glaze (S2228 from Sneyd Colour Works, UK) and fired to 1140°C (2080°F).

Slabbed and decorated earthenware box
Idonia Van der Bilj, UK
Height: 7 in x 5 in (18 cm x 13 cm)

This box is made by rolling colored clay motifs into a clay slab, which is then cut to form the sides, base and lid. Hollow clay coils are made by rolling the clay round a piece of wooden dowelling. Sections are then added to the concave grooving on the edge of the cut slabs. The lid is held in place with clay knobs which are added to the holes cut in the corners of the hollow coils. The clay used is Watts Blake Bearne fine white earthenware, glazed with a transparent glaze at 1140°C (2080°F).

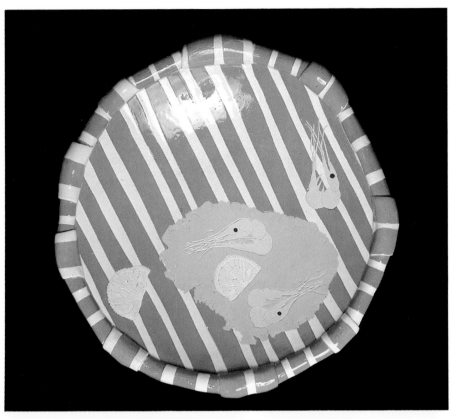

Thrown and slabbed porcelain teapot
Nicholas Homoky, UK
Diamter: 5 x 4½ in (13 x 12 cm)

An unerring quality of line and design, together with a confident handling of the clay, is shown in the making of this teapot. After shaping and slabbing when the clay is soft, it is dried until leather-hard and then incised to take the black clay inlay. Firing is to 1260°C (2300°F) without glazing, after which the vitrified surface is polished with water and Carborundum paper.

LAMINATION

The U.S. potter Dorothy Feibleman's approach to lamination has much in common with the inlay techniques used in cabinet making and marquetry. As well as building up her pots with individual layers and pieces of different colored clays, she also uses many different stains in her work, which contribute to its strikingly delicate effect. The sketch (*right*) shows how carefully this must be planned; the photograph (*below*) shows the cutting and building-up of the different clay layers.

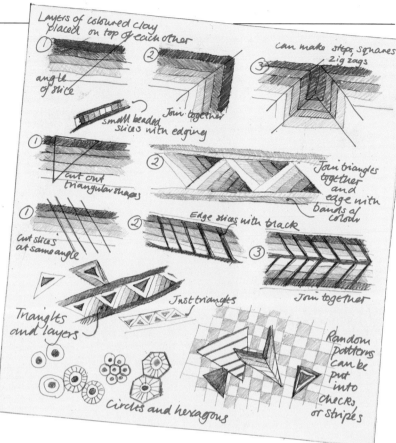

usual way and finished when leather hard. The slabs may be allowed to dry to a leather-hard state and an article made by the slabbing technique described earlier (page 38).

In some cases the colored clay is pressed on or into a damped plaster mold and the sheet of plain, rolled clay placed over the top, and firmly shaped and pressed onto the mold. This may leave slight grooves around the colored areas when dry, but these will be filled when the article is glazed.

Inlay

This is when an impression or recess in a clay surface is filled with another plastic clay or slip and, when both are leather-hard or bone dry, the surface is carefully scraped to leave a sharp outline between the two colored clays. The most important factor is to make sure that the inlay has a lower shrinkage than the clay used for the body of the article. To prevent the inlay from cracking during drying, add fine grog or a non-shrink material such as whiting in the preparation. Depending on the type of ware, it may be fired to stoneware temperatures and remain unglazed, or it can be glazed for either stoneware or earthenware temperatures. This method is most commonly used on tiles as it is easier to scrape them down to reveal the design.

Another form of inlay is marquetry, which is closely related to agateware. It is done by rolling specially shaped pieces of coloured clay into the surface of a rolled clay slab and then placing it over a hump mold. Alternatively the shaped colored clay pieces can be prepared on a board, and

arranged in or on a plaster mold which has been dampened with a sponge. The rolled clay is laid over the top, or inside, the mold and firmly pressed around the colored clay pieces. It is important to make sure that the same clay is used for the stained pieces as for the clay slabs to ensure even shrinkage. When bisqued it can be glazed with a clear or transparent colored glaze.

Agateware and lamination

Agateware is the mixing of two or more colored clays, either freely (as in throwing) or by a careful and controlled structuring of coils or layers of colored clay. There are many instances of this laminated agateware quality in nature and it is a study of this quality which has inspired many potters to become involved in the technique. Shells, rocks and various aspects of the landscape all exhibit the type of lamination which is a source of visual stimulus. Agateware is both a method of decoration and an integral part of the structure of the pot.

Many agateware bowls and dishes are made in a press mold, or over a hump mold. Sometimes a thrown form can have a band or area 'turned out' and an area or strip of agateware inlaid. In some cases the colored seam is visible both on the inside and the outside of the article; in others the layers of agateware are only visible on one side.

As with slip ware, a great deal can be achieved with a limited palette of basic colors. These stains can be added to a clay body in varying percentages to create articles with a richness of tone and color.

LAMINATED BOWL

Here, Feibleman's delicate making and decorative technqiues are combined in the creation of this agate porcelain bowl. Coils of clay triangles and stripes, each of a different color created with body stains and oxides, are built up inside the bisque fired bowl she uses as the form. The bowl, held in a saggar for safety, is tired in an electric kiln in a 12-14 hour firing cycle.

1. The building starts with the rolling out of a thin, even clay sausage with the fingers.

2. A second piece of colored clay is rolled out in the shape of a long leaf with a rolling pin.

3. The sausage is placed on the leaf and slip applied with a sable brush. Sable should be used as it is important that no hairs are left on the clay, as these would drag when this is cut.

4. The edges of the leaf are trimmed and the leaf rolled around the white clay sausage. This process can be repeated, layer upon layer

5. The rod is then cut into thin slices, using a razor blade, the thickness of the slice being determined by the desired thickness of the pot.

6. A bisque-fired bowl is used as the form, lined with an even sheet of white clay, the same thickness as the rod. Mark out the design guide lines with dividers.

7. The untidy edge around the top of the bowl is trimmed away with a sharp craft knife.

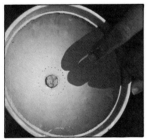

8. The build up of the design begins, starting from the center and working outwards.

9. The slices of rod are laid in with slip, with little effort being made to keep the inside surface clean.

10. Once the design has been completed, the inside surface is cleaned with a metal kidney scraper. A protective mask should be worn.

11. The inside surface is given a final cleaning, first with coarse wire wool and then with fine wire wool.

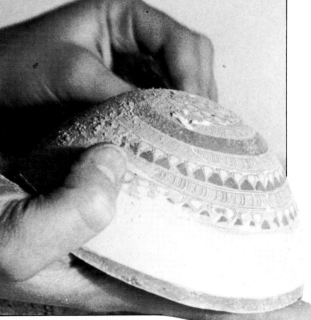

12. The pot is carefully removed from the form and the white liner coating its outside surface is · scraped away with a razor blade. This is easier to use than a knife, because it can be bent to follow the curves of the pot. The surface is then cleaned with coarse and fine wire wool.

LAMINATION AND AGATEWARE

Lamination is an ancient technique which transcends every artistic medium. The effects created on the surface of the article can be bold, or as subtle as a pointillist painting. The fascination of using this method in three dimensions is that the structure and decoration are integral. This technique, applied to clay, is similar to slab and coil building, but it differs by distinguishing every join with a change of color or texture.

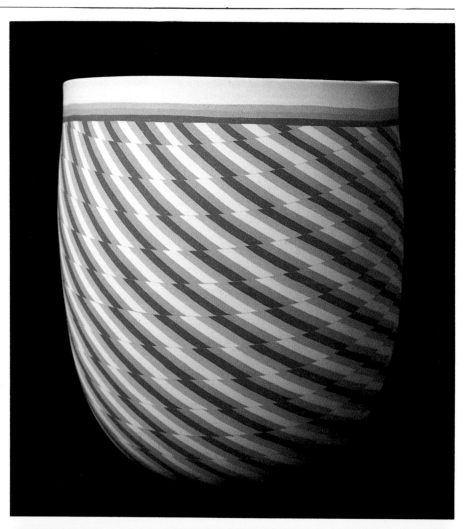

Porcelain agateware bowl
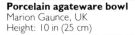
Marion Gaunce, UK
Height: 10 in (25 cm)

The clay for this bowl is prepared in flat slabs and placed in a three-piece press mold for joining. The top edge is added later to give strength and finish to the form. When made, the bowl is dried very slowly in a covered container, which must be free from draughts. The body is David Leach porcelain (page 19), which is fired to 1280°C (2340°F). For making agateware, see page 81.

Porcelain inlaid agateware bowls
Margaret Milne
Diameter: 10 - 12 in (25 - 30 cm)

The clay body recipe used for making these thrown bowls is David Leach porcelain (page 19), stained with a gray body stain. A band is turned from the inside of the bowls when they are leather hard and various strips or sections are firmly pressed in. These are allowed to dry slowly and, when firm, the surface is turned to give a continuous curve to the bowl. The bowls are fired and vitrified at 1280°C (2340°F), but left unglazed. The inlay is made by laying flat square areas of colored clays one on top of the other, and then rolling them into a sausage. The rolled clay is left wrapped up and kept damp for several days. When needed the ¼ in (0.6 cm) thick pieces are sliced off the end and used as inlay.

Turquoise zig zag (top left)
Diameter: 4¾ in (12 cm)
Teapot (top right)
Height: 7 in (18 cm)
Lunar (bottom)
Width: 5½ in (14 cm)

Dorothy Feibleman's early work consisted of bold patterns which allowed control over the stresses inherent between laminations. In her more recent work she has used clay overloaded with chemicals to produce volcanic textures, and she uses the stress created to produce dynamic effects.

Decorating with slip

SLIP, a sieved mixture of clay and water, can be used in many ways to make attractive decorative patterns. This section explains the principles and techniques involved!

Using slip

Slip can be specially mixed or blended, but start by exploring the potential of the natural red and white clays for slips. These clays can be stained with metal oxides to produce a wide range of colors for decoration. Black sip, for example, is made using red clay with the addition of 8-10 per cent manganese oxide. There is endless potential in the basic earth colors and these can be mixed to produce contrasting tones and colors. It is only after much practice and experience that the majority of potters achieve attractive results with other than red, white or black slip. The painting of slips onto ware can be very beautiful and subtle giving an effect like oil or watercolor painting, as well as making bold, incisive patterns.

Slip is made by mixing clay and water to a given consistency and then sieving it through an 80 mesh sieve. It may be poured, brushed or sprayed over the surface of the pot, or the pot can be dipped into the slip. According to the desired effect, the thickness of application is relevant; if the slip is too thin the clay body will tend to show through, especially when it is glazed. Even this can become a feature.

Spotting slip

Spotting slip is a traditional technique, used in parts of Portugal. A piece of wood or metal is dipped into a variety of colored slips and used to 'spot' the slip onto the soft clay. The articles can then be bisque fired and glazed or raw glazed before firing.

Slip trailing

Slip trailing is a fluid medium for drawing on ceramic ware. The slip is trailed from a rubber or clay container with nozzle attachments of varying sizes to limit the flow of slip. The technique is very similar to icing a cake — the article is given a coat of slip and, while it is still wet, a trail of contrasting colored slip is applied to the surface.

Burnishing and scratching slip

This technique is used for decorative, rather than functional ware. The slip is applied when the clay is soft or leather hard and burnished when the surface loses its shine.

Slips can be colored with basic oxides or stains and,

SPOTTING SLIP

This is an ancient and traditional technique, practised by potters in some parts of Portugal. Articles are press molded or thrown and turned and, when in the leather-hard state, a contrasting colored slip is applied to them A variety of tools with different shaped ends are dipped into the slip and pressed gently onto the surface of the clay. A tool with two prongs can be used for speed of application. The traditional colors are white on red or red on a white slip, sometimes with the addition of some brushed copper under the standard transparent glaze. However any colored slip can be used, and the illustration (right) shows a plate decorated with black, red and white. The slip should be the consistency of double cream — fairly thick so that the spotting tool can pick up enough slip.

1. A circular piece of wood is used to produce a flat spot. The breast of the bird is decorated in this way with colored spots of slip.

2. A thin strip of metal gives a thin line of slip, used for drawing in the tail and legs of the bird.

3. A carved piece of a branch with a flat end can produce a variety of shapes, depending on how it is cut.

4. A blunt-edged piece of wood, about the size of a pencil, will produce small spots.

SLIP TRAILING

The planning and spacing of the lettering around the edge of the dish is very important. Crowding of letters would make areas look darker, giving an imbalance of pattern on the dish. Control of the amount of slip which is dispensed from the trailer is also essential and there should be a continuous flow of slip to accommodate the speed at which the potter is decorating.

Points to remember

● It is a good idea to draw out the design on a piece of paper of the same size as the actual article, to make sure that it is practical and will look right on the plate.

● A contrasting colored slip can be applied on top of a line which has already been slip-trailed.

● It is helpful to practise slip trailing on a tile first, so that you obtain the correct weight and accuracy of line.

● A batten of wood can be placed across the wheel to support and steady the elbows when slip trailing onto the article.

1. The dish or plate is revolved on the wheelhead or banding wheel, and the slip trailer is held as still as possible to produce a line of even thickness.

2. As the wheel slowly revolves a zigzag pattern is made around the edge of the plate. Squeeze the slip trailer very lightly to keep the pattern of equal weight around the whole dish.

3. Dots are made on the rim of the dish with the same intermittent pressure on the slip trailer bag to produce dots of consistent shape and size.

4. Any uneven dots or blotches made by the slip trailer can be scratched away with a needle when the slip is leather-hard; fine details can also be drawn in.

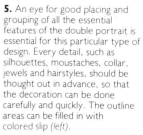

5. An eye for good placing and grouping of all the essential features of the double portrait is essential for this particular type of design. Every detail, such as silhouettes, moustaches, collar, jewels and hairstyles, should be thought out in advance, so that the decoration can be done carefully and quickly. The outline areas can be filled in with colored slip (left).

SLIP TRAILED CERAMICS

Slip trailing is a long established decorative tradition in several European countries and remains one of the primary ways in which the surface of a pot can be enriched. In the UK, for instance, medieval slipware is one of the highlights of the national heritage, its spontaneity and robustness reflecting the rugged vitality of rural life. Such attributes, plus a sense of humor, are also seen in the more illustrative work of the Toft brothers and others of the seventeenth century.

Slipware cockerel dish
William Newland, UK
26 × 18 in (66 × 46 cm)

As with all good slipware, Newland's cockerel is both useful and decorative. The white slip was applied to the red body and the design then trailed with a warm, dark clay. The dish was then glazed with a standard bisilicate glaze before firing.

Sliptrailed royal wedding dish
Mary Wondransh, UK
Diameter: 16 in (41 cm)

The decoration of this dish owes much to Wondransh's studies of William Toft and others, who often used distinctive decorative devices to portray topical themes with a touch of humor. Careful selection of colored slips gives tonal balance and variation of color. The glaze used was a 2 per cent iron lead sesquisilicate, which was fired to 1040°C (1900°F)

according to the design or effect required, more than one color can be brushed or applied at a time. Painting the slip onto the article is done before bisque firing or sometimes on the bisqued ware, and it is usually more satisfactory to apply two coats. When the slipped pot is almost dry (or is bone dry) the design can be lightly sketched on the surface with a pencil and then scratched through the slip to the body of the ware with a suitable tool. All surplus clay should be dusted gently from the surface of the pot.

For the best results with this method, use a fine terracotta, such as Fremington clay (see suppliers, page 199). When this body is fired it gives a good color and tone contrast with the applied colored slips. Red slips generally contain more iron than the red clay of the body.

Recipe for black slip
70 per cent red clay
15 per cent manganese
15 per cent cobalt oxide

Recipe for red slip
85 per cent red clay
15 per cent iron oxide

While cobalt is extremely expensive, a small amount in a black slip will go a long way if used to contrast with the red slip. Production will be on a small scale, because burnishing is a slow process, but the outlay and necessary equipment is minimal for this technique of decoration and, for beginners , can be confined to pressed dishes.

Sgraffito

This is the process of scratching through a pigment slip or glaze applied to a fired or unfired ceramic surface, to reveal the clay body underneath. The clay body is coated with a contrasting slip while the clay is damp and when it becomes leather-hard, the coating is selectively scratched or scraped away with a scribing tool or scraper to produce a decorative design. A different quality of line can be achieved if the coating of slip is left until bone dry. It is also traditional to add washes or areas of basic oxides to the raw clay with a brush when using this technique, and sometimes splashes of colored glaze can be added at the biscuit firing stage. especially when a white slip is used.

Resist

Areas of slip can be prevented from adhering to the clay body using resist techniques of decoration. Pieces of shaped

BURNISHING AND SCRATCHING SLIP

The appeal of this technique, which owes a great deal to non-European traditions, lies in the inexpensive simplicity of the materials required and the minimum of equipment needed to achieve its affects. Despite the basic nature of the technique, richness of decoration and design can be achieved. In these examples, a slip-brushed, leather-hard pot is being burnished with the back of a metal spoon *(right)*, a plastic-film pad filled with cotton wool *(far right)* is being used to polish the burnished surface. A selection of burnishing and polishing tools is shown *(below)*.

The potter Siddig El Nigoumi at work scratching in the decoration of this hand-built, slip-coated burnished and scratched bottle *(above)*, using a steel knitting needle. The scratching was executed once the burnished pot was completely dry. The contrast of matt and shiny surfaces and the depth of the incisions are carefully calculated parts of this technique, the scratched lines and areas emphasizing and complementing the bottle's shape *(right)*.

SGRAFFITO

A broad brush is used to paint red and black slip all over the inside of the dish, while it is still in the leather-hard state *(below)*. The dish is left within the mold, which lends its support until the decoration is complete. The slip is burnished when it is no longer shiny and then it is left to dry, after which the decoration is carried out. During the decorating process, a narrow piece of wood is used as a bridge across the mold to steady the hand, and a steel knitting needle is used as a scratching tool *(right)*.

Points to remember

● The dampness of the clay is very important for scratching and scraping away backgrounds. Only experience will indicate this.

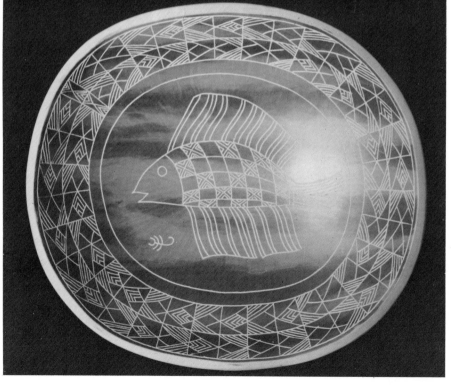

Scratched dish
Siddig El Nigoumi, UK

The dish is decorated with a line of uniform thickness which reinforces the two dimensional character of the design. An exotic fish floats comfortably in the bottom of the dish, surrounded by a line and then a border. A signature punctuates the space left by the fish, and becomes an integral part of the design. The body of the fish is subdivided into rectangles and these are given a subtle variety of weight by the filling-in lines. The fins of the fish are drawn with a slight waviness of line which gives a feeling of gentle motion. The abstract border pattern echoes the movement of the fish. The rectangles are ingeniously sub-divided into diamonds and triangles which are again broken down asymmetrically by lines and spaces. The overall design gives a fine balance between shape, line and texture and exhibits interesting cross-cultural influences from African and Arab traditions.

Scratching and painting This is highly skilled technique, especially when it comes to adding the touches of color *(far right)*. Here, basic oxides of copper, manganese and cobalt are being used to add a half tone, as well as some sparkly, to the red and white contrasting slips. The glaze may be transparent, or have a 1 per cent iron content.

Points to remember
● The white slip must 'fit' the red clay so that it does not shrink at a different rate and crack, lift off or flake.

1. A line is scratched with a metal scriber when a clay is firm but not bone dry. The background has been scraped away with a bevelled hacksaw blade.

2. A looped wire is used as a modelling tool for making darker accents in a linear design. Washes of color may be added before glazing.

3. Clay dust and particles left at the edges of scratched lines are brushed off, otherwise they will be caught in the glaze and give a rough surface to the pot.

paper are dampened slightly and placed on the surface of the moist, firm clay. A coating of slip is then poured over the whole surface and when it has dried to a matt state the paper can be peeled off. If required, more paper and slip can be used to build up layers. Wax resist can also be painted onto the leather-hard clay and a slip coating poured over it. For this method the slip must not be too thick or it will not resist. It is quite possible to combine several of these resist techniques to produce a more complex form of decoration.

Painting and casting slip in molds

The painting of colored slips onto the surface of a plaster mould can be combined with the incising, scratching, or carving of a design into the plaster. When slip cast this becomes a relief pattern on the surface of the article.

It is important that the slips are made from the same clay as the body of the article in order to reduce the chance of variable shrinkage. The surface to be decorated must first be dampened, with a sponge so that the slip, when applied, does not dry too quickly or flake off. When the application of one or more colored slips is complete, the mold is filled with prepared casting slip and left until the necessary thickness is attained. Drain in the usual way and remove the mold when ready. Such articles are glazed with a transparent matt or transparent colored glaze. The technique is best done in a two-piece skin mold if the article is a bowl or dish, and cast through the top of the mold (the base of the article) rather than in an open mold.

It is also possible to stick thin areas or patterns of

Covered cheese dish
Mary Wondransch, UK
Height: 10 in (25 cm)
Diameter: 15 in (38 cm)

A skilful sgraffito decorated dish, inspired by traditional West Country ware. The scale, balance and execution make it an impressive piece. The

characteristic Bideford white pipe clay is used over an excellent red Fremington clay. The dish was glazed with a one per cent iron lead sesquisilicate glaze and fired to 1640°C (2980°F) 1040°C (1900°F).

SGRAFFITO WARE

Scratching a clay surface is one of the oldest of all decorative techniques — it is probably as old as pottery itself. Today, potters use many variants on the basic method of simply marking the clay's surface; these include scratching through slips, glazes, pigments, unfired enamels and wax resists.

Earthenware form
James Tower, UK
Height: 27.¾ in (70 cm)

Knowledge of the behavior of glazes at various temperatures — either singly or combined together — is crucial, or the whole effort and time spent in decoration can be wasted. This large discus-shaped form was hand-built by joining its two halves together, each half having been made individually in the same press mold. The form was glazed and fired twice, the first black glaze contains manganese and the second being of thick white tin. When dry, lines were scratched through the white to reveal areas of the fired black beneath it, which, as the black is softer than the white, flow in firing to give a gentle movement to the scratched lines. These are starting to disappear. The second firing was to 1080-1100°C (1980-2010°F).

Terracotta scratched dish
(below right)
Siddig El Nigoumi
Diameter: 10 in (25 cm)

Here, the whole surface has been scratched to create lines or small areas of the subtly contrasting colored body under the slip. The scratched border area has a balanced, asymmetric quality, which gives the design interest while contrasting with the more geometric quality of the central area.

Sgraffito earthenware dish
(far right)
Mary Wondransh
Diameter: 7 in (18 cm)

The design and background of this white slipped thrown red earthenware dish were sgraffitoed when the clay was cheese hard. Basic oxides were lightly brushed on to the white areas before bisque firing; the dish was then glazed with a lead sesquisilicate based transparent glaze and fired to 1040°C (1900°F).

TERRA SIGILLATA AND MOCHAWARE

The terra sigillata technique is best suited to the decoration of individual pieces, because of the time involved in burnishing and polishing the ware. Though mocha decoration is also used on individual pieces, it is more suited to the decoration of standard ware; however, it is more limited in its immediate effect.

Decorated terra sigillata pot
Fiona Salazar, UK
Height: 16 in (41 cm)

This hand built and shaped terracotta pot had terra sigillata slip applied at the leather-hard stage. Different colored slips were brushed carefully on to different areas either directly, or by masking and spraying. Once the slip had lost its initial shine, the surface was burnished, using a spoon. Salazar's patterns and symbols come from a wide source of collected and drawn imagery, which take their final form when being adapted to the shape. In this, she is following in the footsteps of the early Greeks, who used the technique extensively for decorating vases and dishes.

Slab built porcelain bottle
Robin Hopper, Canada
Height: 14 in (36 cm)

The colored porcelain body of this bottle had slip freely applied to it and was then treated with a mocha solution while still wet. After glazing and firing, enamels were applied as a further decoration. Much of the inspiration for Hopper's work comes from nature and the Canadian landscape, which he expresses either with a neat abstract quality, or more literally. The mocha here, for instance, suggests the growth and structure of trees.

colored clay to the surface of the mold and then fill the mold with casting slip.

Colored casting slip

Taking several colored casting slips, pour them alternately in and out of the mold for short periods until a series of thin layers build up and form an article of standard thickness. When leather-hard or bone dry, the layers may be scratched through or the surface scraped to give an interesting pattern of colored clay laminations.

Alternatively, the colored slip may be trailed onto the surface of the plaster and then the casting process continued with a standard slip. This method gives scope for maximum variety in design, while using a standard shaped article.

More and more small workshops are producing ware by casting, but to this they apply an interesting and varied range of hand-decorating techniques.

Mocha ware

As a decorative technique this can be very elaborate and varied, or it can be used with striking simplicity, as in the 19th-century Staffordshire mugs and jugs made for pubs. The decorative effect is named after Arabian quartz, known as mocha stone, which has a moss or tree-like pattern on it. In ceramics the result is obtained by preparing a dark acid-based colorant called mocha tea, which is applied immediately to a freshly slipped surface of pale colored slip. Stronger colored bands of slip are traditionally added above and below the main area. The clay bodies used are stoneware and cream or white earthenware. According to tradition the designs are either blue, green or black on a pale slip.

Mocha tea is made with tobacco juice, stale wine or turpentine, or a combination of all three, with coloring. It has been suggested that citric juices, coffee, the juice of hops or tansy assist the reaction of the tea, so there is plenty of scope for experiment.

Recipe for mocha tea
25 gms finely cut tobacco   30 gms iron or manganese oxide
1 pt water

Bring the tobacco and water to the boil and allow the mixture to simmer for 30 to 40 minutes. Sieve it through a 200 mesh sieve. Add the iron or manganese oxide and resieve. If the tea is made in advance, it must be resieved before use. It improves if kept in a refrigerator.

An alternative method is to simmer the tobacco in half a pint of water, sieve it through a 200 mesh sieve and store the tea in a screw top jar. When it is required, decant a small quantity into a shallow dish and add whatever pigment you want. You will soon learn from experience that, if it is too thick, the pattern will not form and when too thin it runs

Three Mocha ware beakers.

excessively and gives a weaker pattern. With practice you can vary the range and strength of the colors.

The slip can be made of three parts ball clay to one part china clay. If you are experimenting with other slips the addition of a little deflocculent may assist the reaction.

Terra sigillata

This is the traditional name for a burnished, finely precipitated slip, applied to a low firing clay body. The slip is usually applied with a brush, but it can be poured, sprayed or dipped when the pot is leather-hard. When the slip has dried to a non-shiny matt surface it can be burnished with a hard, smooth object such as a spoon, a pebble or a piece of hard plastic rod.

The slip can be colored with stains or oxides and applied in areas, or in layers. When the article is dry, it is fired to a temperature between 900°C and 950°C (1650°F and 1740°F). It is also possible to apply terra sigillata to a bisque fired pot. The pot to be treated can be made from terracotta clay, white earthenware or a mixture of earthenware and stoneware clay.

Recipe for terra sigillata
Supplied by Fiona Salazar   7.5 grams sodium hexameta
3500 centilitres water   phosphate (SHP)
1500 grams dry clay (white ball clay)

Add the clay to the water and grind up the flakey SHP in a pestel and mortar to add to the mixture. Stir thoroughly and leave for 48 hours.

Dispose of the top level of water and then pour (and keep) the second layer of clay in suspension. The bottom layer of firm clay can be discarded. Take the clay in suspension and add a small lump of calcium chloride to it; stir it well, until the slip is ready for use. When stains are applied to the slip the percentage can be calculated by 'Broignart's principle', or by trial and error. It is always worth testing a variety of slips to ascertain at what firing temperature they begin to lose the burnished shine.

FIGURATIVE CERAMICS

In ceramics, the figurative tradition is still a living element, its origins going back several centuries. The examples here show how diverse the tradition can be, within the broad framework.

Porcelain covered vessel
Rudy Autio, USA
Height: 22½ in (57 cm)

This slab-built and once-fired porcelain is decorated with colored engobes which contain small quantities of basic oxides and stains. The ware is glazed when bone dry with a transparent glaze and fired to 1305°C (2380°F). Some pieces have a second low temperature firing at around 895°C (1640°F), after application of low firing colors. A typical feature of Rudy Autio's designs is the drawing of figures and animals to give a fluid, lyrical quality to the ware.

Recipe for engobes

Silica	1
Felspar	1
Kaolin	1
Nephyline syenite	0.5
Ball clay	0.5
plus basic oxides	

Coiled Raku pot
Agalis Manessi, UK
Height: 10 in (25 cm)

This pot is decorated with oxides and a yellow lead antimoniate glaze under a transparent bisilicate glaze. The clay used for making the pot is 'T' material, a highly plastic white clay containing some 20 per cent of fine sandy grog to dry weight of clay. The firing is to standard raku temperatures and the pot is rolled in long grass when drawn from the kiln to give a light reduction. When cool it is washed and cleaned.

Stoneware bowl, 'Theme of Tenderness'
Eric James Mellor, UK
Diameter: 7¾ in (20 cm)

This sensitive design was created by applying basic oxides to bisque ware using a water colorist's painting technique. The bowl was glazed with elm ash and placed in an electric kiln for an oxidised firing to 1300°C (2370°F).

Ash recipe

Potash felspar	40
Body clay	5
China clay	25
Flint	10
Ash	40

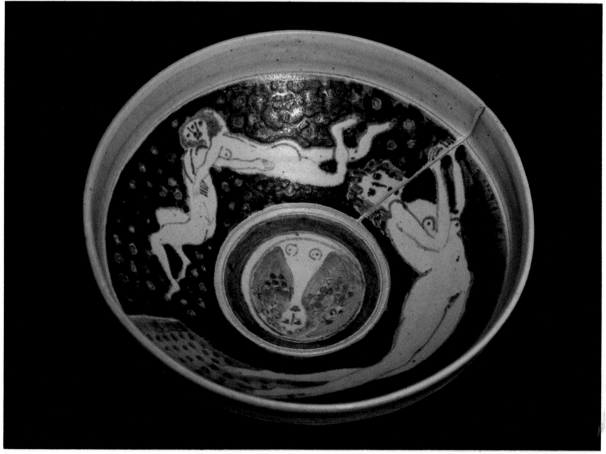

Stoneware vases
Yolande Beere, UK
Height: 5in (13cm) and 7 in (8 cm)

These thrown stoneware vases are glazed with a matt white glaze containing 45 per cent whiting, 45 per cent china clay, 10 per cent ball clay and 4 per cent tin oxide. The figures are painted in with a mixture of manganese and iron oxide and then covered with wax resist. The pots are washed to leave areas of bisque showing and they are reglazed with the same glaze, but this time with 0.5 per cent cobalt oxide instead of the tin oxide. They are fired to a temperature of 1280°C (2340°F).

'Ascot Couple'
Malcolm Gooding, UK
Height: 9 in (23 cm)

In the Staffordshire ceramic figure tradition this piece was slip cast in sectons and joined. The slip was made from Watts Blake Bearne fine white earthenware, bisque fired to 1160°C (2120°F), and glazed with a tin glaze. The gloss firing was to 1120°C (2050°F). Potterycraft water-based onglaze colors were brushed on for decoration and detail, and the whole piece was refired to 760°C (1400°F).

Slab built earthenware figures
Ruth Franklin, UK
Height: 9 in (23 cm)

These male and female dancing figures are made from cut-out rolled and slabbed earthenware clay with a minimum of relief. Underglaze colors are sprayed and painted on after bisque firing, and then the figures are refired with a transparent glaze to 1100°C (2012°F).

Decorating with pigments and glazes

PIGMENTS AND GLAZES are the basic tools of the potter's decorative art. This section explains what they are, how they can be made up and how to apply them.

Decorating with pigments and colors

The basic oxides manganese, cobalt and iron and other oxides can be applied to leather-hard clay, bone dry clay or after raw glazing. The metal oxides can be rubbed, dry, into the surface of the ware or brushed on with a little water or gum. In most cases water is used, but sometimes gum arabic or gum tragacanth is mixed in liquid form to bind the colour and fix it to the surface of the ware during glazing. If a quantity of glue is prepared and stored in a plastic bottle it can be used for adding to glazes, pigments, or for any technique which uses a binder or adhesive.

Oxides in clay

Apart from adding ceramic pigment to give an even color to a clay body, coarse grains of metal oxides can be mixed with the clay body. When the fusing temperature of the clay is reached in the glaze firing, the oxide will flux and bleed into the glaze, giving an attractive decorative effect.

Lustres

These are thin metallic applications which are brushed, sprayed or, if specially prepared, printed onto a once-fired glaze surface. They are salts of metals and require very careful preparation. Because of this they are not commonly used, but some studio potters have made a study of them and use them frequently in production (see page 140). If they are applied with a brush they have a tendency to flow too freely, so they should be put on sparingly, thinly and with speed. Lustre can be painted onto fired majolica glaze and refired in a reduction firing.

Enamels

These are specially prepared pigments which contain sufficient flux to allow them to fuse onto a once-fired glaze surface at a temperature between 750°C (1380°F) and 850°C (1560°F). The technique of applying enamels requires great skill, using fat oil of turps and pure turps as a medium and applying it with soft, shaped brushes. They can also be applied by a brush wash method (using a little oil with pure turpentine), by sponging, or with a palette knife, as in oil painting.

Enamels give the widest possible range of colours for decorating, but cannot be used effectively for large areas except by ground laying (see below). Firing should be slow in the early stages to allow the oil to slowly burn away without disrupting the surface of the pigment. Not all the colors mature at the same temperature so that higher firing colors should be fired in the first firing. When firing with enamels, plenty of ventilation is necessary, both for the kiln and in the kiln room.

Ground laying

This is a technique in which an even area of enamel is applied to a once-glazed and fired surface. It is generally combined with various forms of printed design, such as litho or silk screen transfers, engraved designs or printed and hand-coloured tiles. Areas not to be ground laid are painted out with a water-based resist for easy cleaning when the ground laying is finished and dry. This can be a sugar, treacle, or another water soluble mixture which takes easily to the fired glaze surface. The resist can be stained with ink or water colors. When the resist is dry the area to be

Burnishing fired luster After specially prepared lusters have been applied and reduction fired, it is necessary to gently burnish the painting with lambs wool and pumice powder upon cooling. This procedure reveals the full color quality of the final luster by removing all traces of the vehicle or medium that held the luster during firing.

BODY STAINS

Lucy Rie decorates most of her work by exploiting the natural instability of copper and manganese oxides, which characteristically fuse and flow at stoneware temperatures. These oxides are used as surface coating, in glazes or by being mixed with the throwing clay.

Agateware pots
Lucy Rie, UK
Height: 8in (20cm); 13in (76cm)

The spiral agateware design of these pots, which superbly emphasises the clay's form and its movement and structure during throwing, was achieved by juxtaposing, but not mixing, two clays. Porcelain clays have been used in the two outer pots while the centre pot was made with stoneware. Further interest has been given to their form by the varying interval between the light and dark clays. Frequently shaping her pots by beating them after throwing, Rie gives variety to her work by varying her use of different glazes. Firing was to 1260°C (2300°F).

Thrown shaped and fluted stoneware bowl
Lucy Rie, UK
Height: 7 in (18 cm)

Rie's success with a potentially limited palette and firing conditions is illustrated by this pot's subtle form, flute and glaze treatment and the effect of oxide during firing. Mixed with the body before throwing and fired in an oxidised atmosphere, the manganese oxide has fused and flowed during firing to 1260°C (2300°F) into the slip and matt glaze previously brushed onto the unfired pot.

LUSTER AND PRECIOUS METALS

A metallic luster effect is quite often obtained in the course of firing glazes with a varying oxide content. However a real luster only achieved by following particular techniques and firing procedures, using specially prepared metallic salts. Traditionally lusters are the salts of copper and silver, used singly or together in kaolin or ocher. The mixture is used to decorate ware which has already been glazed and fired with a soft tin glaze. Firing is most successful in a wood-fired kiln with a short period of reduction. The maximum temperature for the firing is around 660°C (1220°F). When cool the ocher or kaolin is burnished off, using pummice powder and a pad of sheep's wool to reveal the areas of luster. Those potters who are prepared to develop their own lusters and firing techniques are few in number, but once they master the technique it may become a major aspect of their production. For those interested in using lusters, several manufacturers have produced a wide range of commercial lusters which can be fired at low temperatures.

Enamel and gold dragon jar
Roger Michell, UK
Height: 26 in (66 cm)

The jar was thrown and turned with press molded additions. After bisque firing it was glazed and fired with a transparent lead glaze and then decorated by painting and air brushing the enamels onto it. It was then decorated with burnished gold. Depending on the firing temperature of the enamels, the gold is usually fired in the second firing at a lower temperature.

Luster fruit bowl
Roger Michell and Danka Napiorkowska, UK
Diameter: 22 in (56 cm)

This slip-cast earthenware bowl was made with Watts Blake Bearne fine white earthenware clay and bisque fired to 1120°C (2050°F). It was glazed with a low solubility lead glaze and fired at 1040°C (1900°F). Areas of the surface were then resisted using white gouache and sprayed with various colored commercial lustres. The second firing was to 750°C (1380°F).

Thrown luster bowl
Margery Clinton, UK
Diameter: 11 in (28 cm)

After making the bowl and bisquing to 1100°C (2010°F), it is glazed with a tin glaze. Prepared salts of silver or copper mixed with glaze are applied with a sponge to the unfired glaze. The bowl is then fired to 1020°C (1870°F) to complete the glaze firing and reduction takes place when a temperature of approximately 700°C (1290°F) is reached. On other occasions the luster pigments are used as decoration and then fired in exactly the same way.

Luster vase
Alan Caiger-Smith UK
Height: 11 in (28 cm)

This extremely attractive vase was painted with strong, rich lusters. The basic lusters silver and copper were painted onto a soft lead and alkali tin glaze and fired in a reducing wood-fired kiln. The inglazed blue pigment was applied later and not reduced. The same wood-fired kiln is used for firing standard ware using willow wood because it gives a long, soft, hot flame and a particular quality to the glaze achieved by no other type of fuel. Poplar wood is also suitable for such firings.

SCRATCH PIGMENT

Raw, dry clay can be scratched with a fine or a thick, pointed tool. It is then painted with oxides and the surface area is gently scraped to leave pigment in the scratched lines or marks. The article can then be bisqued and glazed using a clear glaze, a colored clear glaze or a semi-opaque glaze.

Points to remember

● When scratching, a piece of lambs wool (attached to the leather) is excellent for gently dusting off the surplus clay dust.

● When applying pigment, do not have it too pale, but just strong enough to give a positive line when the article is fired or glazed.

1. A design is sketched onto the surface of the dish with a pencil, prior to scratching. The dish is placed on a banding wheel for ease of movement.

2. The dish is held in the mold to support it during scratching. A wooden batten can be used to rest the hands on while you are decorating.

3. A heavier tool is used to make impressions for textured areas.

4. Pigment is brushed into the indented and textured areas.

5. A flexible kidney is used to scrape the pigment from the unscratched areas. The lambs wool pad can be used to dust the area afterwards (right).

ground laid is brushed evenly with a mixture of ground laying oil mixed with enough spirit of turps to give reasonable flow, but not so thin that the coating runs. The article is left for 40 minutes or more for the layer to become slightly tacky (it can be tested with the finger tip). Use a fine silk or nylon buffer to dab all over the surface until it acquires an even, tacky texture. Take a carefully folded dry cotton wool pad and dip it into a volume of sieved enamel Dust gently over the tacky surface with a circular motion, until the whole area is covered with pigment. Refill the cotton wool pad at intervals and when the operation is complete shake off any surplus powder. Take great care that no loose strands of cotton wool come into contact with the tacky surface otherwise the coating will be blemished and uneven. Throughout the process work in a completely dust-free atmosphere or room. Take particular care that your clothing is not wool or any fluffy material from which fine particles can be constantly released into the atmosphere to settle on the tacky surface. If possible wear a nylon coat or overall. When the coated surface is thoroughly dry, and this may take some 24 hours, wash the resist off gently in cold water with a cotton wool pad and fire the articles at the necessary enamel firing temperature.

Decorating with glazes

According to how it is used, glaze color and texture can give a decorative quality to ceramics. Like slip, it can be poured, sprayed, brushed or trailed and areas of glaze can be sharply defined, or merged to give a soft effect. Matt or shiny glazes can be contrasted and pigments can be applied to either. Alternatively, one glaze can partly overlap another to form a third color or texture.

Reactive glazes

A soft, colored glaze can be first applied to pots or tiles and then overglazed with a harder glaze. The soft glaze will break through the hard one during firing and give an area of mixed glaze texture and color.

Spray glaze decorating

With spray glazing the surface is first glazed and fired with a colored glaze. The article is then warmed with a blow

WAX RESIST

This technique needs to be well thought out before it is used for applying decoration. It can be used on raw, dry clay as well as bisque ware. It can also be used on top of glaze already applied to an object to retain or mask out certain areas and reglaze others, or for applying pigment onto the unresisted areas. Resist can be purchased as a cold-water soluble solution, or made from a selection of waxes heated with turpentine or similar solvent. A mixture of beeswax and candle grease could be used. The resist must not be too hard when set, or too tacky — the former tends to flake off and the latter fails to resist cleanly.

Points to remember
●Never place the container with the wax directly onto the source of heat, but place it instead in a container of water for melting.
●When scratching through wax prior to applying pigment, do not brush the clay dust off with a dry brush as it will adhere to the wax and reduce its capacity to resist. Shake the dust off if possible, or blow it away from you gently with an empty slip trailer. Wear a mask to avoid inhaling any dust.

1. The raw dry clay dish is painted with 'brush wax' — a cold water-soluble resist. The painted areas are light in tone and are not clearly defined.

2. Lines are scratched through the resist to the clay. Be firm, but gentle as too much pressure will break the dish. (Do not use too fine a point).

3. Pigment is applied to the unresisted areas and the scratched lines. It should be applied quickly with broad brush strokes.

4. The pigment is scratched with the blade of a knife in the unresisted areas of the dish. This contrasts with the dark lines scratched in the resist areas.

heater or placed in, or on top of, a hot kiln which is firing. Another slightly softer but stiff, colored glaze is sprayed over the top. When completely dry, the glaze can be scratched away where desired to leave patterns or shapes. It is then refired. More than one glaze can be sprayed on before scratching to give a wider range of colors. The skill is in firing the second glaze to the correct temperature so that it is fired into the glaze (inglaze), but do not fire it too high, otherwise the image will break up and blend with the first glaze.

Tube lining

This method of decorating ware is not unlike slip trailing, but is it carried out on a bisqued surface, using a matt glaze mixture. The success of the solution will depend on several factors. The first consideraton is to be sure to use materials with the minimum shrinkage, such as kaolin, flint whiting or fine grog to prevent the surface cracking as it dries. Secondly the line, or area of tube line should adhere firmly to the ware so that it does not smudge when the glazes are applied. Adhesion is achieved by the soda in the

5. Another wax resist dish is treated with pigment. There is a certain excitement with this method of application as the unwaxed areas suddenly become black and reveal shapes that are not always part of the premeditated design. The technique develops a sensibility to positive and negative shape and the ability to integrate them into a design.

SPRAY-GLAZED CERAMICS

The application of glaze over an already fired glaze, and the technique of scratching through one to the other can be used on a large number of shapes or surfaces. Application of the glaze can be with a brush, spray gun or it can be poured, though greater control is by spraying.

Landscape with hens and rooster

Ann and Kenneth Clark, UK
Height: 24 in (75 cm)
Width: 32 in (90 cm)

One of several panels designed for a wholefood butcher's shop in which farm animals were to be depicted in a rural setting. The inner panel of tiles was first sprayed with an overlapping series of colored glazes ranging from blue to mauve, and then green to iron red on standard white tiles. After firing, a second dark blue-green glaze was sprayed and allowed to dry. A little glue was added to the top glaze to assist adhesion, and prevent chipping when scratching the design through the glaze to reveal the colors underneath Gauging the thickness of glaze application is crucial in order to get good definition when scratching as well as strength of tone. At this stage any details may be picked out with pigment brushed on. The technique can be expanded by spraying more than one color at the second glazing and it may often be necessary to have a third stronger, or different colored glaze to complete the design. The tiles around the border were silk screen, printed onto bisque with an inglaze yellow and then spray glazed with a pale transparent blue glaze. The background tiles were a warm off-white.

Section of landscape panel with cows

Ann and Kenneth Clark, UK
Height: 32 in (81 cm)
Width: 72 in (183 cm)

This is another section of the butcher's shop panel, using the same techniques as for the other panel. Because of the subject it was more difficult to achieve the tones from near to far distance.

TUBE-LINED CERAMICS

Glaze on a bisque surface can be extremely attractive. Prevent crazing by avoiding the use of materials that shrink and apply the tube lining firmly to avoid smudging.

Earthenware decorated jar
Moorcroft Pottery, UK
Height: 3 in (8 cm)

The outline of the design is first applied to the leather-hard pot with a tube liner, filled with slip made from the same clay as the body. When bisqued underglaze colors are painted onto the areas like watercolor painting with a graduated intensity of color. These colors may be hardened on by firing before glazing with a transparent glaze. A similar technique can be used on bisque fired ware with a special tube-line mixture. Colored glazes are then applied to the outlined areas, instead of underglaze colors.

A selection of Victorian tiles
(below) Most of these tiles have been decorated using the tube-line technique with the application of colored glazes. In some areas more than one color has been used and the colors allowed to flow together. The relief decoration on two of the tiles has been achieved by using a tile die made from an original relief mold.
1. Clear turquoise glaze has been applied thickly and this has flowed into the lower areas during firing, thus emphasising the form.
2, 3, 4, 5. Tube line designs with applied colored transparent glazes.
6. Colored glaze has been applied to the relief areas, possibly with a brush.

1	2	3
4	5	6

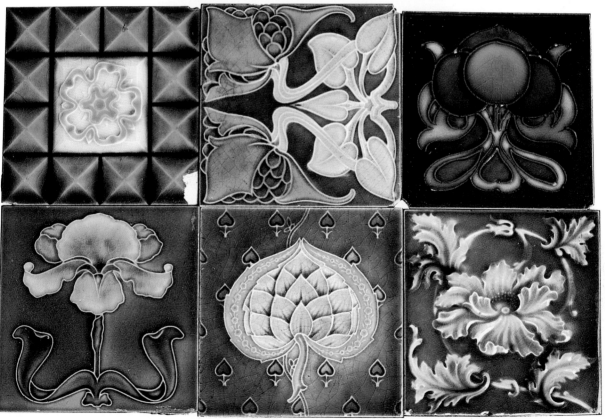

TUBE LINING

Tube lining involves working on a bisqued surface with a matt glaze decorative mixture. The design can be sketched out with a fibre-tip pen (left) in preparation for the actual lining, the design for which can be treated freely or formally, with clearly defined areas of color. The technique was frequently used, as here, for the decoration of tiles; it is also suitable for large murals and panels.

Points to remember
- Using a slip-trailing tool and nozzle means that large areas of the colored glaze can be applied quickly.
- The mixture should be just fluid enough to flow from the nozzle freely, giving an easy, continuous line. If it is too fluid, it will tend to crack on drying, as the lining will be too shallow.

1. The outline of the design is drawn on a bisque-fired tile with the tube-line mixture. The thickness of line is determined by the size of the aperture in the nozzle. The potter is aiming to create a free-flowing line, so that the lines she is creating are as much a part of the design as the areas of color.

3. The aesthetic aim is to use the line to create texture in the design, as well as delineating an area for glazing.

4. Areas are filled in with thick turquoise glaze, using an ⅛ in (0.3 cm) aperture nozzle in a slip trailer. Practice enables the potter to keep the glaze flowing.

5. A large background area of glaze is filled in with slip trailer as the design nears completion.

6. Specific features are defined with a brush and pigment. When the glaze has dried, a water-charged sable brush is run down the joints and the tiles divided.

alkaline frit, or by using soda ash or sodium carbonate. A little ball clay should be added so that the mixture flows easily when thick, but still keeps its adhesive quality. Finally the mixture must have sufficient flux to allow it to fuse at the required firing temperature for the glazes. The fluxes are supplied by the ball clay, alkaline frit and, to some extent, by the whiting.

Before applying the tube line, damp the surface of the ware with a sponge. Use a nozzle which is finer than one used for slip trailing (0.5 or 1 mm aperture should be adequate). When the tube line is dry, the glazes can be applied with a brush or trailed from a slip trailer into the outlined areas. If the tube line lifts off when drying, just touch the section with a wet camel hair brush and the moisture will activate the soda and renew adhesion.

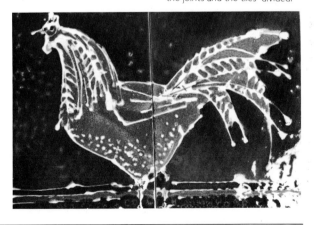

MAJOLICA

Inglaze painting is the potter's term for the application of pigments onto a raw, unfired glaze either before or after the article has been biscuited. When a white opaque tin glaze is used, the technique is called majolica painting, though it can be used to equal effect on color transparent glaze. When fired, the pigments permeate the glaze to create the final effect.

Points to remember

●The underlying glaze should not be too soft. Because of the fluxing action of most basic oxides during firing, the effect will be ruined if this is so.

●Stains or underglaze colors should be mixed with a little flux or base glaze before use.

●Do not apply the glaze too thinly. If you do, the oxide will saturate the glaze when it is applied and the end result will be black, not the anticipated color.

1. A palette knife can be used to grind the colors into a fine powder. If necessary, base glaze or flux can be added and ground at this stage.

2. The jug is placed on a banding wheel and this makes it easier to brush on the bands of color around the base.

3. A broad brush is used to add the larger areas of color. This is easier to apply if the wrist is steadied by resting it on the left hand.

4. The heavier areas of color are applied with a broad brush. As the design becomes more intricate, increasingly smaller brushes should be used.

5. The motif on the side of the jug is built up gradually, first using broad brush strokes.

6. Long strokes are done with a long medium brush, which holds sufficient paint for the strokes. The black oxides will reveal their true color of firing.

7. The thinnest and longest brush strokes are added with a long narrow brush to complete the qualities of contrast in the composition. After applying the band to the top of the jug, another full brush stroke defines the line of the handle.

Recipe for tube lining mixture
Firing temperature 1060°C - 1100°C (1940 - 2010°F).

Plain
35 gms china clay (kaolin)
15 gms black ball clay
35 gms flint
3 gms whiting
3 gms borax frit
3 gms high alkali frit

Black
35 gms china clay (kaolin)
15 gms black ball clay
35 gms frit
3 gms whiting
3 gms borax frit
10 gms high alkali
8 gms manganese dioxide
3 gms cobalt oxide
4 gms iron oxide

dry. When dry the outlined area is filled with other colored glazes and then fired to the desired temperature. Again the maturing temperature of the glazes is critical to prevent the two glazes combining. This technique is used mainly for earthenware.

Clay tube line and underglaze colours
For decoration on smoothly turned, thrown or cast forms the design is drawn in outline with fine tube-lined slip on the leather-hard pot. When the clay is bone dry or bisqued, these outlined areas are painted with underglaze colors, over which a transparent glaze is applied.

Underglaze colors
Underglaze colors are generally applied by brushing,

Glaze trailing
This technique is used to give a rich amalgam of colored glazes to the surface of tiles or dishes. The outline of the design is generally trailed with a dark glaze and allowed to

GLAZE BRUSHWORK

The brush can express deliberation or immediacy. It can give a fine line or a broad line and is used for applying slip, pigment or glaze.

Decorated earthenware plate
Plate: Ian McKenzie, UK
Decoration: Fiona Salazar, UK
Diameter: 11 in (28 cm)

This plate shows the richness of a freely decorated pattern, using a simple motif which flows across the form. The colors are mainly underglaze stains and glazes with some pink enamel onglaze. The glaze is a lime zinc matt which harmonizes well with the underglaze colors, and the firing is to 1060°C (1940°F). The design has much in common with some of the all over Persian decorated dishes.

Stoneware platter
Milton Moon, Australia
Diameter: 6 in (15 cm)

A sensitive rendering of inglaze brushwork on an oxidized stoneware platter. Decoration is with basic oxides onto a nephyline syenite glaze and the ware is fired in an oxidizing kiln at 1280°C (2340°F).

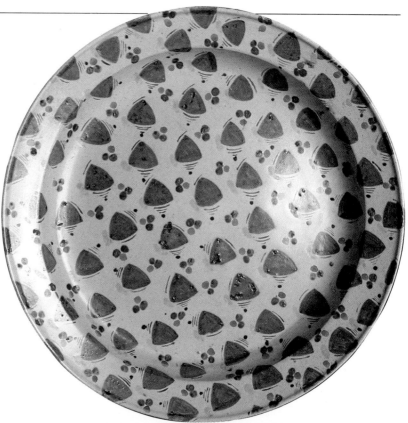

Glaze decorated stoneware bowl
Janice Tchalenko, UK
Diameter: 14 in (36 cm)

The bisqued bowl is decorated with a magnesia semi-shiny white glaze. When completely dry, colored glazes are brushed and trailed onto the glaze, and the bowl is given a reduction firing to 1280°C (2340°F). Colored glazes used are copper red, blue, matt pink, yellow and green. Many designs are based on flowers, and others are inspired by rich Persian fabrics and ceramics. The painter, Matisse had also been a strong influence.
Recipe for white glaze

Potash felspar	55
China clay (kaolin)	15
Quartz	15
Whiting	10
Talc	5

Hand built decorated porcelain
Agalis Manessi, UK
Height: 15 in (38 cm)

There is considerable harmony in the method of making the vase and the interpretation of the decoration. It suggests that the flower was very much a part of the whole from the moment of conception and one feels that the marks of the brush have the same deliberation as the contours of the vase. The body used was David Leach porcelain (page 19) fired to 1250°C (2280°F) with a tin/dolomite glaze. Oxides used in the decoration are copper, nickel, rutile and chrome.

Wood-fired, inglaze decorated bowl
(below left)
Alan Caiger-Smith, UK
Diameter: 12 in (30 cm)

An example of masterly and direct handling of a broad brush to fully exploit its qualities. The brush strokes are used to create a design which is abstract, but gives equal consideration to the decorated and undecorated areas of the whole. The iconography of the brushwork is an integral part of the design. The glaze is a lead-frit based 10 per cent tin glaze on a red bisque body, fired to 1060°C (1940°F). Decoration is with a pink stain and mixed basic oxides.

Hand-built decorated stoneware vase
(above)
Stephen Benwell, Australia
Height: 16 in (41 cm)

This coiled and slabbed vase is made from light-colored stoneware clay. When dry, the clay was decorated with oxides and ferro glaze stains, which were lightly brushed onto the surface, after bisquing the vase was glazed with a dolomite glaze and given an oxidized firing to 1290°C (2350°F).

Decorated porcelain boxes *(above)*
David Leach, UK
Diameter: 4 in (10 cm)

Painted with a dolomite glaze and reduction fired to 1280°C (2340°F), these boxes were decorated by an overglaze incorporating blue and iron pigments and red nephyline syenite glaze, applied thick from a slip trailer. The red glaze is composed of 50 parts low calcium, high iron red clay and 50 parts nephyline syenite. To reduce plasticity and contraction, which causes it literally to crawl off the glaze over which it is applied, the red clay had to be calcined to 600°C (1110°F) before its mixture with the nephyline syenite.

Decorated thrown porcelain bowl *(below)*
John Sweden, New Zealand
Diameter: 19 in (48 cm)

This bowl's fluidity and freedom of decoration is reminiscent of early Chinese painting, while the pattern of flowers and butterflies shows how Sweden is influenced by his rural working environment. The bowl was glazed with a pale green felspathic glaze and reduction fired in a gas kiln to 1300°C (2370°F).

Lidded earthenware pot
Geoffrey Parkinson, UK
Height: 9½ in (24 cm)

This thrown pot was made with white earthenware clay and painted with a lime zinc matt glaze applied over a black underglaze decoration its humoros shape and design suggest Greek influence while the pot's form is complemented by the lively drawing, where the piano echoes the contour of the musician's foot and the knob.

sponging, stippling or spraying onto a bisqued surface with a light oil or oil and spirit based medium. This could be pure turps mixed with fat oil of turpentine or a proprietary brand of medium obtainable from a ceramic color merchant. Before glazing the color should be fired on at a temperature of 800°C – 950°C (1470–1740°F) to fire away the oil and adhere the pigment to the ware prior to glazing. If this is not done the oil could erupt through the glaze in the early stages of firing.

Glazing is usually done with a clear transparent glaze or a transparent colored glaze.

Underglaze pencils and crayons
These may be bought from suppliers but a substitute can be made by mixing stains or underglaze colors with china clay, extruding the mixture in pencil form and firing to the required degree of firmness for handling.

Another method is to mix the color with plaster of paris and cast it into holes pressed into soft clay to form finger size chalks for drawing on bisqueware. Once the decoration is complete, cover and fire with a thin coating of transparent glaze. One of the most versatile and reliable transparent glazes is Harrisons Glaze 3622/6 which has a wide temperature range, firing from 1040°C to 1150°C (1900°F to 2100°F).

Inglaze decoration
Inglaze is when coloring pigments are applied under a glaze, onto the glaze before firing, or onto a once-fired glaze surface. The ware is then fired to a temperature at which the color fully permeates the glaze. Applying pigments to the glaze before firing has long been an established practice and includes the majolica technique (painting on to unfired opaque white glaze).

Glazed tiles can be overprinted with pigment or glaze and then fired until the print becomes inglaze. This is very different to decorating with enamels, which flux and only adhere to the surface of the glaze.

Crystalline glazes
There are two basic methods of producing crystalline glazes. The first is to saturate the glaze with coloring oxides, such as iron, manganese, zirconium or cobalt and then allow them to cool very slowly so that crystals are formed. This method produces fine crystals which will give a texture, sparkle or opacity to the glaze and can be applied to both earthenware and stoneware. For earthenware the critical temperature for crystal forming is around 800°C; for stoneware it is also 800°C (1470°F).

The second method is also dependent on slow cooling, but the composition of the glaze is of equal importance to producing the right reaction for the forming of the large umbrella-like crystals (which can be up to 3 inches in diameter). The two factors governing the formation of the crystals are that the glaze should be soft and fluid, with a low viscosity (and little or no alumina which gives viscosity), and it should contain a refractory ingredient such as titanium or ilmenite or some form of calcium or zirconium. These refractory substances do not melt in the glaze, but on cooling, act as a seed or nucleus from which the crystals grow. The glazes are fired quickly to a stoneware temperature (1260°C/2300°F)) to melt the ingredients and then rapidly cooled in 1120-1140°C (2050-2080°F). This temperature is held for about two hours and then dropped to 1080°C (1980°F), where it is held for a further two hours before the kiln is switched off.

As the glaze is fluid during firing and will run off the pots, adequate precautions will be necessary to protect the kiln shelves or to collect the glaze. The pot should be well supported from the inner base and be placed clear of the container or surface collecting the molten glaze. It is obviously easier when producing crystal glaze, to use a horizontal surface such as a tile, rather than a vertical form.

The form of the pot is important in creating suitable areas to show the crystal formation. The glaze may be dipped, sprayed, poured or brushed, but brushing and spraying give the best opportunities for varying the thickness as required, especially on the shoulder of the pot. The glaze needs to be thicker at the top of the form as it will flow downwards. While not essential, it is a great help to have digital kiln controls for the temperature in order to control, and gauge accurately, the periods and temperatures of cooling.

A basis from which to develop a satisfactory glaze firing to 1260°C (2300°F) would be:

Soda, potash or borax frit	45-62%	Zinc oxide	22-27%
Flint	5-20%	Titanium dioxide	5-9%

Above This section is of a plate with crystal glaze as a decorative technique. The fine crystals add their own distinct qualities of texture to the glaze. The largest crystal is 4 in (10 cm) across.

MIXED MEDIA

No other period in history has seen such a diversity of techniques in making and decorating pottery than the present. The desire for novelty and discovery is now the main motivation for experimenting with new methods of pottery making, although sufficient time and money play an important part in indulging these interests. For all the facilities available today, the best work is still the most simple in style and sympathetic in the use of available materials.

Bone china bowl
Angela Verdon, UK
Height: 5 in (13 cm)

These bone china bowls have been incised and pierced after they have been fired to a temperature of 1080°C

(1980°F). They are then fettled and rubbed with wet and dry abrasive paper and painted with body stains. The second firing is to 1220°C (2230°F).

Raku fired, broken and reassembled bowl
Rick Dillingham, USA

This Raku-fired bowl is reminiscent of the Oribe period in Japanese pottery. The ware had a lively, asymmetric quality which makes use of the juxtaposition of disparate images — many derived from fabric designs. This bowl has been broken after firing and the sherds decorated individually (without reference to the rest of the piece) with pigments and gold before refiring and reassembling the pieces.

Stoneware dish
Brian Gartside, New Zealand
Diameter: 15 in (38 cm)

Several colored glazes have been used in the decoration of this dish. The glazes are poured on, or applied by other methods and the glaze is scratched through. The dish was fired to a temperature of 1240°C (2260°F).

Decorated thrown black bowl
Kenneth Clark, UK
Diameter: 8 in (20 cm)

The bowl is thrown with a black clay and, after bisque firing to 1120°C (2050°F), it is trailed with an opaque white glaze. It is then thinly glazed all over with a high alkaline turquoise glaze and gloss fired to 1060°C (1940°F).

Recipe for glaze
P 2250 Alkaline frit	90 gms
Flint	27.00 gms
China clay (kaolin)	4.50 gms
Copper oxide	4.00 gms
Nephyline syenite	13.50 gms

Salt-glazed and decorated porcelain vase
Jane Peiser, Canada

The vase is hand-built and inlaid with colored clays as well as areas of agateware. The commercial stains used in coloring the inlay are, as far as possible, the same color before and after firing. The vase is salt-glazed and given an oxidized firing to 1305°C (2380°F). Similar pieces are often refined at enamel temperatures, using transfers and enamels.

Porcelain plate
John Glick, USA
Diameter: 18 in (46 cm)

This example shows a lively, direct use of
mixed media together with a range of
techniques. Aside from the asymmetrical free
shaping of the plate's edge, a number of
colored slips were applied by sponging, and
then areas of the surface were scraped away.
The rolling of patterns and surface combing
were other techniques used. When bisqued,
the plate was glazed and reduction-fired to
1305°C (2380°F).

Porcelain pinched shallow bowl
Mary Rogers, UK
Diameter: 6½ in (17 cm)

For this exquisitely fine, pinched porcelain
bowl, the behavior of the clay has been
exploited to great advantage. The edge was
allowed to fray in a controlled manner and
then pigmented in such a way that the matt
glaze was stained and permeated to resemble
colour at the edge of flower petals. A
delicately patterned clay ammonite was
worked in the base.

Thrown Raku dish
Brian Gartside, NZ
Diameter: 15 in (38 cm)

Brian Gartside works with an extensive range of materials, techniques and media. His diverse visual interests are seldom stated in figurative or descriptive terms; much of his work is decorated with what he calls environmental symbols. This dish was Raku fired to 1000°C (1380°F) and then salt-smoked with the addition of acrylic decoration.

Lidded stoneware container
John Sweden, NZ
Diameter: 4½ in (12 cm)
Height: 3 in (8 cm)

The bamboo brushwork design, applied as a wax resist, embraces and unifies the whole form. The container was first glazed a pale green/grey and decorated with wax resist. A deep green to rust red khaki glaze was then applied thickly and fired in a reduction gas kiln to 1310°C (2390°F).

Recipe for khaki glaze

Blue china stone	60
New Zealand ball clay	16
Wollastonite	7
Talc	6
Silica	11
Titanium	40
Red iron oxide	7

Fire in a reduction kiln to between 1285 -1355°C (2345 - 2470°F) for both recipes.

Recipe for green/grey glaze

Sletley potash felspar	26
New Zealand china clay (ultra fine)	13
Wollastonite	27
New Zealand ball clay	6
Talc	3
Silica	26

Thrown and turned teapot
Roger Michell, UK
Height: 6 in (15 cm)

The technique used for this teapot required it to be fired three times, but this body also stands up extremely well to raw glazing and firing, if a suitable glaze is used. Made from Watts Blake Bearne fine white earthenware, the teapot was first biscuit-fired to 1120°C (2050°F), with a three-hour soak. After glazing and firing to 1040°C (1900°F) with a low solubility lead frit glaze and a two-hour soak, it was sprayed with enamel to give the geometric pattern. Some hand-painted enamel was also applied before the third firing at 750°C (1380°F).

Tiles

WITH CERAMIC OR TILE MURALS, the first consideration must be the suitability of the proposed design in its architectural context, whatever the final image or treatment of the ceramics. Assessing this involves scale, color, relationship to other surfaces, lighting and maintenance. The method of fixing must also be taken into account and sometimes the possibility of future removal to another site.

The most satisfactory projects are those in which the maker and designer are the same person. This means that the mural will be designed with the knowledge of exactly how it will be made and what colors will be used. This can reduce the cost of developmental work. The ability to draw and supply an adequate sketch is essential in any case, as clients are reluctant to commit themselves to large sums of money without seeing a rough and possibly pieces of glazed ceramics to show the final finish, before starting work.

DESIGNING A PANEL

The brief for this mural was that it should illustrate subjects relating to Norwegian rural and farm life. Having discussed the color scheme and subject with the client, a selection of sample tile glazes was assembled and quantities of each color made up and tested. These were then used on small sample tiles to see how they reacted with each other (right). Small sections of the design were also executed in miniature (far right) to show the general style and decorative theme in context. At the same time, a scale watercolor sketch was submitted for approval with the glaze references for each tile (below). Having checked all the colors, and techniques once more, the final mural was then made. The details were first outlined by trailing with dark brown glaze; when dry, the spaces between were filled in with the appropriate colored glazes, using the same techniques and tools. The tiles themselves were 8 in x 12 in (20 cm x 30 cm) unglazed and stoneware tiles, supplied by a tile manufacturer.

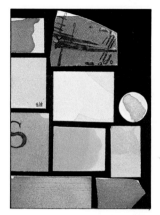

Tile number

Glaze code for reference when decorating tile.

TILE DECORATION

The examples here show how varied tile decoration can be.

In the top row *(from left to right)*, the Victorian tile is decorated with tube line or molded relief to hold years of colored glaze. After the areas of color are filled in the entire tile was coated with clear glaze. The William De Morgan copper luster brush painted tile was one of a series decorated in this color and in this way. The glaze trailed design was created directly onto a white glazed and fired commercial tile. The glazes

were colored with basic oxides or glaze stains, all formulated to fire at the same temperature.

In the middle row, the Lancastrian tile is influenced by the Persian technique of broadly modelling relief areas, which are then glazed and more clearly defined by luster brush decoration. The William De Morgan hand-painted underglaze design was subsequently glazed with an akaline glaze to give the flowers their turquoise blue color. The group of small luster tiles by Alan Caiger-Smith used copper- and silver-based lusters on a white tin glaze. The tiles were fired in a wood-firing kiln.

In the bottom row, Danka Napiorowska's bathroom tile panel shows the use of stencil, while the encaustic Victorian tile's medieval

theme was extremely popular in its day. The Persian tile inspired De Morgan to develop his Persian-style glazes and some of his designs.

FIXING AND HANGING PANELS

The most important thing to consider when hanging tiled panels is the security of the fixing. There are various alternatives which can be used; these include strong adhesive, cement and screwing. The choice of method depends largely on the panel's thickness or weight. With concrete and brick walls, check that the wall will take the weight of the ceramic and then fix directly; if the panel is to be hung, it should be fixed first to a thick ply support, using screws and adhesive, and then hung using one of the methods shown here.

Points to remember
●Only fix thin tiles directly to plastered walls. Heavy tiles must be hung on a panel.

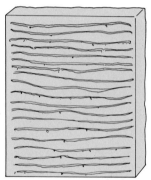

The ceramic slab (above) has been grooved on the back to provide a key for the fixing agent. The grooves are cut when the slab is cheese-hard, as it will then not bend while being handled. The depth of the grooves should be related to the thickness of the slab.

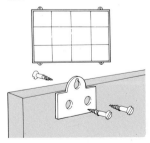

Mirror brackets are a good way of fixing these framed tiles to a wall (above). The brackets should be fixed to the wooden backing before the tiles to establish the right length for the screws.

This slab (below) has had holes drilled in it to take screws. The screws should be countersunk, so that their heads will be below the slab's surface. Small ceramic plugs are then colored and fitted to conceal the screws.

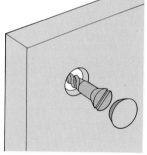

This is an efficient and easily adjustable method of hanging heavy ceramic panels. Holes are drilled into the clay at the leather-hard stage and heavy galvanized or mild steel wire inserted. The holes must slope upwards. When the clay is fired, the ends of the wires are bent into a loop to be hung from screws in the wall (below).

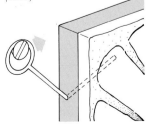

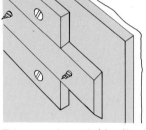

This mounted ceramic (above) is being fixed wood to wall by dovetail battening on the back of its support through a single batten screwed to the wall. For a large panel, an additional plain batten of equal thickness, to the lower half of the panel, should also be fitted to keep the panel equidistant from the wall.

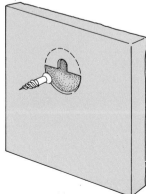

Individual heavy tiles or plaques can be hung over a screw head in the wall using this method (above). The recess is cut out with a knife fitted with a curved blade.

The panels (above) have had heavy-duty nails embedded in them while soft. When the panels dry, the nails will be firmly in place, so providing ideal stability for the eventual support.

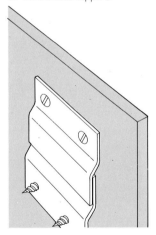

Another way of fixing a heavy mounted ceramic panel to a wall is to use bent mild steel strips (above). These can be almost as wide as the panel. This is a firm hanging method, which will support very heavy panels and, at the same time, is easy to remove. Sufficient tolerance must be left in the strips to take up any slight bowing in the backing wood panel, while the wall needs to be extremely level.

'The Garden', ceramic panel
Alan Lloyd, UK
6 ft × 5 ft (1.8 m × 1.5 m)

This panel is made from pieces cut out of stoneware clay and fired at various temperatures from 850 - 1200°C (1560 - 2190°F). As none of the pieces are glazed, the drawing texture and subtle variation of colored clay and pigments provide visual impact and serve to balance the composition. Colors range from pale terracotta and buff to dark brown, the pigments brushed or sprayed on using underglaze colors and oxides. Smooth clay is used so that at the leather-hard stage the motifs can be drawn and cut, giving the surface a textured quality.

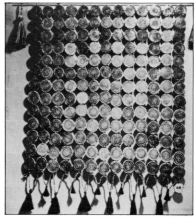

Hanging screen of porcelain dishes *(above)*
Les Blakebrough, Australia
3 ft (1 m) square

This screen illustrates the richness that can be achieved using clay and pigments alone. Each tiny porcelain disc (7 cm in diameter) was pressed with another disc to give a decorative pattern. When dry, iron and cobalt oxide in various strengths were washed over each surface, giving a higher intensity in the recesses. When the discs were fired to porcelain temperature (1300°C/2370°F) the color fused and reacted with the vitrified body, making glazing unnecessary.

Ceramic and lacquer panels
Les Blakebrough, Australia
10 ft × 18 ft (3 m × 5.5 m)

This is one of a set of two panels designed for the entrance of the main theatre auditorium of the University Centre in Tasmania. Each unit is composed of 12 tiles 18 in (45 cm) square and 1½ in (3 cm) thick, mounted on 1 in (2.5 cm) thick plywood panels. Each panel is bolted to a steel support pipe 4 in (10 cm) in diameter. The tiles were made by mounting a wooden die on a radial arm and passing it across the surface of the clay. They are, composed of sillimanite kiln shelf body fired to 1250°C (2280°F), unglazed, but given a cobalt wash. The lacquered panels were made by lacquering and silk screening the design onto composition board and then adding gold leaf and burnishing.

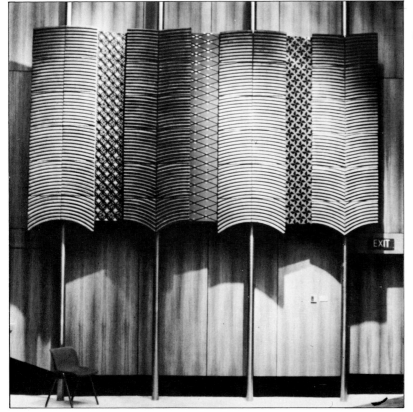

SCULPTURAL CERAMICS

In the past 10 years ceramics has moved further into the field of fine art. In many ways the potential of clay and glaze has added scope to the sculptor's vocabulary and is another medium to add to his already extensive range. Forms of expression cover the figurative and the abstract, but a sculptural ceramicist such as James Tower, still makes use of the hollow pot form to convey his ideas. Others are less creative and fail to detach the concept of form from the functional with the result that their work is neither useful nor successful as an art form.

Earthenware animal bicycle
Ruth Franklin, UK
Diameter: 28½ in (71 cm)

This slab-built sculpture is almost two-dimensional. It is made with Saint Thomases clay (Potclays) and biscuit fired to 1120°C (2050°F). It is then painted with acrylic colors. The sculpture is supported with flat wooden battens, fixed to a blue perspex base. The graphic element blends successfully with the form,
suggesting an animal, bird and bicycle within one piece.

Stoneware bust
Jill Crowley, UK
Height: 18 in (46 cm)

The hollow bust was coiled and modelled, and then painted with slip-type glaze which gives a dry to matt surface. Underglaze colors have also been applied to the surface and the sculpture fired to a stoneware temperature of 1250°C (2280°F).

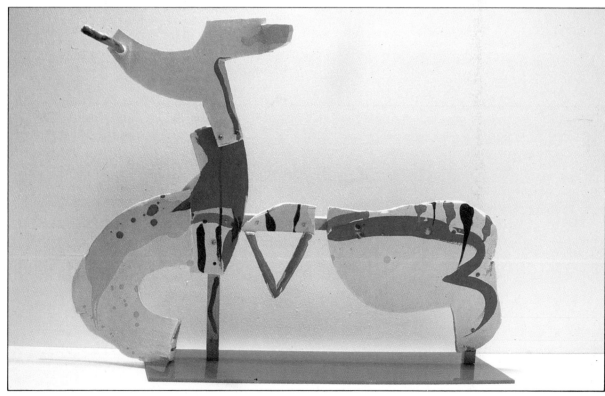

Sculptural form (right)
Ruth Duckworth, USA
Height: 6 ft (1.8 m)

Ruth Duckworth has drawn inpiration from organic form to make this agateware sculpture. This is a work made for a pastoral environment and the shapes have an affinity with trees and other vegetation. Her work always displays an appreciation of the inherent qualities of stoneware and porcelain, combined with a subtle use of color, texture and lamination which complements the form.

Sculptural Form for the Reserve Bank of New Zealand, Auckland (below)
Roy Cowan, New Zealand
Height: 7 ft (214 cm)

The form was made with a white stoneware body in three interlocking sections and given a salt-glaze firing to 1280°C (2340°F). The colors are blue grey to white with a deeper blue at the edges. Inside is a saturated red-iron column and inside that a steel pillar which holds the form together. The structure has a degree of flexibility to withstand the shock of earthquakes and other hazards. The form has a great richness which contrasts with the smooth surfaces of the interior of the building. It has a similarity with the Maori-ancestor panels which are found in meeting houses and are familiar to most New Zealanders.

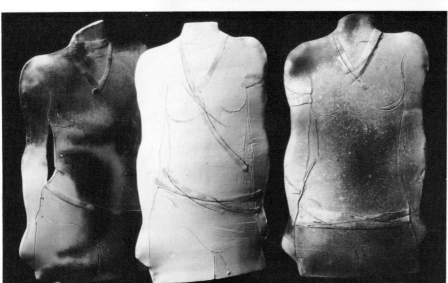

Raku and porcelain torsos
Christie Brown, UK
Height: 20 in (50 cm)

The clay in these shallow slabbed torso forms is characterized by gently shaped relief and incised drawings, executed while the clay was soft for added definition.

They were all bisque fired to 1140°C (2080°F) and the two made in Raku body carbonized by sawdust firing them to 750°C (1380°F). The center porcelain torso was waxed after bisque firing.

Printing techniques

PRINTMAKING TECHNIQUES are used by many modern potters for decorative purposes. This section outlines the main processes and shows you how to utilize them.

Silk screen printing

In this method of printing, ceramic colors are mixed with an oil-based medium and printed through a nylon mesh, using a tool called a squeegee. The image may be printed directly onto the screen or applied to the mesh using a photo-sensitive emulsion with a clear plastic backing, on which the image originating from a drawing, photograph or design has been fixed. The image can be printed directly onto a ceramic sufrace, such as a tile or onto transfer paper. It can also be printed onto a gelatine pad over which the ceramic form is rolled to pick up the printed image. As color is pushed through the negative shape of the stencil on the screen, the image is printed onto the surface underneath. The squeegee is a piece of slotted wood into which a half-inch (5cm) thick strip of flexible rubber or polythene which is held in a groove in an oblong piece of wood. The rubber strip forces the color through the mesh onto the ceramic or transfer paper.

The frame is made of wood or metal with a piece of nylon mesh stretched tight over the face and it is either clamped or attached with glue or staples. The gauge of the mesh will vary according to the intended use, weight of color required and the particular materials to be printed. The thread of the mesh is either mono-filament or multi-filament. This means that each cross-thread of the weave is a single strand of nylon or several twisted or spun together. The threads and the spaces between them vary in size, but

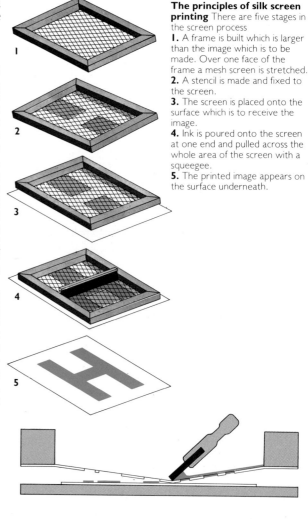

The principles of silk screen printing There are five stages in the screen process
1. A frame is built which is larger than the image which is to be made. Over one face of the frame a mesh screen is stretched.
2. A stencil is made and fixed to the screen.
3. The screen is placed onto the surface which is to receive the image.
4. Ink is poured onto the screen at one end and pulled across the whole area of the screen with a squeegee.
5. The printed image appears on the surface underneath.

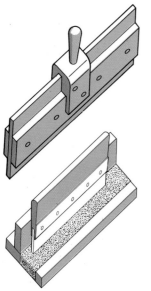

The squeegee Most squeegees consist of a synthetic polyurethane blade set into a wooden handle.

Left and above When the frame is laid down prior to printing, the screen mesh must not come into contact with the surface which is to receive the image. There should be a small gap between the mesh and the printing surface. When using the squeegee (above), it should be held at an angle of 45° to the screen. Take care to apply pressure evenly.

A silk screen press in action
(left). The screen is held in a
metal frame during the process of
printing onto transfer paper. The
surface under the paper is a grid
of small holes over a vacuum box
attached to a vacuum motor
under and attached to the
printing table. The vacuum is
operated by the foot pedal;
alternatively, it can be operated
by a contact and break point on
the printing frame. The printed
transfers are hung to dry on the
steel rack on the right; they
should be left for at least 24
hours.

Silk screens *(below)* vary in
weave and consequently in
strength. The basic taffeta weave
is strong and durable, but not as
strong as the full multi-filament
weave *(bottom)*, which has a
thread added to every strand.

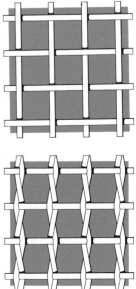

MAKING A SCREEN

There is a wide range of frames and screens which can be made or bought. For most purposes, however, a screen attached to a wooden frame is quite sufficient.

Points to remember
● Make sure that the cloth of the screen is 3 - 4 in (7.5 - 10 cm) larger than the frame.
● Ensure that a strong, permanent bond is achieved, otherwise the image could become distorted during printing.

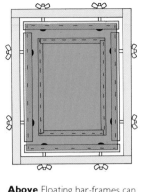

Above Floating bar-frames can be used for stretching a frame. The bars are attached to the frame by bolts and butterfly nuts and are adjustable.

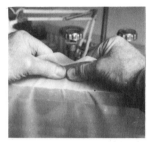

1. Staple the mesh from the center of one side of the screen moving out towards the corners. Repeat the process along the opposite side so.

2. When attaching the fabric, staple through a thin strip of card to avoid tearing the mesh. Trim off the surplus fabric around the edges of the frame. Fold the

fabric around the corners of the frame. Secure the folds with staples.

the one constant factor is the number of apertures to the square inch or centimetre. These are stated as 40, 80, 100 and 300 mesh, but as there is no standard classification of thread sizes, you must be careful when choosing the mesh for a particular purpose. The size of mesh will vary according to the thickness of the deposit required and the sharpness of the line or outline to be printed. You may be printing an area of thick glaze, using a coarse mesh with a resultant variable outline, or printing very fine detail using a fine thread. Very close, fine mesh is used for luster or precious metals. The three most desirable qualities when printing glaze are crispness of image outline, strength or weight of color and thickness of deposit.

Metal mesh screens are used for very long print runs, but for the work of small studios, wooden frames are adequate. They should nevertheless be well made and thoroughly varnished or primed to prevent water absorption during washing which can warp the frames. If wooden frames are used, the nylon can be hand-stretched and stapled, or stretched in a special frame and the mesh glued to the face of the screen with a two-part resin adhesive. If you are stretching the frame by hand, make sure the piece of nylon cloth is 3 to 4 inches (8 to 10 cm) larger than the frame, the wood of which should be soft enough to take the staples easily. Using a staple gun, attach the mesh right across one end and then reverse the screen and, starting from the middle, stretch and staple it tightly for the width of the frame. Now take up the tension and staple right down one side, leaving the opposite side to be

stapled. This should be done starting from the middle and working outwards, making it as tight as possible before the insertion of each staple. Fold the corners and staple down; trim off any surplus cloth.

Once stretched, the nylon must be cleaned thoroughly to remove any possible oil or spirit-based contaminant. To clean off any water-based dirt, scrub with liquid bleach. As a precaution, use Acetone as a solvent for any dirt which is spirit-based. Lastly, scrub the back of the mesh (which takes the image) with a scouring bleach such as Vim, Ajax or a similar brand. This is to give roughness or bite to the nylon surface which, being new, is very smooth and less likely to take the photo image or emulsion easily.

Indirect photo stencil: Whatever the image it will need to be an opaque black positive on a piece of clear transparent film. This must be exposed to the light in a vacuum frame or under clear glass against a photo-sensitive emulsion with a clear plastic backing. The distance of the image from the light source should be about 30 inches (76 cm) when you are using two Mercury Vapour light bulbs of 500 watts each. The exposure time is three to five minutes, depending on the strength or thickness of the emulsion. After exposure, take the film with the emulsion and place it in a solution of four parts water and one part hydrogen peroxide (with a strength of 20 volumes) for one minute. Wash the film gently in a large sink with luke-warm water, using a shower attachment, and hold the exposed film at an angle so that the residue runs away easily. After about one minute the image will begin to appear where the emulsion

INDIRECT PHOTO STENCIL

Indirect photo stencils are made away from the screen and attached to it after they have been exposed and developed. The stencil is usually manufactured in the form of a two-layer film. One of these layers consists of emulsion; the other layer is a transparent backing sheet which is removed after exposure.

1. Place the film positive on the exposure screen, emulsion side up. Cover it with a sheet of sensitized gelatine.

2. Center the positive image under the gelatine. Expose the film to ultra-violet light for between three and five minutes.

3. Put the gelatine in a solution of four parts water and one part hydrogen peroxide. Leave it for about one minute.

4. Wash out the film with luke-warm water. The unexposed gelatine washes away gradually and the image emerges.

5. Place the film on a flat surface and lay the screen on top.

6. Lay pieces of newspaper over the mesh of the screen to absorb the excess moisture.

7. Work over the printing area with a roller to force the fabric onto the stencil. Remove the newspaper and allow the screen to dry.

8. Peel away the transparent backing sheet leaving the image on the mesh of the screen. If the film starts to come away as well, the screen must be allowed to dry further. Finally, the area of the screen which is not covered by emulsion surrounding the image must be covered with gummed paper.

has been washed away. When all of the image has been dissolved place the piece of film on a bench, emulsion side uppermost, and lay the screen carefully on top. Now place some cut pieces of newspaper to cover the mesh inside the screen, and rub evenly all over so that the newspaper absorbs the moisture from the emulsion as it adheres to the screen. Remove and replace the newspaper two or three times until all the moisture is absorbed.

Place the screen, with the backing and emulsion fixed to the face, in a warm, dry place for one or two hours until completely dry. Then, taking one corner of the clear backing film, very gently peel it off the mesh. If the film begins to come away as well then it is not dry enough and should be left to dry out further. The area of mesh not covered by the emulsion surrounding the image will need to be covered with broad strips of gummed paper, or by painting the mesh with stopping out or touching-up liquid (available from screen material suppliers). It is possible to paint stopping-out fluid directly onto the screen, leaving the required image, which can be printed when the liquid is dry. You can also purchase a stencil film and cut your image with a fine stencil knife, but this will not give the same precision or scope as a photo image.

As the sensitized film is costed by area, you will only want to use a piece which is 1½ - 2 inches (3.8 - 5 cm) wider or longer than the image. The rest of the screen can be filled in with painting or using masking paper, as already described. If the gummed paper is too close to the image,

DIRECT PHOTO STENCIL

When using direct photo stencil, the mesh of the frame is coated with a photo-sensitive emulsion. This is exposed to a light source which passes through a positive transparency. The areas which are exposed to light are hardened and become impervious to ink.

1. Draw a coating-trough, filled with light-sensitive emulsion, up the screen to lay an even coating of emulsion on the mesh.

2. Dry the coated screen in a dark room. Place the positive transparency on the exposure unit with the image right-reading as you look at it.

3. Place the light-sensitive screen over the positive. Expose to the light for 10 to 12 minutes.

4. After exposure, wash the screen out with water. The emulsion will have been hardened by the light except for in those areas which have been protected by the positive image. These areas will be washed away.

the thickness of the paper can lift the mesh away from the printed surface to give a blurred outline to the print.

Direct photo stencil: Another method of transferring the image to the screen is to impregnate it with a photo stencil solution in a dark room, excluding all ultra-violet light. Use a simple wooden trough to hold the solution and transfer it by pouring it on to the screen, which is resting at a slight angle to the vertical (see illustration).

The solution is made in two parts, composed of a Bichromate sensitizer, mixed with an equal quantity of PVA based solution and water. This can be stored for further use and has an approximate shelf life of three months, if kept away from the light. The advantages of this indirect method is that it gives a much tougher coating to the image than direct stencils and will stand continuous printing with little wear, as the emulsion is in the mesh and not on the surface.

The positive film is placed against the screen and exposed to the light for 10 to 12 minutes and then the screen is washed with warm water until the image is clear. All stencils for ceramics are relatively easy to clean off the screen with bleach and are usually water soluble. Indirect film only needs two minutes in bleach before being cleaned. However the direct stencil can take soaking for an hour or more in bleach before being removed. Only very specialized stencils need spirit-based cleaning solvents.

Direct printing

This method is mainly used for printing on glazed or bisqued tiles. For bisque tiles you can print with the basic oxides, underglaze colours or with glaze, depending on the mesh of the screen. For glazed tiles you can use enamel colors, basic oxides or another glaze. It is possible to print a resist to either surface. Lusters and precious metals, which are supplied in paste form, can be printed onto a glazed surface using a very fine mesh. In both transfer and direct printing, overprinting is possible, but great care must be taken when registering the second image, so that one image is lined up with the other. You must also take into account when printing on tiles that they may vary slightly in size and that you may not get a constant and accurate register with a second print. It is possible to print directly onto the surface of a cylindrical shaped vessel, but this will require special equipment, which is mainly used in factories.

Indirect printing

It is possible to place an image onto a cylindrical surface with reasonable accuracy by first printing the color onto a geletine pad, and the rolling the bisque ware over the surface to pick up the ink. This is called indirect printing and is used mainly for mugs, beakers or vases. The gelatine pad should be raised well above the printing table in order to give room for the handles of articles when printing. An image can also be printed onto a small block of gelatine and used as a stamp for printing by pressing onto a ceramic surface. For indirect printing do not forget to reverse the image before applying it to the screen.

DIRECT PRINTING

Direct printing is used mainly for printing on glazed or bisqued tiles. While it is possible to print directly onto the surface of cylindrical vessels, special equipment is required.

Points to remember
● Pull the squeegee at a constant speed and keep it at a constant angle.

3. Mask out the areas of the screen which are not going to be printed.

1. Position the tile on the printing bed in the position which you require.

2. Lower the screen and check the registration. This is vitally important if you are going to print more than one color. You can make registration marks on a sheet of paper taped down on the printing bed.

4. Prepare the colors which are to be used by grinding the powder and mixing with an oil medium.

5. Test the consistency of the color. The texture should be even and just thin enough to pour.

6. Pour some color into the screen at one end. Make sure that the line of color extends beyond the edges of the image.

7. Position the squeegee close to the frame behind the color. Stand at the other end and pull the squeegee towards you, at an angle of about 45°.

8. Lift the screen and remove the tile.

9. Dry the tiles either by standing them upright or by stacking them in a rack. Once they are completely dry, you can repeat the process.

INDIRECT PRINTING

Indirect printing is used mainly for placing images on cylindrical surfaces. It involves printing the image on a gelatine pad and then rolling the article over the surface of the pad.

Points to remember
● The image on the gelatine must be reversed.
● Make sure that the image is not longer than the circumference of the object.
Screen the image onto the gelatine pad. Place the gelatine on a block to facilitate the rolling of the vessel *(left)*.
Place the article on the gelatine pad and then roll it away from you *(below left)*
Remove the article from the pad, once it has been rolled beyond the image *(right)*.

Transfer printing: Sometimes it is more convenient to print the image onto transfer paper and then apply the transfer to the ceramic ware. Transfer paper has a dried film of water-soluble gum on one side, onto which the ceramic color, and then the overprinted cover coat of clear plastic film, is printed.

Start by cutting the transfer paper so that it is approximately 1½ inches (3.8 cm) larger than the image to be printed (unless multiple images are being printed on a large sheet). When the printed image is dry on the paper it will be overprinted with the cover coat. When it is dry the paper is immersed in water until the glue or gum is dissolved. The image will then float off, or slide away, attached to the film or cover coat. It is then transferred to the surface of the glazed ceramic ware and gently pressed down and squeezed with a very soft rubber kidney. If the transfer is left for too long in the water and the image floats from the paper, there will be insufficient glue left to adhere the transfer to the ceramic surface.

If you do not have a vacuum table to hold the transfer in position during printing it must be peeled from the back of the screen after the printing process, taking care not to smudge the surface. This also applies to the printed cover coat. When printing either color or cover coat, the mesh will need to be just clear of the printing surface. All transfers must be printed and dried in a dust-free atmosphere.

When the article is dry it will need thorough washing and wiping with a soft cloth, or cotton wool, using warm water. This is done to clean off all soluble glues which hold fine dust or traces of color. If left, these can somteimes leave a halo of color or tone around the fired image.

Stencil printing

This method is employed when a heavy deposit of glaze is printed onto a tile. A simple shape is cut out of a stiff plastic or formica sheet of between 0.5 and 1.5mm thick, which is glued to a wooden frame. The glaze to be printed is mixed with water to a stiff, but fluid, state and squeegeed, while the screen is in contact with the tile, onto the ceramic surface. The printing surfaces and apertures of the screen need to be treated with a water-repellent, such as polishing wax, otherwise they tend to heal up and reduce the printing area. More than one color can be used, and more than one printing can be done, once the first print is dry.

Should you wish to print with an image which only covers part of the bisqued tile area, it is possible to spray another color over the whole tile to give a full glazing. Alternatively, the tile can be glazed with a single color and then an image printed onto the surface when the first coat is dry.

Firing transfers and prints

Adequate room ventilation is essential at all times when firing ware in which an oil-based medium and cover coat has been used. The fumes, though not toxic, are irritants when breathed in and are best avoided. All printing and transfer work will initially need a slow firing to allow all the

TRANSFER PRINTING

Transfer printing is a simple technique, suitable for decorating all forms of glazed ceramics. Its use enables a design to be reproduced in large or small numbers, whenever desired.

Points to remember
●When printed and dry, transfers should be stored between pieces of greaseproof paper, as they have a tendency to stick together.
●Prolonged storage is not advisable, as the covercoat will not keep indefinitely.

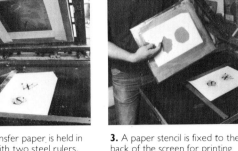

1. Readying the screen with squeegee and pigment for printing onto transfer paper. When printing, the screen should be just clear of the surface of the transfer paper.

2. The transfer paper is held in position with two steel rulers, stuck in place with sticky tape.

3. A paper stencil is fixed to the back of the screen for printing the covercoat over the transfer. The paper is held to the mesh of the screen by the tacky covercoat.

4. Covercoat is poured onto the screen before printing. Keep the can be closed when not in use and only use a little at a time, as it dries very speedily.

5. The covercoat is printed through the paper silhouette.

6. After printing, the coverage and section of the stencil on the screen is clearly seen.

7. The covercoated prints are hung to dry on special metal racks.

medium and overcoat to burn away. This means that as much air as possible should be allowed to pass through the kiln in the early stages of firing. If, at this point, the temperature rise is too rapid, the medium in the print will literally boil and break up the surface of the print. It may take at least two hours on a low kiln setting before the atmosphere is clear.

Decorem printing

This is essentially a reproductive technique using a photographic process. The design element is contained within the photo image to be reproduced, as the process has little flexibility. As with silk screen printing, the image is supplied as an opaque black positive on clear film. It has the quality of reproducing very fine, half tone, solid area or line with great accuracy.

The Decorem solution can be used as supplied, or diluted with Decorem thinners. Place the solution in a metal or glass container (do not use plastic) when in use. Before using the solution strain it through filter paper, using a glass or metal funnel, to eliminate any dust or foreign matter which might impair its application. Do not wear woollen clothing when working with this medium as the finest particles can settle in or on the solution when it is being applied to the tile or ceramic surface. Only mix sufficient for your immediate needs and store the surplus in a dark glass bottle or tin, keeping it away from the light.

Pour a sufficient amount for the areas needed, into a glass or ceramic container and apply to the glazed surface

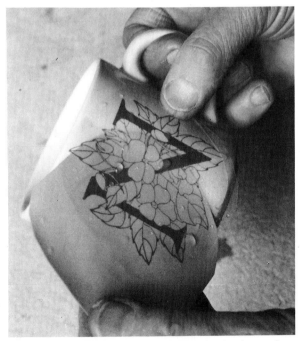

8. The transfer is soaked in water until the image begins to slide of the paper, when it is applied to the mug. Soft glue on the underside of the covercoat and image ensures that the transfer adheres firmly. The transfer should be fired at 750°C (1380°F).

depending on the warmth of the atmosphere. If you are coating tiles, they must be kept level until dry as the solution tends to flow. When the Decorem is dry and the article is at room temperature, place the image on the surface of the treated ceramic, facing the light source. This can be done using a vacuum frame or a good substitute, such as attaching a large plastic bag containing the image and ceramic ware to a vacuum cleaner suction pipe to extract the air. It is then exposed to ultra violet or mercury vapour lamps (total 30 amps) for one minute. If a pale print is needed reduce the time to 50 seconds. The lights in the light box should be approximately two feet from the image using four, 125 watt high pressure mercury vapor lamps or two, 125 watt high pressure mercury vapor lamps and two ordinary ultra violet bulbs. When using half tones, cut the positive as close as possible to the ceramic to ensure a really close fit.

When the surface has been exposed prepare a mixture of the pigment to be used with Decorem mordant and ethyl alcohol (for quantities you should consult the instructions given with the Decorem solution). The mixture is applied with a broad brush and left until dry. Wash the surface with cold water and clean off the surplus color and reveal the required image. It is the mordant and the alcohol which softens the areas of the image and accepts the pigment in the applied solution.

The ceramic is now ready to be fired, but should be thoroughly dry before placing in the kiln and fired to the normal temperature for litho or enamel pigments. This can vary from 740°C - 850°C (1360°F - 1560°F) according to the color. If the tiles are not thoroughly dry before placing in the kiln they will sweat and the moisture will affect the image. There are various types of positive that can be used — line screen or block, any ordinary photographic negative showing contrast, half tone using 60 - 100 screen or full tone positive made from photographic negative.

Decorem is only affected by radiation in the ultra violet region of the spectrum and not by visible light, so that you may work with 60w or 100w tungsten lamps. As a precaution lights and windows can be covered with a special orange, transparent filter to effectively remove ultra violet radiation.

If after firing the image is too light it may be overexposed or if the image is too dark then under exposure will be the cause.

If you are not using photographic positives it is possible to place any object, such as dried grass or leaves, on the treated tile and expose it to the ultra violet light. This is a method which gives flexibility to the manipulation of an image and, with care, you can apply several colors. Alternatively, the whole process can be repeated several times using a different color each time as well as a separate firing for each colour.

Stencil printing Here, a circular tile is being stencilled with glaze, which is printing through a pierced rigid plastic sheet attached to the wooden screen frame. When drilling the holes in the sheet, ensure that they allow the maximum amount of glaze to flow through during printing, but without clogging. The technique can be used either to print onto an unfired glaze, or onto a bisqued surface, over which another glaze may be sprayed.

with a 1½ - 2 inch (3.8 - 5 cm) wide soft brush. Make sure the surface is first cleaned thoroughly with acetone or meths, but wear a mask and rubber gloves when doing this.

Apply the solution evenly to the surface and do not allow it to settle. If applied too thickly it can give a crazing appearance, and if too thin, will not accept a high enough density of pigment. This process may be carried out in natural light, but when it has been completed place in a dark box, or room until dry. This can take an hour or more,

CERAMICS WITH PRINTED DECORATION

Egyptian tiled bathroom
Danka Napiorkowska, UK
6 in x 6 in (15 cm x 15 cm)

The decoration of this tile panel is done by brushing or spraying enamel colors through a stencil. The same stencil can be used for more than one image, using a selection of colors. Firing was to 750°C (1380°F) with a final half hour soak. Colors range from yellow and orange to dark and light blue, green and grey.

Decorem tiles
Kenneth Clark Pottery, UK

Three examples of decorated tiles for a mural in the Harrow Civic Centre. Each tile depicts a scene from the life of the town, supplied by newspaper cuttings and photographs from the archives. The technique illustrates how fine line and tone can be used as a method of ceramic reproduction. One tile is green, another sepia and the third is magenta.

House plaque 'Partridge Wood'
Ann Clark, UK
Diameter: 12 in (30 cm)

A hand-made plaque rolled from 'T' material and trimmed on a throwing wheel when leather-hard. After glazing with a white glaze and firing to 1120°C, (2050°F), it was silk screen printed using a single enamel color and fired to 800°C (1470°F). Panels may be fixed onto the wall with adhesive or can be screwed on. The screw holes are made in the clay at the leather-hard stage. The lettering and design are hand-drawn before being photographically transferred to the screen.

'Black sheep restaurant' mug
Decoration: Ronald Searle, UK
Mug: Kenneth Clark, UK
Height: 3 in (8 cm)

The image was first screen printed onto a gelatine pad and the mug rolled across it to pick up the pigment. The mug was glazed white inside when raw and fired to 1120°C (2050°F), then spray glazed with a 6 per cent iron glaze and fired to 1060°C (1940°F).

LETTERING

Despite a constant demand for lettering few potters have any extensive knowledge of or skill in this art. A guide to lettering is depicted on the facing page. Numerous different lettering styles are employed in ceramics but specific styles are governed by different techniques. For instance, single letters may be cut from or pierced through a thick slab of clay or modelled in relief. They may be slip cast in a mould or press moulded. Other techniques include brush painting, silhouette painting, printing or by pressing relief letter dies against hard clay.

The photograph *(right)* shows a potter embellishing a dish with the lettering reproduced on the facing page. Vegetable dyed watercolors are used to sketch out the letters which are then painted onto an unfired opaque white glaze with oxide. The picture *(below)* shows the dish resting on sponge to protect its glaze. In the photograph *(bottom)* the border of a large dish is lettered with a slip trailer made from bicycle tubing attached to a cork with an inserted nozzle.

CERAMICS WITH LETTERING

Lettering can be an extremely effective decorative device. The oval plaque *(below)* was rolled and cut from 'T' material and the design was carefully picked out on the smooth clay surface, after first working it out on tracing paper. The paper was then placed on a thin sheet of clear plastic on the clay, the latter stopping the moisture from the clay dampening and buckling the paper. When the clay was bone dry, the letters were painted with a dark oxide and the plaque bisqued to 1120°C (2048°F). It was then sprayed with a thin tin glaze, enabling the color to impregnate it to give a soft quality. The glaze firing was at 1060°C (1904°F). The circular, white glazed plaque *(bottom)* was slip cast and spray-glazed with a blue-green second glaze after warming. When dry, the inscription was scratched through the surface glaze to the white glaze underneath. The final firing had to be carefully controlled, because, if it were too hot, the definition would be lost and the two glazes would merge. To assist adhesion and prevent the glaze chipping during scratching, a little liquid gum was added to the top glaze. The inscription on the clock *(right)* was scratched into the clay at the leather hard stage, after having first been roughed out on the surface with a thin wooden scriber. After bisque firing, the clock was given a coat of clear glaze and fired to stoneware temperature.
All designs by Ann Clark.

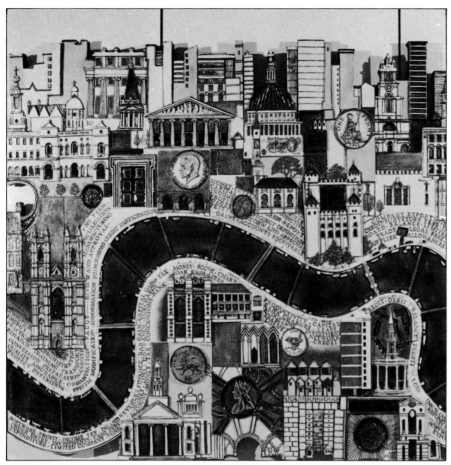

London panel
Ann Clark, UK

Many potters use well-known styles of lettering or type face, adapting them to their particular needs. The methods they use to apply them can similarly vary; examples include pressing, brush painting, scratching, carved relief, or clay or glaze techniques. In the London panel, individual pieces of metal type were pressed into the clay while it was firm, but not excessively hard. When dry, pigment was brushed into the recessed letters and the piece was the bisque fired.

Relief house number
Anne Spencer, UK
Diameter: 10 in (25 cm)

The relief numbers on this turquoise blue and white plaque were cut from leather hard 'T' material; the white clay was finely grogged.

Tiled toilet panel
Ann Clark, UK

To meet the problem of graffiti, Ann Clark used a variety of techniques to create her own artistic impression of the subject. These included scratching through areas of glaze on glaze and trailing with colored glazes, while, in some areas, pigment was simply brushed onto the surface. Smooth glazing meant that unwelcome additions could be easily washed off the tiles.

5
KILNS AND FIRING

A kiln is an enclosed construction in which the ceramic ware is placed and heated, using one of a selection of fuels, until the heat penetrates and fires the ware. Combustion or radiation takes place inside or beneath the chamber and the excess fumes escape through a flue or chimney in the kiln. Heat must be allowed to circulate freely around the ware while it is firing. The kiln is constructed with various forms of fire brick, or a refractory ceramic, and may now be lined internally or have within its construction a heat-resistant ceramic fiber element.

A kiln may be no more than a hollow brick cylinder through which the heat passes, or it may be an enclosed chamber, in which the air circulates. It can be a 'through' or 'updraft' kiln, or a 'downdraft' kiln, in which the heat circulates and then passes down through an aperture in the floor of the kiln and out through a chimney. In some kilns the heat surrounds an enclosed muffle (inner chamber containing the ware) and in others it is in direct contact with the pots. The fuel used for firing may be gas, oil, coal, wood, coke or electricity. The most primitive form of pottery firing is the bonfire technique which is still used in many parts of the world. A hole dug in the ground is another ancient method of firing pottery in which the pots and fuel are stacked together inside. When the fuel is ignited, the pots are cooked, and then removed from the ashes when cool.

The principles of firing

What happens when clay is fired is quite simple to understand. The aim to apply sufficient, controlled heat for long enough to enable specific chemical and physical changes to take place. Though this sounds scientific, the process itself is not; there is always a certain degree of unpredicability which is part and parcel of the art of creation. While the techniques of firing should be strictly observed, even these cannot guarantee total, constant success. What is important is to be aware of the need for as much control as possible.

There are two atmospheres for firing ware in a kiln. If combustion in the kiln is unrestricted, with plenty of air or oxygen, it is called an oxidizing fire. However, if the air intake is restricted, a reducing atmosphere is created and the resulting unstable carbon monoxide gases combine with the oxygen in the metals of the clay body and glaze, reducing them to a lower oxide and altering their color during firing.

Choosing a kiln

Throughout the world there are many suppliers and manufacturers of oil, gas and electric kilns, as well as those which use solid fuel. Kilns vary considerably in size and proportion so that if you intend constructing one to a particular design, consult someone who has a similar model and is completely satisfied with its performance. Make sure that they have used the kiln for the particular type of ware and firing you have in mind, and with the same fuel.

The decision to build or purchase a kiln will depend on several factors — the type of ware you intend to make, the quantity of ceramics to be produced, the space available for a kiln or kilns, the type of firing envisaged, available finances, personal knowledge of kiln construction and building restrictions or local regulations governing pollution. A list of suppliers dealing with kilns, and books on how to build your own are given in the appendix.

Before choosing a kiln, weigh up the comparative costs of fuel, such as town gas, bottled gas, fuel oil, electricity, wood, or other forms of solid fuel. Remember that this is not a constant factor as very often the cheapest fuel at a particular time will increase in price and become the most expensive. For those interested in small scale stoneware production and in making both reduced and oxidized stoneware, a small portable cylinder, gas-fired fiber kiln, is a good choice.

Another important factor to consider when installing a kiln (unless it is outside) is room ventilation. If possible, avoid working in a room where a kiln is in use because of the fumes. Depending on the type of firing, these can act as an irritant, or they may even be toxic. Adequate ventilation is particularly important in a reducing atmosphere, because of the release of carbon monoxide. Some form of exhaust fan, either into a chimney or through to the outside is essential. Gas and oil fired kilns must be fitted with special chimneys to carry away poisonous gases.

Blue veined Raku pot
Harvey Sadow, Jr., USA
8 in x 8 in (20 cm x 20 cm)

This ceramic form is from a series entitled 'Other suns and guiding lights' — clay landscape vessels which capture and move the light across the form, texture and color of the pot. This is an excellent example of the rich color possible with a multiple Raku firing. The pot is hand thrown and fired to temperatures ranging from 880°C - 950°C (1610°F -1740°F).

The blue color is given by copper oxide.
Collection of Betsy Beasley, New York

Types of kiln

A KILN is probably the most expensive initial investment made by any potter. This section defines the different types, together with their advantages and disadvantages.

Electric kilns

For beginners the most satisfactory and easy to manage is an electric kiln, but make sure that ceramic fibre is used extensively in its construction in order to reduce fuel costs and heat wastage. Ceramic fibre insulation has now reduced the external size of kilns, as well as heat loss and fuel consumption. As the elements wear they get darker in color and eventually show small dark eruption spots on the coils. At this stage it is a good idea to replace them before they fail during a firing. It is safer to renew all the elements, rather than just one or two, so that unnecessary strain is not put on the old ones, causing them to wear more quickly. Heavy duty element wire is needed if you intend to fire regularly to stoneware temperatures.

Electric kilns have a safety advantage and give a cleaner combustion, but they will not give much scope for reduction firings, if required for stoneware. This is possible in an electric kiln, but it is not good for the elements as the atmosphere corrodes the metal in time. Special elements can be fitted, but on the whole a gas, oil or wood fuelled kiln is better suited to reduction. However a great deal can be achieved and produced with regular firings in an electric kiln of between 1.5 and 3.5 cubic feet (0.042 and 0.999 cubic metres) capacity.

Before installing or buying an electric kiln, check the availability of sufficient electricity and the cost of installing cable, as many kilns need three-phase supply, which can be expensive to install and is usually only laid on to business premises. However with modern fiber insulation, many larger kilns only use single-phase for firing. The ease of access for installing any kiln should also be considered, as should the mobility of the kiln in case of a move to new premises. The kiln should be small and mobile or constructed in such a way that it can be dismantled easily.

Gas kilns

The use of bottled gas has increased enormously with the advent of the mobile, quick-firing, knock down fiber or light brick and fiber kilns. This has allowed for a wide range of firings — from reduced lusters and Raku to porcelain and stoneware. If desired, these can be fired more slowly in a gas kiln to produce well-fired and mature glazes. Larger and more durable gas kilns can be installed for firing by town gas, or from gas stored in large cylinders but make sure you

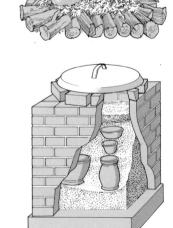

Types of kiln
Outlined briefly are some of the different types of kilns, from the most primitive to those which are electronically controlled.
Bonfire kilns (top left) Firing hand-made pots in the open, using straw, wood, brushwood or other combustible materials, is one of the oldest of all firing methods. Many systems are used; the simplest is to lay the pots carefully on a bed of brushwood, cover them lightly with more brushwood and set the whole alight. After preliminary heating — pots can also be preheated individually by burning straw inside them — heavier wood is added to raise the temperature until the pots are sufficiently fired. Alternatively, pots can be built up into a large domed pile and covered with wood, grass and a top layer of earth; a small funnel chimney is left at the top for hot coals to be dropped down to set the wood and grass alight. The optimum temperature is about 900°C (1650°F).
Sawdust kilns (left) are round or square brick structures, with a kiln shelf or dustbin lid on top which can be raised as required

to regulate the draught. A steel drum can also be used as a sawdust-kiln if sufficient draught holes have been made to assist combustion. The pots are set apart as the sawdust is loaded in and then ignited from the top with paper and checked until the sawdust is steadily smouldering, but not burning. Firing can take up to 24 hours.

Woodfiring (above) can be done with large or small kilns and many types of wood, but the wood should preferably be dry and seasoned. If you are firing and glazing, start with a small fire and gradually heat the contents until the kiln is dull red. Wood can give a fierce heat but if it is well controlled it gives a distinctive quality to both earthenware and stoneware glazes. Wood is being used more and more because of the shortage of fossil fuels; successful sawdust and forced air burning kilns have also been developed and these will fire to stoneware temperatures.

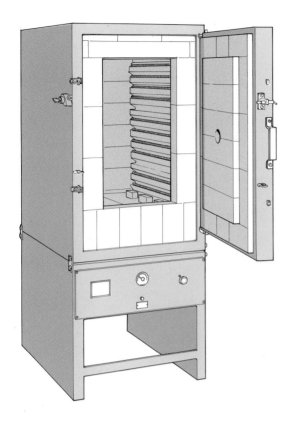

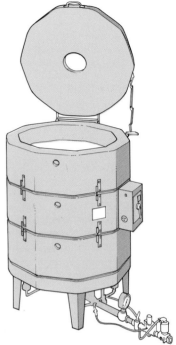

Gas and electric kilns Modern gas, electric and oil-fired kilns cost less to make and run than they did as recently as 10 years ago. The chief reason for this is improved insulation, due to the introduction of lightweight, thin ceramic fibre as an insulator. Lightweight, highly refractory bricks can also be used with the same advantages of reducing heat loss and hence lowering costs. The kiln *(right)* is an American Torch Gas Kiln, which is fired with natural or bottled gas. The construction is chiefly of thermal mass bricks in a stainless steel jacket. One interesting feature is its four interlocking sections, which enable the size to be varied. This is important, since small kilns heat up more quickly than large ones, but, equally, cool down more rapidly. Firing can be to 1300°C (2370°F), with either oxidizing or reducing atmospheres, operating on the updraft principle. This gives more variation in temperature from the bottom to top than would a downdraft kiln. Because ventilation is through the lid, an extractor fan should be used if the kiln is being operated indoors. Good firing safety devices are built into the burners. The standard electric kiln *(left)* is fitted with a series of elements that radiate heat. Among its safety features is a device designed to automatically switch off the kiln, if it is opened during firing. Extra ventilation is necessary.

have an efficient flue or chimney. Every precaution should be taken to prevent the accumulation of unfired gas which can be ignited as gas explosions are not unheard of.

When firing with gas it is important to avoid the direct impact of the flame on the pots. Therefore the kiln is constructed in such a way that it leads the flame around the interior chamber and general combustion is created. The ware may be fired in ventilated, but enclosed, fireclay containers (saggars) or the kiln can have a full or semi muffle construction to protect against the direct heat of the flames.

The main advantage of a gas-fuelled kiln is that you can control the temperature by restricting or increasing the fuel input. Consequently this type of kiln is well suited to reduced stoneware firing as the intake of air into the chamber can be reduced, or some form of solid fuel can be introduced to create a reducing atmosphere.

Oil-fired kilns

The fuel for these kilns can vary from crude oil or used car sump oil to kerosene. One method of using it is drip feed firing, but these fuels can also be combined with a continuous forced air supply which creates a fine spray of combined air and fuel to give prolonged, intense flames. The flames must not make contact with the ware, but should have room to disperse or strike against a highly refractory brick or ceramic baffle. Increasingly potters have problems with smoke pollution in urban areas, as Bernard Leach did in St Ives. He originally built his kiln outside the residential district, but over the years the town spread and encompassed his pottery. Many local councils have by-laws governing the output of smoke and fumes and neighbours began to complain about the black smoke which poured from his chimney during reduction firings. Many articles and books have been written giving plans and instructions on building all types of kilns and indicating the regulations and laws which apply.

Wood-firing kilns

Wood, when dry, is a cleaner burning fuel than oil or coal and can give a fierce heat. Depending on the type of kiln, some wood will burn slowly while others ignite rapidly and give off an intense heat. It is traditional towards the end of a wood firing to put bundles of dry brushwood into the kiln at intervals. This produces sudden bursts of heat which travel up or along the kiln in waves to flux and mature the ware farthest from the firemouth. Between stokings the firemouth is cleared of ash to allow plenty of air to enter and take the heat into the kiln before another bundle of brushwood is fed in. It is not uncommon to use wood at the end of a coal or oil firing, provided that the method of stoking the firemouth is suitable.

The quality of glazes is greatly enhanced by wood firing, giving a softness and maturity, aided by the gases and composition of the burning wood at high temperatures. This is a particular feature in high temperature stoneware firings when wood is fed into the kiln when it is white hot, giving off gas, smoke and ash in a burst of combustion. The ash combines either with the glaze or the unglazed body to give a reaction of rich color and finish. Beautiful oranges and greens can be obtained in terracotta earthenware wood firings when a lead-based glaze is used; the ash also gives attractive flecks to the glaze.

Alan Caiger-Smith of the Aldermaston Pottery near Reading in England has an excellent wood-fired kiln which is used for both Majolica firings and luster reduction. The plans for his kiln can be purchased from him.

Solid fuel kilns

Coal, coke, charcoal, sawdust and peat are all fuels used for high or low temperature firings. There can be problems with coal due to the sulphur in its composition giving a dry scum to either glazed or clay surfaces. Sawdust and peat are used in slow, low temperature firings to give varied reduced, oxidized and carbonizing effects. This is most effective when firing burnished red terracotta ware. Excellent results can also be achieved using cow dung as fuel. Some people rinse the pots in milk or buttermilk after firing, while they are still hot, thus using the casein in the milk to seal the clay. The high cost of charcoal makes it uneconomical to use this type of fuel. Another fuel used for aiding firing is a mixture of up to 25 per cent sawdust or coke dust with a plastic red clay. This fuel fully ignites and burns at about 900-1000°C (1650-1830°F). The coke dust is a common addition when making hand-made bricks.

Temperature gauges

The heat in the kiln must be controlled during a firing and the rise in temperature registered. Many kilns are fitted with recording instruments attached to a heat probe (or probes) in the kiln called a pyrometer. This will tell you the temperature of the air in the kiln at a specific time or in a particular area of the kiln. Another method, important in the glaze firing, is to use a set of cones which are specially designed to melt at different temperatures. These pyrometric cones are made from ceramic materials and, according to their composition, will melt and bend at the correct temperature. The cone indicates what the heat in the kiln is doing to the ceramic body or glaze and this process is referred to as 'heat work'. The relevant cone is placed inside the kiln and its progress is observed through a spyhole in the door of the kiln. When it begins to melt you know that the critical temperature for the ware to be fired has been reached. Cones should be placed as far into the kiln as is practical and away from spyhole draughts. When the body or glaze reaches its maturing temperature, the increase of heat should be gradual to allow it to penetrate the ware and complete all the chemical reactions. If the heat is too sudden, the outside layer of the ware will be fully fired and the inside underfired. This applies to all types of ware.

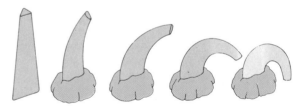

KILN FURNITURE

Kiln furniture is used for stacking and separation of articles during firing. Useful items include tile cranks (1), props (2), props with castellated tops (3), stilts (4) and saddles (5). Use of this furniture means that the maximum amount can be fired at one time. The furniture itself is made from refractory material, purpose-designed to withstand high temperatures. Pyrometric cones (above) are used as a guide to internal kiln temperature; each cone is made from a specific composition which melts at a given temperature. Large flat kiln shelves are supported by the props and used as platforms for stilts, cranks and other supports. Shelves are often brushed with a coating of 50 parts china clay and 50 parts alumina so that dripped glaze can be easily removed. For cone conversion temperatures, see page 199.

EFFECTS OF FIRING

Ceramics offer unlimited possibilities to those who wish to experiment and make beautiful articles in preference to functional pots. By combining a graphic element with various firing techniques and an infinite range of color possibilities, a vast range of creative ideas are possible. All over the world potters are experimenting with new techniques. All the pieces illustrated on this page are from New Zealand, where there is a very active potting community.

Thrown and Raku fired dish
Brian Gartside, New Zealand
Diameter: 15 in (38 cm)

This dish shows a dramatic use of both Raku firing and acrylic colors. Most of Brian Gartside's decorative work is inspired by ideas and feelings drawn from the natural world. This influence can either be apparent in the decoration or application of glaze, or in manipulating the clay. Raku firing is to 1000°C (1830°F).

Saggar fired porcelain pots
Cecilia Parkinson, New Zealand
Height: 6 in (15.2 cm)

These examples show some of the color effects which potters can achieve by firing the ware in saggars. The thrown porcelain shapes were first bisque-fired in an electric kiln to a temperature of 1240°C (2260°F). The saggars are made from a stoneware body with a 20 per cent grog addition and fired to 1240°C (2260°F). The pots are placed in the saggars with a mixture of sawdust, oxides and sulphates of metals and fired to 1100°C (2010°F) in a gas kiln. Much depends on the firing, but certain effects can be achieved by the right choice of materials.

Bisque and glaze firing

THIS SECTION explains the principles of the two firing methods used for many types of ware. Bisque firing takes place before glaze is applied; the final firing occurs after this.

Bisque firing

The bisque is the first firing of the ware, before it has been glazed. It changes the chemical composition of the clay and gives the pottery durability, while leaving it porous enough to absorb the glaze. With many forms of ceramics the bisque and glaze firings can be done together, making a saving in time and cost. This applies mainly to production stoneware and to certain simple plain or decorated forms of earthenware. Unglazed ware, such as garden pots and certain cooking utensils, may only need a bisque firing, or possibly firing to a semi-vitrified state.

Unglazed vitrified tiles are fired once in stacks, and tiles to be glazed and decorated are first bisque fired in stacks or packed closely on their edges. The bisque firing is at a higher temperature than the subsequent glaze firing. This is to make the clay body hard and strong before the application of the lower firing glaze (practically all glazed tiles are fired in this way).

For more involved ceramic ware, a bisque firing may be necessary before glazing and storing or for convenience, especially when more elaborate decorating techniques are to be used. If the article is raw glazed, breakage from handling can be a problem. Before placing the pots in the kiln they should be thoroughly dried out in a warm atmosphere or a well-ventilated space.

The crucial factors in a bisque firing are firstly, the giving off of chemically combined water and secondly, what is called the critobalite conversion factor. The mineral silica comes in various forms which are termed phases. These can change during firing from one type to another. This happens, for example, when the free silica (quartz) in its crystalline form is transformed into free silica of the cristobalite phase. Cristobalite alone during firing both expands and contracts by 3 per cent with the contraction taking place at the crucial cooling temperature of 226°C (439°F). The desirability of cristobalite in a clay body is that it gives an extra shrinkage to a body when glaze fired and cooled at 226°C (440°F) and this will reduce crazing. The amount the body contracts at this temperature will depend on the percentage of cristobalite in the clay body. With 10 per cent in a body, the contraction will be 1 per cent, which is greater than that of an ordinary earthenware body (being approximately 0.7 per cent) and sufficient to cause compression. This shrinkage is referred to as the cristobalite squeeze and is crucial in white earthenware bodies. Crazing occurs when the shrinkage of a glaze is higher than that of the body.

The actual forming of the cristobalite takes place about 1100°C (2012°F) and the amount of free silica formed is governed by the amount of time the body is soaked. Soaking is done by keeping the body or glaze at a specific temperature during firing for a given period of time. Once some cristobalite has been formed it acts as a catalyst for the formation of further cristobalite.

It is possible to purchase cristobalite to add to a clay body. Additions range from 1 per cent to 10 per cent and are tested by applying and firing a thick coating of glaze.

Packing the kiln for bisque firing

The kiln should first be cleaned and all the kiln furniture checked for damage. Packing for bisque firings can be as dense as required, with articles stacked one inside the other or lip-to-lip; this makes bisque firing economical on kiln space. An article with a lid can be fired with the lid in place as it will not stick to the pot during firing. Make sure that the pottery is well supported all the way up and that the articles are evenly distributed for weight. A layer of sand or grog between the pots will help to space them and, at the same time, distribute the weight more evenly. When a large area of the article is in contact with the kiln|shelf a thin layer or bed of sand will aid the firing and shrinking of the ware. Bone dry pots are extremely strong and, when biscuited, can be stacked very high with the largest and heaviest at the bottom.

Bisque firing must begin slowly in order to allow the chemically-combined water to escape as it changes into steam. If the firing begins too rapidly the sudden pressure of the steam will blow large flakes from the walls of the ware. This conversion of steam takes place at a temperature between 450°C (840°F) and 600°C (1110°F) when the kiln begins to become a dull red. It is at the 200°C - 400°C (390°F - 750°F) stage that organic matter in the clay begins to decompose and fire away. Other impurities such as fluorine, and sulphur trioxide (which combines with moisture to form sulphuric acid) do not begin to fire away until the a temperature of 900°C (1650°F) or higher is reached.

The higher the bisque firing, the more difficult the glazing, as the porosity is progressively reduced. However, if the bisque firing is near vitrification any distortion will already have taken place and there should be few failures at the lower temperature glaze firing. If low temperature alkaline glazes are used it is advisable to give the ware a high bisque firing to strengthen it. However with reduced porosity this makes it difficult to hold the thick glaze application, but preheating the ware on or in a hot kiln, or with a blow heater, will help greatly. The glaze must be applied thickly and is best sprayed onto the ware. In order to dry it as quickly as possible the article should be heated on top of a firing kiln, in front of a blow heater or heated

Packing kiln for bisque firing
Pieces can come into contact with each other and lids kept on pots during a biscuit firing, the first firing which dries and hardens clay prior to glazing, so they will not stick together. It is often necessary to support individual pots on small piles and here the leg of the figurine, a delicate part of the piece, is also given support.

sufficiently in a kiln immediately prior to glazing.

Whether the final firing or the body is bisque or glaze, it should come near to the point of vitrification. This will vary according to the type of ware or composition of the body, but the following is a reasonable guide to vitrification temperatures.
Terracotta ware, bricks and red tiles: 900 - 1040°C (1650 - 1900°F)
General earthenware: 1040 - 1140°C (1900 - 2080°F)
Fine earthenware: 1100 - 1200°C (2010 - 2190°F)
Stoneware: 1200 - 1280°C (2190 - 2340°F)
Porcelain: 1240 - 1340°C (2260 - 2440°F)
Bone china: 1230 - 1240°C or 1280 - 1290°C (2240 -2250°F or 2340 - 2350°F)

Glaze firing
Apart from raw glaze firing, when the bisque and glaze firing is combined, the glaze firing cycle is the reverse of the biscuit firing. In the early stages the rise in temperature can be rapid and steady, but it needs to slow down as the melting and maturing temperature of the glaze is reached. This allows the glaze to fully combine chemically with the body and adhere to the surface of the article. At the same time a chemical reaction takes place in the glaze which affects the color and texture of the ware. The following temperatures will serve as a basic guide.
Earthenware: 1000 - 1180°C (1830 - 2150°F). The glaze firing of red clays seldom exceeds 1100°C (2010°F). **Fine, white earthenwares** range from 1060 -1140°C (1940 - 2080°F) with the clay body composition or function being the deciding factor.

Stoneware: 1200 - 1300°C (2190 - 2370°F). Most stoneware glazes mature between 1240°C (2260°F) 1300°C (2370°F), but it does vary according to the clay body.

Porcelain: 1280 - 1350°C (2340 - 2460°F). Here the glaze fuses with the body and is no longer a layer on the outer surface, as with stoneware and earthenware.

Oxidized and reduced firing
The atmosphere within the kiln has a marked effect on the appearance of the fired ware. In kilns where there is sufficient oxygen to allow complete combustion, such as an electric kiln, the atmosphere is described as oxidizing. Adequate ventilation is present in the kiln so that oxygen is available to combine with the hot metals in the clay body and glaze. The gas given off is carbon dioxide.

In a fuel-burning kiln the fuel is burnt within the chamber itself and this results in hot carbon being produced. If the carbon is fed with air, or oxygen, then an oxidizing atmosphere is created.

The principle of reduction firing is to restrict the supply of oxygen (but not fuel) to the area of combustion. Instead of giving off carbon dioxide, the fuel gives off the unstable gas, carbon monoxide or free carbon which, when hot enough, will take oxygen from the metals present in the body or glaze. The metal oxides most strongly affected are iron and copper which are reduced to their lower oxide form of cupric and ferrous oxide. Heavy and continued reduction is necessary to reduce these and other oxides to their lower form.

Copper oxide or carbonate will give varying deep reds with a reduction firing and pale blue to green celadons are obtained with the addition of approximately 2 to 5 per cent iron oxide to an appropriate stoneware glaze. When 10 per cent iron oxide is added and applied thinly to the ware, a rich rust red is obtained in the reduction firing and if thickly applied a jet black.

Reduction generally begins at a temperature of about 1100°C (2010°F) , when the oxygen atoms in the glaze and body become unstable. Reduction should not begin at too low a temperature, otherwise the free carbon will impregnate the unfired glaze making it grey or black.

**Stoneware Forms 'Uluru'
series**
Marea Gazzard, Australia
Height: 30 in x 24 in x 10 in
(76 cm x 60 cm x 25 cm)

This is a series of large sculptural
forms which are coiled using a
stoneware/Raku mixture. No
attempt is made to smooth the
surface, as a textural quality is
later given to the surface when
treated with slip pigment. When
leather-hard to dry the surface is
selectively sprayed with Albany
slip made from an American clay
having a high flux content. The
nearest English equivalent is
Fremington clay. It is also
treated with copper and
manganese dioxide. When the
pots are bone dry they are once-
fired to 1280°C (2340°F). They
suggest the hot, dry texture and
form of weather-worn rocks
found in the heat of Australia.

Hand-shaped stoneware dish
Ewen Henderson, UK
15 in x 11 in (38 cm x 28 cm)

Ewen Henderson's pots are slab-
built layer and coil constructed.
He starts with a basic stoneware
body, and then adds other clays
and materials such as red clay,
bone china clay, earthenware
clays and various raw materials
and oxides. Pots are once-fired
to 1260°C (2300°F) with a
nephyline syenite glaze which is
either brushed all over or onto
particular areas. He sometimes
likes to experiment with his
materials by taking the pots
almost to the point of collapse in
the firing process to test the limit
of his materials.

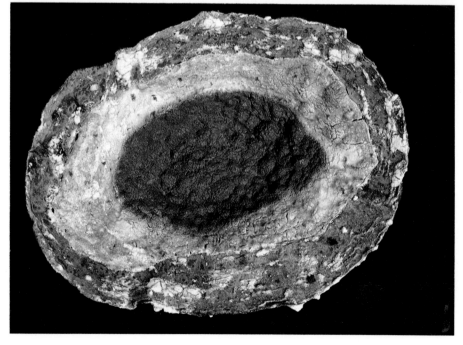

Japanese Bizen pot
Height: 2½ in (6 cm)

A pot made using a particular local clay from one of the many pottery districts of Japan. The pots are wound in twisted rice straw and fired in saggars. The ash from the straw reacts with the reducing body to give the particular color effect.

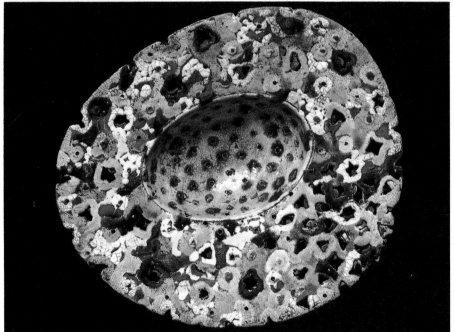

Raku dish
Ian Byers, UK
Diamter: 12 in (30 cm)

Hand-shaped and press molded dish made with Raku body. After bisque firing the wide rim area has been glazed with a range of colored glazes which include white yellow, black, yellow-green, a little red and the turquoise in the center hollow. When it is fired to 920 - 1000°C (1690 -1830°F) and reduced in dry softwood sawdust, the small areas of body which are not glazed are reduced to a rich black which gives added emphasis to the texture of multi-colored glazes.

Reduction can be induced by the addition of silicon carbide to the glaze. This is called local reduction because it only affects the glaze, not the body, and it takes place in an oxidized kiln firing rather than in a reducing atmosphere. This method of reduction is used for reducing copper when approximately 0.5 per cent is added to a glaze. The reduction firing begins at about 1000°C (1830°F), but to maintain the reduced color a stabilizer, such as tin, must be present during the firing in small quantities while the carbon dioxide and monoxide gas bubbles from the silicon carbide are given off.

Two points to remember with a reduction firing: if you are firing with a muffle kiln then some form of combustible material has to be fed into the muffle at the appropriate temperature. Secondly, care must be taken to provide adequate ventilation for the clearance of excess carbon monoxide fumes.

Packing a kiln for glaze firing

However you pack your glazed articles, it is wise to give the kiln shelves a coating of bat wash first to protect them from drips of glaze and to make them easier to clean. This wash can be made with equal proportions of kaolin and flint, or kaolin and alumina mixed with water, and brushed on. Because of the porosity of earthenware, it is advisable to glaze the footring with the rest of the article and support the pot with a stilt on a shelf when firing. Porcelain is often raw glazed and once-fired so that it is wise to set the article on a clay sleeper, made of the same clay as the pot. This is a thin, flat disc of clay which will shrink at the same rate as the pot and prevent the footring from fusing and sticking to the kiln shelf. If this is not done there is often a series of chips around the footring when it has been fired. Because of the intense heat, pots should not be stilted in a stoneware firing, but fired directly on their footring. It is sometimes the practice to fire thick, heavy stoneware pots, using sea shells as a support. In a glaze-firing kiln the pieces must not touch one another as they will stick together when the glaze melts.

Eight to nine hours is a reasonable period for a glaze firing, but it depends very much on the size of the kiln and the type of ware.

Salt-glaze firing

Another method of firing which is less commonly used, but gives a distinctive quality to body and glaze is salt-glaze firing. This is a single firing which combines the bisque and glaze firing. Salt naturally absorbs moisture so there should be no need to wet the salt before use. In the firing the soda combines with the alumina and silica of the hot pottery body.

While most salt glaze firings are reduction firings, you can get a particularly fine quality of white body with a clear

Stacking kiln for glaze firing As the pieces can stick together when the glaze melts, it is important to keep them apart. The pieces are stacked on kiln shelves covered with bat wash, which protects the shelves from dripping glaze. They should be stacked evenly in both firings to ensure even heat distribution.

salt glaze in an oxidized firing. This is an area waiting to be explored and developed, having been neglected since the 19th century.

In a reduction firing, reducing begins heavily at around 950°C (1740°F) for a good hour and then continues with light reduction until 1250°C (2280°F) is reached. There is then a period of oxidation and salting begins at a temperature of 1260-1280°C (2300-2330°F). The salt is introduced in small quantities over an approximate period of 1½ hours, until 1300°C (2370°F) is reached; a good soak finishes the firing.

As a temperature of 1250°C (2280°F) is being reached the salt deposits from previous firings on the inside of the kiln begin to volatilize and form a thin coat on the ware. Various effects and colors can be achieved by applying different pigments and colored slips to the unfired ware which react with the salt or soda during the firing. Great care needs to be exercised in the siting of the kiln as hydrochloric acid fumes are given off during the firing and can be injurious to plants, humans and animals. The safe form of soda for glazing (sodium bicarbonate) is much weaker than salt (sodium chloride), so that it is very difficult to get a really good deposit to settle on the ware during firing. The salt fumes do not deposit well in enclosed shapes so that these forms need to be glazed inside before packing. Only articles like very shallow dishes will attract a thick enough deposit.

Anagama fired stoneware pot (left)
Bruce Martin, New Zealand
Height: 12 in (30 cm)

This pot was fired in a large Japanese Anagama type kiln at temperatures between 1280-1300°C (2340-2370°F). The firing process takes seven and sometimes 10 days to complete, while the kiln takes an equally long time to cool down before unpacking is possible. Ash has fluxed with the pot's shoulder, either by falling on it, or as a result of continuous stoking of the kiln near this point.

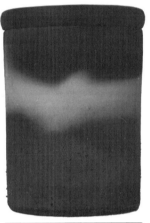

Saggar fired jar (above)
Una Sharples, New Zealand
9in x 4in (23cm x 10cm)

Made of red earthenware pipe clay, this thrown and lidded jar is a beautiful example of the saggar technique of firing pots. Many variations of this technique exist. This pot was partially buried in a saggar, which was a third filled with fine sawdust, and fired at 1150°C (2100°F). Results vary, depending on how compressed and fine the sawdust is and how deep the pot it buried in the saggar. This pot has a light grey band at the center a smooth black band at the top and a black reddish base.

Thrown porcelain jars (left)
John Glick, USA
Diameter: 5 in (13 cm)

These jars display an attractive, lively and plastic sense of throwing, while the incised and scratched decoration shows sympathy to their forms. Both were fired to 1300°C (2370°F) in a reducing atmosphere, after having been glazed with a red copper glaze. The basic glaze and copper content, together with skilful control of the firing largely determined the quality of the red glaze.

SALT-GLAZED CERAMICS

This is a technique in which wet salt is introduced into the kiln at a temperature of approximately 1260°C (2300°F), at which the sodium (flux in the salt) volatilizes and combines with the red hot clay body. In the process it gives off highly toxic and polluting hydrochloric acid fumes. This method of salt-glazing is a well-established tradition which has been used for domestic ware, as well as for building and industrial work; several potters, however, now use a method of spraying a solution of sodium bicarbonate and water into the kiln at high temperatures to achieve a similar result.

Salt-glazed, slip-trailed plate
Janet Mansfield, Australia
Diameter: 10½ in (27 cm)

The bowl was trailed with an iron based slip and given a salt glaze firing, with periods of reduction and oxidation. The slip was sprayed on at the bone dry stage, and the interior of the pot glazed at the leather-hard stage. The plate was fired in a gas kiln to 1300°C (2370°F). The marks from shells, which were used for stacking the pot, are visible in the bottom of the bowl.

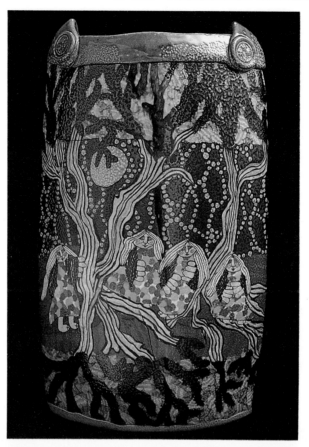

Hand-built vase
Jane Peiser, USA
Height: 12 in (30 cm)

Most of the decoration on the vase is inlaid, but some parts are agateware. The main body, as well as the inlay, is a standard porcelain body. Colors are commercial stains and, when mixing them, it is important that the unfired and fired color of the clays are as alike as possible, so that the stains can be used in a similar way to paints. When dry, the pot is salt glazed to 1300°C (2370°F). Low-fired overglaze has been added to certain areas in a subsequent firing.

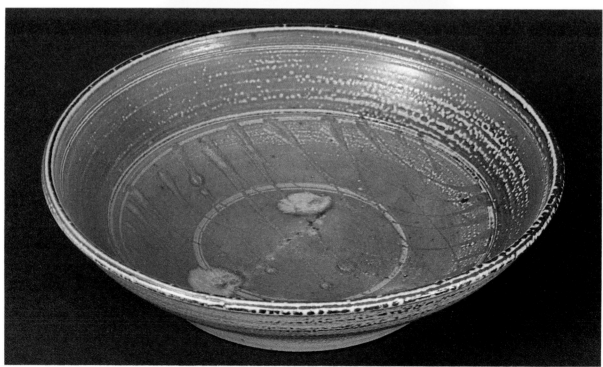

Salt-glazed dish
Carl McConnell, Australia
Diameter: 17 in (43 cm)

The dish was thrown and decorated with a manganese slip over which a glaze pattern was trailed with a ladle. It is one of four dishes which were set in stacks in the kiln with sea shell supports to separate them. The dish was then fired to 1335°C (2435°F) in a reducing salt glaze kiln. The richness of color was achieved by the reaction of the slip with the glaze, and added contrast was given by the freely ladled glaze decoration. Carl McConnel has been deeply influenced by his visits to Japan, and he is one of the few potters outside Japan who are skillful enough to be successful in using such a complicated technique.

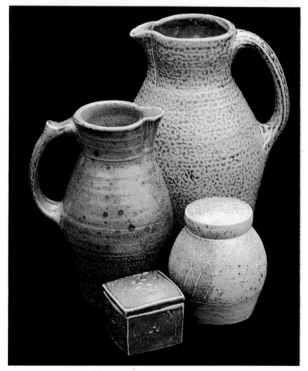

Selection of salt-glazed stoneware
Sarah Walton, UK

In this selection of salt-glazed jugs and jars *(left)*, all the pieces are raw-glazed and once-fired. The large jug has a thin porcelain slip which is heavily salted to give the rich orange-peel effect. The smaller jug is decorated with a china clay and ball clay slip. The round-lidded jar is slipped with a high china clay slip and fired at approximately 1280°C (2340°F).

The rich color of the lidded box is achieved by using a slip with a high kaolin and ball clay content and a heavy reduction firing. The section of the edge of a salt-glazed dish *(above)* shows oxide decoration on a background of slip. The dish was given a heavily reduced salt-glaze firing, details of which are given on page 186. Success in salt glazing depends largely on the careful control of salting and firing the ware.

6
TOOLS
AND
EQUIPMENT

There are various approaches to selecting equipment and tools for use in pottery. You may decide that apart from a kiln for firing, you will work with the minimum of equipment and thus keep costs low. You can rely mainly on hand preparing and making and still produce work of great richness and variety using techniques from hand-building, burnishing and slip-casting to tile decorating and hand-making of panels. The basic equipment you will need for these purposes is a kiln and furniture (the shelves and supports), plaster for press molds, a banding wheel, buckets and bowls, simple scraping, scratching and cutting tools and shelves or bats for drying articles. Materials will include a supply of one or more types of clay, some basic pigments and stains for coloring, and possibly a limited selection of raw materials for experimental work with glazes. If you are contemplating earthenware glazing and firing, you should start with a good reliable frit also.

If your interest in ceramics is general rather than specific and you will be using a much wider range of techniques, you will need a greater selection of equipment. Firstly a small kiln of just over 1 foot cubic capacity for firing tests and small orders, and a medium to large kiln of approximately 7.5 cubic feet for a larger output. Work could include throwing as a limited activity, and for this purpose some of the equipment already mentioned would be needed. The use of industrial techniques would necessitate a clay blunger for mixing casting slip, a possible jolley attachment to the wheel and a compressor, spray booth and spray gun for more accurate and detailed application of glazes or pigments. A silk screen printing table is necessary for all forms of printing on tiles and a vacuum table for printing transfers. You will also need an adequate selection of screens and silk together with light box and photo transfer materials, should you want to do the complete process on your own premises. One or more squeegees are essential for printing techniques.

You will need adequate space for storing ware before and after firing and, if possible, a special area for storing, mixing, drying and handling plaster for molds. For all areas of activity a large sink with a hot water supply is necessary together with bowls and sieves for preparing slips and glazes. Depending on the space available, it is a very good idea to have one or two trolley working benches of different sizes. These should be the same height as your fixed benches to allow for flexibility and speedy rearrangement of working areas. Extra equipment could be a hand-operated tile press, a tile-cutting machine, and a second blunger for preparing a coarse-bodied clay slip. Investment in a viscometer for checking casting slip would be advisable. This should act as a guide to the equipment necessary for specific types of ceramics, but most potters will also need a wide range of hand tools which they will depend on to a great extent in all their work.

If your production is going to be centered on throwing, you would need an electric or kickwheel, possibly a larger kiln and a pugmill for mixing or recycling clay. You will also need big bins and buckets for glaze making, and a good stock of throwing clay if you are not preparing it yourself from raw materials. You would need plenty of shelving for storing and drying ware before and after firing, and a reasonable area for packing, as well as some scales to weigh cartons or boxes for consignment.

Hand tools

Whatever kind of pottery you are making, you will need a selection of tools for cutting, turning, scraping, fettling and modelling the clay. This is the basic and essential equipment for any potter, although there are many other hand tools available for more complicated techniques and for specialist work. It may be useful to drill a hole in the end of some of your hand tools so that they can be hung up within easy reach.

Firstly you will need a cutting wire. Experience will tell you the correct thickness of wire for cutting thrown pots off a wheelhead as well as for cutting slices from a large block which has become leather–hard. Cutting wires can be purchased from an equipment supplier, but you can make your own quite easily. Twisted picture hanging wire attached with a toggle at each end, (made of wood or some object with a hole in it, such as a large button, washer or metal nut), can be used for cutting. Cheese cutting wire wears well and is strong, but it tends to be too springy for cutting moist clay. Wire from electrical flex will also work if not too soft or thin. Try twisting several strands together, joining them at one end to a piece of wood or a washer and placing them in a small lump of hard clay, stuck to the centre of the wheelhead. If you grip the other end firmly in your hand and set the wheel in motion, you will have a twisted cutting wire in a few seconds. Clear nylon thread is also good for cutting clay and is surprisingly strong.

Piano wire, bound to a shaped piece of hardwood which

At the far end of the workshop the author throws a bowl on the electric wheel. In the foreground tiles fresh from the kiln are being checked from the cranks on the right. In this studio screen-printed and hand-decorated tiles, murals and some individual pieces of earthenware, stoneware and porcelain are produced. Method, and a degree of orderliness, are essential if work of a professional standard is to be maintained. The equipment used is basic and relatively unsophisticated. Trolleys, because of their flexibility, are used extensively for storage and as work surfaces. Immediately in front of the wheel the silk screen printing table can be seen. Daylight and non-strip lighting is used and, for health reasons, the workshop is kept as free from dust as possible. At one end of the studio a spray booth is set conveniently into the chimney breast so that the chimney acts as an air outlet.

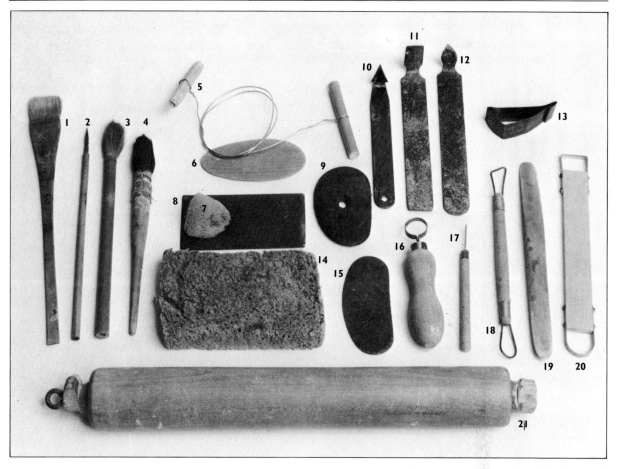

has been tempered in a flame, is ideal for cutting clay strips for handles.

You will need both natural and synthetic sponges for fettling and finishing dry clay pots and for cleaning benches and equipment. Natural sponges are best for mopping up when throwing pots on the wheel, but synthetic ones are adequate for cleaning surfaces and general mopping up.

Modelling and turning tools

A selection of boxwood tools for incising, hand-building and modelling will be needed, together with wire modelling tools and a range of steel turning tools. These come in all shapes and sizes, but a basic turning tool can be made by bending and shaping a metal strip from a packing case if you want to improvise. The metal tools will need constant sharpening, and for this purpose you can use a power grindstone. Boxwood, being close grained, can be filed and used as a template when throwing, giving detail to profiles or shaping the rims of plates.

Steel kidneys of varying gauge and size are used in mold shaping, and when turning and trimming the inside of a bowl. They can also be used for burnishing the surfaces of pots as they revolve on the wheel, as well as for scraping uneven plaster surfaces, such as the inside of plaster molds for dish pressing. Wooden kidneys, (or any metal or wooden tool with a thin edge) can be used for turning, if the

HAND TOOLS

A basic selection of hand tools for beginners (above).
1. Broad Japanese hake brush for covering areas with pigment or glaze or making broad to thin brush strokes.
2. Sable or similar haired Japanese brush for fine lines.
3, 4. Mopbrush for slip or oxides.
5. Twisted wire with toggles.
6. Wooden kidney for shaping.
7. Natural sponge.
8. Strip steel scraper.
9. Wooden rib for throwing.
10. Pointed steel turning tool.
11. Square-ended steel turning tool.
12. Oval steel turning tool.
13. Turning tool made from steel packing case.
14. Synthetic cleaning sponge.
15. Stainless steel flexible kidney.
16. Loop turning tool.
17. Needle in stick.
18. Wire ended modelling tool.
19. Boxwood modelling tool.
20. Metal ended turning tool.
21. Rolling pin for rolling clay.
Another tool necessary for a beginner is a pair of calipers for

measuring the width of plates, lids and jars. A good thin steel knife for cutting clay, fettling, or cutting holes in slabs or pots is another useful tool.

Tools for shaping and modelling (right).
1, 2, 3. Hardwood ribs for throwing and shaping.
4. Rubber kidney for smoothing surfaces.
5. Steel looped tool for paring clay or for turning.
6. Wooden-handled turning tool.
7. Boxwood modelling tool.
8. Circular tapering file.
9. Flat bootmaker's knife for cutting clay and fettling.
10. Double-ended forged steel modelling tool.
11. Curved and double ended serrated forged steel modelling tool.
12. Double-ended, leaf-shaped forged steel modelling tool.
13. Double-ended forged steel, serrated modelling tool.
14. Square-ended and sharpened modelling tool.
15. Thin flexible steel strip for smoothing clay surfaces.

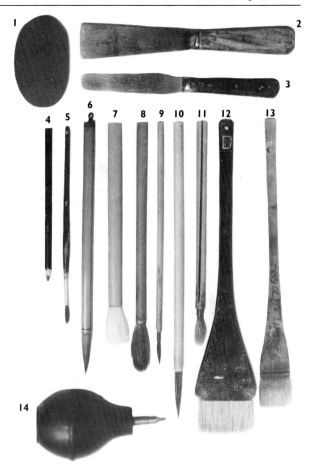

clay is not too hard. Rubber kidneys can be used to smooth the inside of bowls when throwing on the wheel and for cleaning glaze out of bowls before sieving. Hard rubber kidneys are good for sieving glazes and the thin flexible red rubber kidneys are ideal for applying silk screen or litho transfers to fired ware. These red rubber kidneys improve with use. Secondhand dentist's instruments make excellent modelling tools, when ground down and shaped.

Scraping and cutting tools

Narrow and wide fishtail paint scrapers are excellent for many tasks in pottery. A wide scraper is used for cleaning plaster slabs and boards when wedging the clay, as well as for cleaning the wheelhead during throwing. A narrow paint scraper is good for mixing and stirring color and medium when screen printing and for preliminary mixing of color and medium on a glass, marble or tile palette.

Stiff steel scrapers have many uses, including the cleaning of particles from flat surfaces. The end of the tool can be used for a cutting instrument for slicing stiff clay and scraping and levelling leather-hard clay surfaces, such as tiles. Two scrapers used together are very good for lifting or cleaning up spilt glaze and raw materials which are not to be wasted. Flexible steel scrapers of various lengths are used for shaping the surface of curved relief clay models before casting them in plaster. The stiff scrapers are then used to

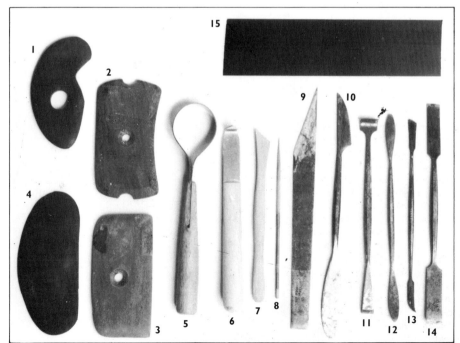

Brushes and knives (above)
1. Very soft rubber kidney for smoothing transfers when fixing them.
2. Square-ended scraper for stirring and mixing colors.
3. Palette knife for mixing and grinding colors.
4. Pencil.
5. Sable brush.
6. Long-haired tapering brush from Japan.
7. Japanese mop brush.
8. Full bodied brush for long full brush strokes.
9. Small thin Japanese brush for details and thin lines.
10. Long-haired Japanese painting brush.
11. Medium brush for painting or applying glaze.
12. Wide Japanese Hake brush.
13. Narrow Japanese Hake brush.
14. Slip trailer with metal nozzle for tube lining or slip trailing.

WHEELS

The two basic wheels used by potters are the kick wheel (below) and the motor driven wheel (right). The former is used in the main by professionals, but the choice between the two is largely a matter of aesthetics, rather than practical preference. For some potters, the act of standing and actually kicking a wheel while making a pot is an integral part of the art's unity and character. For others, the power wheel means they can concentrate on what their hands are doing, helped by the easy control of the wheel's speed. When choosing a kick-wheel, the points to look for are operator comfort and ease of kicking, as it is important to establish a steady rhythm. When selecting a power wheel, check that the speed control is satisfactory, so you can easily speed up or slow down the wheel when desired, and that the motor is powerful enough to cope with a heavy weight of clay while maintaining a constant speed at all stages of centering.

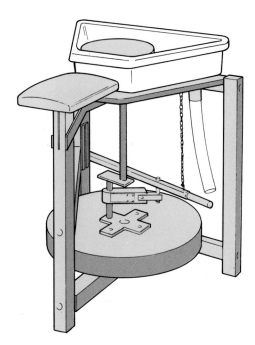

trim and level the plaster as it is setting, or when the casting is complete.

Fettling knives are used for cutting clay slabs, smoothing uneven surfaces when slab building, and for fettling and trimming cast articles. Bootmaker's leather cutting steel blades or knives, if kept sharp, are excellent for cutting clay and sheets of plastic, for sharpening wooden tools and many other cutting jobs. Putty and palette knives are used for cutting, stirring, mixing and scraping.

Slip trailers
These are used for dispensing slip or glaze, and are best if made of rubber. However most slip trailers are made of plastic, which is rather inflexible and can be a strain on the hands, if used frequently. You can make your own trailer from a section of rubber bicycle inner tube, fitted to a cork with a nozzle inserted. The cork and the end of the tube can be held in place by a thick rubber band. A cook's icing bag can also be used as an improvised slip trailer, or you can just use a strong piece of paper, rolled to a cone shape, for dispensing slip.

It is also difficult to obtain a wide variety of nozzles with specific hole sizes, unless you have them specially made. An alternative is to make your own, using a section of plastic tube (from an electrical wire flex) and inserting it into the end of any nozzle which is too large so that you get a finer trailing line.

Brushes
Potters use a wide range of brushes for practical work as well as for decoration. They are available in many shapes and sizes, from small nylon shaders to large, thick glaze mops and flat lacquer brushes for laying on larger areas of color. Price is now a very real consideration so choose carefully when purchasing them.

Sieves
Sieves are essential in pottery, but they vary enormously in price and quality. The perfect sieve has yet to be designed at a reasonable price. Unless a sieve is used for a specific color or glaze, the problem is contamination, due to the impossibility of thorough cleaning. Most potters will need a 40 to 60 mesh sieve for coarse material, and 80 or 100 mesh for glazes and, if very fine results are required, either a 150 or 200 mesh. The most suitable are brass test sieves, but the expense is prohibitive. The best standard mesh to use is phospher bronze, from which a homemade sieve can be made. Take a six-inch (15cm) diameter (or larger) plastic tube or piece of drainpipe, heat the end and place it onto the mesh which is on a flat metal plate. The tube will stick to the mesh and the excess mesh can then be cut away, as with a pie crust, leaving a circular piece.

Miscellaneous tools
A selection of blades is useful in a pottery. A steel hacksaw blade, measuring 1-1½ in (2.5-4cm) wide by ⅛ in (0.3cm) thick, is excellent for scraping, turning and various other

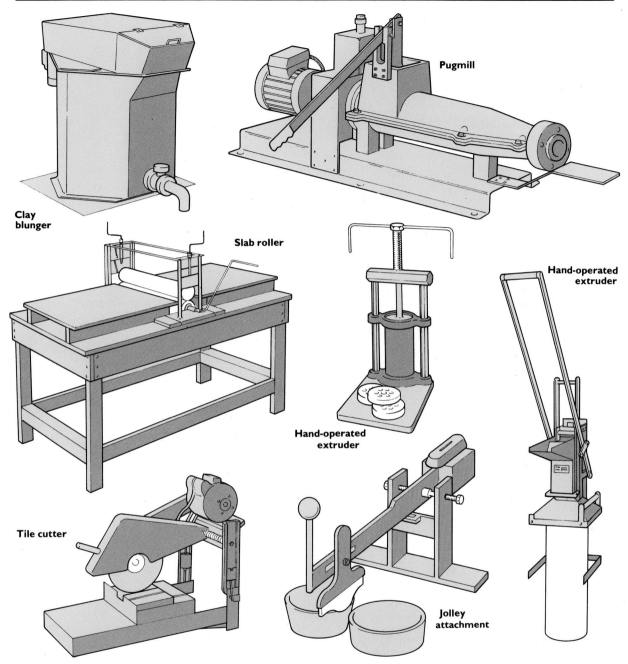

Pugmill

Clay blunger

Slab roller

Hand-operated extruder

Hand-operated extruder

Tile cutter

Jolley attachment

SEMI-INDUSTRIAL EQUIPMENT

The equipment shown here is found in many professional studios, but is not essential for amateurs. A clay blunger or mixer should be operated at slow speeds to thoroughly mix raw clay, which is then thin sieved and dried out or made into casting slip. Pugmills are equipped with intermittently angled fins to mix and extrude clay. The machine's size is determined by the volume of clay to be

processed, or the frequency with which it is used. Shape tiles are extruded by a machine with a worm thread, used to force clay through a die. Slab rollers are used in the production of large garden ware, hand-made tiles and individual slab-constructed forms. Hand-operated extruders of this pattern are used to manufacture coils, handle lengths and hollow forms with various profiles. Tile cutters are used mainly for production tile cutting: they will cut ceramics, stone and marble, but not metal. The jolley attachment is driven by a power wheel and can shape concave and convex articles in plaster molds. Its templates

or discs can be made from mild steel, hardwood, or plastic. Another type of versatile hand-operated extruder will extrude an 8-in (20-cm) diameter cylinder, coils, or any other profiled extrusion.

SPRAYING EQUIPMENT

Spray equipment can be used for slip, glaze or pigments and it provides a high degree of control over the thickness and gradation of deposit. However there is a limit to the thickness that will pass easily through a spray gun. Whatever is being sprayed should first pass through a 100 mesh sieve. The spray booth should be connected to an outside vent or chimney to prevent any glaze escaping into the room. Filters should be regularly washed for the best results, and compressors should be robust enough for using over long periods, so do some research before choosing one to buy. Noise can be a problem so, if possible, keep the compressor in another room and bring an airline to the spray booth. Some people prefer gravity-feed spray guns, while others use the attached cup. They should be thoroughly cleaned and oiled after use.

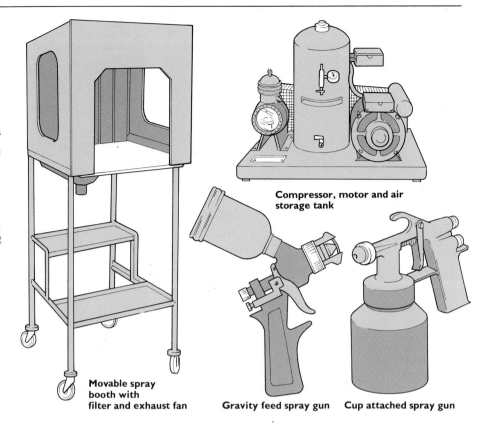

Compressor, motor and air storage tank

Movable spray booth with filter and exhaust fan

Gravity feed spray gun

Cup attached spray gun

clay techniques; it can also be filed and used as a knife. Narrower blades of half an inch are used in sections for scraping clay surfaces and in plaster modelling and mold making. A short section of band saw blade will produce a rough surface on leather-hard or dry clay and surform blades, which have an abrasive surface similar to a cheese grater, are excellent for paring and shaping clay or plaster.

Metal and wooden rulers are handy for the potter. Thin, flexible steel strips, measuring 1-1½ in (2.5-4cm) by 1/16 in (0.16cm), and up to one metre (3ft) long, have many uses, including providing a straight edge for cutting. A six-inch (15cm) steel ruler is invaluable in model making, and for trimming plaster and producing a flat surface. Wooden slats can be used to produce the correct thickness of clay when it is being rolled or for resting sieves on when sieving glaze or slip onto bowls or buckets.

The best kind of rolling pin is one commissioned from a wood turner and made from well-seasoned timber which will not crack if damp. It should not be too hard, but have some degree of absorbency. If all the factors are right it will be an investment for a lifetime. You will also need a pastry size rolling pin and a metre length roller to cover all your needs.

Several tools are very useful for preparing slabs of clay. The first is a large, perspex or wooden set square for making right angles. When levelling leather-hard slabs, moisten the surface with a sponge and use a wooden batten or the long edge of a wide perspex ruler or set square to level the surface, working across it from 180° in opposite directions. A large flexible chef's pastry knife works well to smooth flat clay surfaces when moistened.

One of my best investments was a milk shake mixer bought from a kitchen caterer's supply shop and still in constant use for mixing small quantities of glaze or slip. Alternatively a metal rod with a plastic paddle head, bought as a paint mixer and attached to an electric drill, saves a great deal of effort when mixing liquid materials.

A triangular steel or alloy frame, or circular section with extended corners is best for supporting sieves when working and if you can afford it, a vibratory sieve for dealing with large quantities of glaze.

A small ball mill is invaluable for blending several oxides together or grinding oxide to a finer texture for adding to glaze or for decorating.

Many potters have a Dod box for extruding coils or strips, or varying sections for handles and for building. The dyes can be made from perspex, wood, brass or mild steel.

If you are involved in tile or mural work then a tile cutting machine will soon pay for itself in time saved. You will still need the various hand tile cutting tools as illustrated for cutting small tiles and test pieces.

Tongs for holding pots or dishes are best made from sprung steel acquired from a wire mesh manufacturer, or by using unwound mattress springs.

Always have a coarse and fine oil stone for sharpening large nails or pieces of iron for a variety of uses in pottery as well as for sharpening knives and metal edges.

Fine tapering round files are very good for making narrow holes in clay (for example when making Egyptian paste beads) because the files have a textured surface.

MISCELLANEOUS EQUIPMENT

The basic equipment needed for hand-building is sieves, scales, buckets, a banding wheel and some hand tools. Once a potter is involved in general ceramics the type of equipment needed will be dictated by the technique being used. An essential piece of equipment is some form of balance scales, suitable for weighing quantities of oxides when performing tests using from 0.01 of a gram to about 5 grams.

For those who are earning their living by their craft, time is money, so the use of motorized tools is recommended, because of their capacity for saving time. This particularly applies to mixers, vibratory sieves and ball mills. Another valuable motorized tool with many uses is a portable electric drill for drilling holes in clay, wood or walls. A paddle paint-mixer can be fixed to this for stirring small quantities of glaze or slip. A type of glazing tongs similar to sugar tongs is the most useful, but you may have to get them specially made with double points on one arm and a single on the other. Plastic bowls of all sizes are essential in a pottery, especially small bowls, with a

diameter of 6 - 10 in (15 - 25 cm), for doing tests. A ball mill can be useful for mixing color very thoroughly with clay and for finely mixing oxides for decorating or pigment with glazes. A large set square is essential for cutting large slabs of clay and for checking vertical construction.

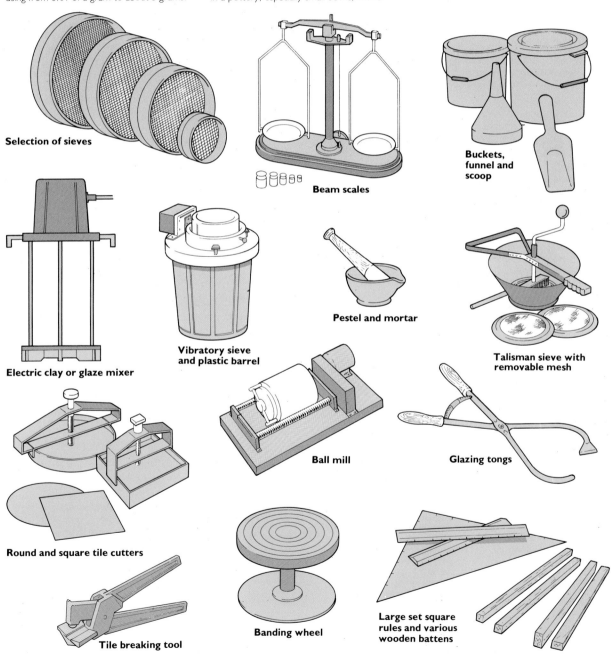

Selection of sieves

Beam scales

Buckets, funnel and scoop

Electric clay or glaze mixer

Vibratory sieve and plastic barrel

Pestel and mortar

Talisman sieve with removable mesh

Round and square tile cutters

Ball mill

Glazing tongs

Tile breaking tool

Banding wheel

Large set square rules and various wooden battens

Health and Safety

ATTENTION TO HEALTH AND SAFETY is particularly important for potters who will be handling raw materials as these can vary from mild irritants to those which are highly toxic or poisonous. They will also be using complex, and sometimes dangerous, machinery for the many processes involved in ceramic work.

Many potters are very conscious of their own health and diet, but are sometimes less vigilant about working conditions and environment. Common sense and the development of good habits for protection will eliminate the risk of accidents. The following points on safety should be adhered to at all times.

1. All moving parts of the machinery should be enclosed so that there is no chance of clothing, long hair or hands getting caught in it. You should be particularly careful when using equipment, such as a pug mill or blunger.

2. Hand held electric drills or mixers should be used with great care as they can easily become entangled with loose clothing, causing serious injury.

3. Never handle electric plugs for machinery with wet hands as you could get an electric shock.

4. Make sure you have plenty of help when moving machinery. It is not worth risking injury from a heavy weight falling on top of you.

5. Always have starting and stopping switches within easy reach of the machinery you are operating so that you can control it without difficulty.

6. When using a gas-fuelled kiln, take every safety precaution as gas explosions are not unheard of. Make sure there are no combustible materials in the vicinity of the kiln and keep the kiln room well ventilated.

7. Ideally, any kiln should be in a separate room as the fumes which escape during firings can be injurious to health.

8. Be careful not to overload shelves (particularly those with cantilevers) with heavy biscuit ware, raw materials or finished pots as they could collapse causing injury or damage.

10. Store all raw materials in closed containers.

11. Pay particular attention to hygiene after using raw materials.

12. Always wear goggles when doing any kind of grinding of raw materials.

13. The fumes given off during some firings can be harmful to the lungs. As many low-firing enamels, lusters, gold and pigments are mixed with a wide range of mediums the fumes expelled as these fire away need to be extracted by fan, or there should be adequate ventilation. The plastic cover coat used with transfers gives off fumes of a particularly obnoxious nature in the early stages of firing. Too many potters work in proximity to their kilns when firing and have inadequate ventilation. There is an excellent booklet on Health and Safety in ceramics, which can be obtained (see bibliography).

TOXIC RAW MATERIALS
Care should also be exercised when using and handling the following.

Bold headings refer to basic materials that are toxic; compounds that contain the basic materials as a constituent are listed below the headings.

Sodium Oxide
Soda felspar, pearl ash, nitre
Calcium oxide
Whiting, dolomite
Magnesium oxide
Magnestite, dolomite, talc
Lithium oxide
Spodumene, lepidolite
Strontium
Strontium oxide, strontium carbonate
Aluminium oxide
Felspar, clay
Titanium oxide
Rutile
Raw leads
Lead carbonate. lead oxide (red lead)
Lead sulphide (galina)
Litharge (yellow lead)

Barium
Barium carbonate, barium oxide
Boron
Borax (sodium borate), boric acid
Calcium borate frit, colimanite
Cadmium
Compounds
Chromium
Chromium oxide
Cobalt
Cobalt oxide
Fluorine
Fluospoar (calcium fluorides) traces in minerals.
To remove fluorine from the kiln atmposphere, good kiln room ventilation is essential
Nickel
Nickel oxide
Selenium
Selenium compounds
Silicon
Quartz (sand), flint
Cristobalite (also present as free silica in most clays)
Vanadium
Vandium pentoxide

Zinc
Zinc oxide
Manganese
Manganese compounds are also regarded as injurious to health
Antimony
Antimony oxide

While many potters use what are called 'low-solubility lead frits', which by themselves do not present a health hazard, they can become toxic with the addition of certain oxides, such as copper and chromium. This can greatly increase the lead solubility as a health risk, especially if acid foods are stored in receptacles glazed in this way. The reason lead frits are still used in glazes is they can give a wide firing range, a low melting range, smoothness and high gloss. They also give enriching qualities to colors and, if used correctly, are highly acid resistant. The compounds of barium antimony and zinc are also toxic by nature and

most of the basic coloring oxides, such as copper manganese, cadmium, and cobalt tend to be toxic. Regular mopping up and vacuuming is the best protection against these health hazards. Rubber gloves should be worn when handling soda compounds which are not fritted and some form of respiratory mask should be worn whenever you are handling powdered glaze materials. If in doubt about any materials, contact the supplier responsible for labelling all the raw materials.

Suppliers

THE TYPES OF CLAY given in this book are standard, although many countries give their own names to local equivalents. These may vary slightly in composition, depending on where they were found, and the firing temperature may alter slightly accordingly. However your supplier will be able to advise you on this. Most countries have their own clay preparation and supply firms and the clays are classified as to type, for example earthenware, stoneware, porcelain, with the relevant firing ranges given by the supplier. Special clays, such as ball clay, china clay or kaolin, porcelain, bone china and certain prepared clays, are often imported. This is the practice in New Zealand, Australia, Canada and South Africa, with England being the main exporter. As raw materials of the same type vary throughout the world it is common for the large suppliers to import from many sources and blend the ingredients so that a more standard and constant material is available to the majority of customers.

The greatest care should be taken when preparing special bodies, such as bone china and porcelain. Bone china, in particular, has such a critical melting and slumping temperature that thorough testing and firing will first be necessary. For porcelain bodies plasticity and translucency are important qualities and the most plastic china clay available should be used and tested. Frits vary from country to country, but are generally classified as high-alkaline, high-lead content (as in lead sesquisilicate) or low-solubility lead frit, borax based or a combination of bases. Nearly all suppliers give a chemical analysis of frits.

When formulating glazes decide whether to use a local felspar or an imported one. It is now the practice to list equivalents for materials in different countries, so once again consult your supplier if there is no indication. Finally, methods of firing ware are numerous and the potter can make his own choice, but the fuels used for firing kilns are standard.

UK SUPPLIERS

Pottery Crafts Ltd.,
Campbell Road, Stoke-on-Trent ST4 4ET, England.
Tel: 0782 272444
(The largest supplier of kilns, wheels, equipment clays, glazes, colors, stains, moulds etc. in the U.K. An amalgamation of Podmores, Wenger and Harrison-Mayers. Agents in many countries.)

CLAYS AND RAW MATERIALS

Watts Blake Bearne Ltd.,
Park House, Courtney Park, Newton Abbot, Devon, England.
(Range of prepared clays.)

Medcol (Stoke-on-Trent)
Sun Street, Hanley,
Stoke-on-Trent.
(Colors, minerals, supplies, clays.)

'Macaloid'
from Steetley Minerals Ltd
Gateford
Worksop
Nottinghamshire
Tel: (0909) 474551
(Excellent suspender, superior type of bentonite)

Morgan Refractories Ltd.,
Liverpool Road, Neston, Wirral, Cheshire.
Tel: 051-336 3911
(Supppliers of 'T' material excellent for large letters and relief mural work.)

Potclay's Ltd.,
Brickkiln Lane, Etruria, Stone-on-Trent, U.K.
Tel: 0782 29816
(The largest range of clays in Europe. Also raw materials, glazes, oxides)

Molochite from
Varcoes Sales Co. Ltd.
St. Austell, Cornwall.
(EHB-BC or best available)

Ferro (Great Britain) Ltd.,
Wombourne,
Wolverhampton WU5 8DA,
Tel: 0902-894144
(Wide range of ceramic raw materials, clays, glazes, equipment and machinery)

Sneyd Oxides Ltd.,
Sneyd Mills, Leonora Street, Stoke-on-Trent ST6 3BZ, England.
Tel: 0782 89431
(Glazes, stains, oxides, slipstains, enamels and underglaze colors)

Blythe Colors Ltd.,
Creswell, Stoke-on-Trent, Staffs. ST11 9RG.
Tel: 07818 5959
(Wide range of glazes, stains, enamels, lusters, raw materials, mediums of all types of decorative colors)

Allied Colloids Ltd
P.O Box 38
Low Moor
Bradford
Yorkshire
(Suppliers of 'Dispex' Deflocculents for the ceramic industry)

VARIOUS MACHINERY AND EQUIPMENT

Edwards & Jones Ltd.,
Globe Engineering Works, Uttoxeter Road, Meir, Stoke-on-Trent ST3 7QD, England.
Tel: 0782 316181
(Heavy duty pugwells and extruders)

'Errut' Products Ltd.,
Jubilee Close, Townsend Lane, London NW9 8TT.
Tel: 205 9773
(Sell an excellent small compact portable tile cutting machine, and heavier cutting machines)

Clipper Manufacturing Co. Ltd., Thurmaston Boulevard, Barkby Road, Leicester LE4 7JB, England.
Tel: 0533 767847
(Tile and masonry cutting machines and equipment)

'Pyrometers'
Kilncraft (Sheffield) Ltd.,
111 Arundel Street, Sheffield S1 2NT, U.K.
Tel: 0742 23279

Honeywell Ltd.,
Charles Square, Bracknell, Berks. U.K. RG12 1EB.
Tel: 0244 024555
(Suppliers of Heat Process Controllers)

Auto Combustions Hoistract Ltd., Harcourt, Halesfield 13, Telford TF7 4EW, Salop, England
Tel: 0952 585579
(Swirlamiser kiln firing equipment for oil or gas)

Deancraft (Craft Division of Blythes)
Deancraft Ceramic Supplies, Lovatt Street, Hanely, Stoke-on-Trent ST4 7RL, U.K.
Tel: 0782 411049
(Machinery, equipment, clay, glazes, colors)

Dragon Ceramex,
5 Nomix Park,
Congresbury, Avon BS19
5HB, U.K.
Tel: 0934-833409
(Hand-operated clay forming
extruder. Hollow sections 8"
diam. Pipes, bricks and tiles)

The DeVilbiss Co. Ltd.,
Ringwood Road,
Bournemouth BH11 9LH,
England.
Tel: 020-16 3131
(All compressor and spraying
machines and equipment.
Fans, booths, etc. and spray
guns (gravity feed)

Transatlantic Plastics Ltd.,
672 Fulham Road, London
SW6 5RX. England.
Tel: 01-136 2271
(Polythene bags, light and
heavy duty. Plastic sheeting)

Commercial Data Services,
Hill House, Amersham,
Bucks., England.
Tel: Amersham 4105
(Sell comprehensive lists of
specialist manufacturers and
suppliers throughout the U.K.)

Norton Industrial Ceramics
Ltd.,
King Street, Stoke-on-Trent
ST4 3LY, England.
Tel: 0782 44821
(Manufacturers of tile and
pottery cranks, stilts and
spurs)

Desoutter Ltd.,
319 Edgeware Road,
Colindale, London NW9
6ND, England.
Tel: 205 7050
(An excellent range of
grinding, stapling, drilling
and other tools, using
compressed air)

Gallenkamp Ltd.,
P.O. Box 290, Technico
House, Christopher St.,
London E.2.
(Beam balance scales, weights
and laboratory equipment)

'Handovers'
6 Angel Yard, Highgate
Village, London N.6.
(Hand-made Sable Brushes)

Davis Industrial (Filters) Ltd.,
Imperial Way, Croydon,

Surrey CR9 3DR, England.
Tel: 686 7561
(Foam plastic spray booth
elements for filtering glaze.
Hard wearing, long lasting
and easy to clean by gentle
washing)

Brindus (Industrial Services)
Ltd.,
56 Great Queen Street,
Dartford, Kent DA1 1TW,
England.
Tel: 32 20305
(Standard rubber gloves —
wholesale)

Mundet Cork Products,
Vicarage Road, Croydon,
Surrey.
Tel: 688 4142
(Cork sheets or cut to size.
Also all sizes of bungs)

Stanhope Chemical Products
Ltd.,
37 Broadway, Welwyn
Garden City, Herts. AL7
1JW, England.
Tel: 07073 24379
(Toucan masks — washable
and comfortable to use)

Industrial Glove Co. Ltd.,
Nailsea, Bristol BS19 2BX,
England.
Tel: Nailsea 2037
(Gloves, Goggles, Ear Muffs,
Respirators and Dust Masks)

British Gypsum
3 Brook Street
Stoke-on-Trent
Staffs ST4 1JN
Tel: 0782 48972
also
Beacon Hill
Newark
Nottinghamshire NG24 2JQ
Tel: 0636 703351
(Manufacturers of plasters)

Ells and Farrier Ltd
5 Princes Street
London W1
Tel: 01-629 9964
(Supplies of various gauge
nylon thread)

Cuttercraft Ltd
Maindstone Industrial Centre
St Peter Street
Maidstone Kent
Tel: 0622-674 170
(Metal silhouettes for cutting
and pressing out flat clay
shapes)

'Brushwax'
Technical Art Products
40 Beachwood Road
Sanderstead
Surrey
Tel: 01-657 5422
(Good water-soluble cold wax
resist)

Whitfields
Albert Street
Newcastle-under-Lyme
Staffordshire
(Suppliers of Hebor plaster)

East London Building
Merchants
Victoria Park Wharf
Old Ford Road
London E3
Tel: 01-981 2614
(A wide range of plasters)

Potters Mates,
Malcolm Hedley-Saw Cust
Hall,
Toppesfield, Halstead, Essex.
Tel: 0787 237 704

Pilling Pottery,
School Lane, Pilling, Nr.
Garstang. Lancs. PR3 6HB
Tel: 039-130 307
(Kilns, power and kick
wheels)

The 'Leach' Modified Pottery
Wheel,
Woodley's Potters Wheel
Ltd.,
Newton Popplesford, Devon
EX10 0BJ, England.
(Kickwheel)

KILNS
Cromatic Kilns Ltd.,
Park Hall Road, Longton,
Stoke-on-Trent ST3 5AY,
England.
Tel: 0782 313947
(Gas and electric kilns. Quick
fire kilns and all accessories)

Kiln & Furnaces Ltd.,
Keele Street, Tunstall, Stoke-
on-Trent ST6 5AS. Staffs.,
U.K.
Tel: 0782 813621
(All types of kiln and
equipment)

Lazer Kilns,
Unit 32/33 off Selby Street,
London E.1. England.
Tel: 377 2174
(Low cost firing natural or
bottled gas fired fibre

insulated kilns. Also range of
electric kilns, and digital
pyrometers)

Acme Marls Ltd.,
Clough Street,
Hanley, Stoke-on-Trent ST1
4AF, England.
Tel: 0782 260848
(Kiln furniture refractories)

F.G.H. Controls Ltd.,
The Wynd, Letchworth,
Herts. SG6 3EN, England.
Tel: 04626 72821
(Manufacturers of
multifunction process
programmers for kilns)

The Industrial Pyrometer Co.
Ltd.,
66-67 Gooch Street North,
Birmingham B5 6QY,
England.
Tel: 021-622 3511
(Temperature controllers —
programmers — electronic.
Electronic & digital —
thermocouples and
temperature fuses)

Fordham Thermal Systems
Co. Ltd.,
Carter Street, Fordham, Ely,
Cambs.
Tel: 063-872 650
(Ceramic fibers)

J.W. Ratcliffe & Sons
(Engineers) Ltd.,
Rope Street, Off Shelton New
Road, Stoke-on-Trent ST4
6OJ.
Tel: 0782-611321/3
(Claimed to be the largest
manufacturers in the U.K.
with a wide range of ceramic
equipment, but not kilns)

Moler Products,
Hyth Works, Hawkins Road,
Colchester.
(Ceramic Kiln Fiber)

P.B. Sillimanite Co.
Atlas Works, Atlas Road,
Willesden, London.
(Refractory kiln walls)

SILK SCREEN SUPPLIES
Sericol, Sericol Group Ltd.,
24 Parsons Green Lane,
London SW6 4HT, England.
Tel: 736 3388
(All silk screen equipment
and material from nylon
mesh to printing tools)

Brittains Converters Ltd.,
Ivy House Paper Mills,
Commercial Road, Hanley,
Somerset ST1 3QS, England.
Tel: 0782 25380
*(Large manufacturer of
decalomania paper for
ceramic transfers)*

W. Bennett & Co. (Rubber
Stamps) Ltd.,
Waterloo Road, Cobridge,
Stoke-on-Trent ST6 3HT,
England.
Tel: 0782-23937
*(All types of stamping and
printing equipment, gelatine
pads, mediums and stencil
cutting services. Materials for
rubber moulds)*

Executive Photoprints,
Farnworth Park Ind. Estate,
Wellington Street,
Farnworth, Bolton BLA
7BY, Lancs. U.K.
*(Reasonably priced quantities
of self-adhesive color prints
for catalogue sheets or hand-
outs)*

Pamela Moreton Ceramics
(Silk Screen)
22B Holt Road, Cromer,
Norfolk NR2 79JW,
England.
Tel: 0263 512629
*(Supplies short or long run
ceramic transfers. Supplies
screen printed ceramics to
commission. Also design and
artwork service)*

CPS Holborn Ltd.,
74-81 Banner Street, E.C.1.
London, England.
Tel: 253 4579
*(Efficient quick service for
applying silk screen images to
customers screens)*

E.T. Marlet Ltd.,
Deer Park Road, Wimbledon,
SW19, London, England.
Tel: 540 8531
*(All silk screen materials and
equipment)*

Oliver Product
Developments Ltd
Water Lane Storrington
Pulborough
West Sussex RH20 3EA
Tel: (09066) 3397)
*('Potta' hinge clamp bracket
and good basic screen
printing equipment)*

'Decorem' process
Arts Loisirs Culture
15 Rue Jules-Ferry
91390 Marsang-sur-Orge
Paris
France
Tel: 904 68 45
*(Special photographic printing
technique materials)*

US SUPPLIERS

Hammill & Gillespie Inc.
P.O Box 104
Livingston
New Jersey 07039
Tel: (201) 994 3650
*(Grolleg white firing plastic
china clay, true Albany slip
clay, Gerstley borate — 200
mesh)*

Lockerbie Mfg Corporation
PO Box 695
Beaumont
California 92223
Tel: (714) 845 5855
(Momentum kick wheel)

Mason Color and Chemical
PO Box 76
East Liverpool
Ohio 43920
*(Largest and cheapest ceramic
stain manufacturer, starting
at 5lb of color)*

Peter Pugger
9460 Carmel Road
Atascadero
California 934222
Tel: 805 461 3334
*(Mix pug and extruders, pug
mills)*

AD Alpine Inc.
3051 Fujita Street
Torrance
California 90505
Tel: (213) 775 6503
(Quality kilns)

Bailey Pottery Equipment
Corporation
CPO 1577
Kingston
New York 12401
Tel: 800 431 6067
914 339 3721 (local)
*(Bailey tile extruder,
extruders, slab rollers)*

Solduer Pottery
Equipment Inc.
PO Box 428
Gilt
Colorado 81652

Tel: 800 525 3459
876 2935 (local)
(Wheels)

Bluebird Pugmills
PO Box 2307
Fort Collins
Colorado 80522
Tel: 800 525 5372
303 484 3243 (local)
*(also Blue bird tile machine
-model 1050)*

Westwood Ceramic Supply
Co.
14400 Iomitas Avenue
Dept. B067 City of Industry
California 91746
Tel: (213) 330 0631
(General Supplies)

Robert Brent Corporation
PO Box 968
Healdsburg
California 95448
Tel: 800 358 8252
*(Wheels, extruders, trolleys,
slabbers etc)*

Amaco
American Art Clay Co. Inc.
4717 West Sixteenth Street
Indianapolis
Indiana 46222
Tel: 800 428 3239
317 244 6871 (local)
(Wheels, colors, pencils)

Skutt Ceramic Products
2168 SE Steele Street
Portland
Oregon 97202
Tel: 503 231 7726
(Kilns and other equipment)

Shimpo West Inc.
14400 Louritas Avenue
City of Industry
California 91746
*(Smallest and most efficient
pug mill, and other
equipment)*

'Jiffy Mixer'
1342-3H Bell Avenue
Tustin California 92680
Tel: (714) 669 9907

Scott Creek Pottery
482 Swanton Road
Davenport
California 95017
Tel: (408) 426 5091
('Super duper' expansion box)

Randall Pottery Inc.
Box 774

Alfred
New York 14802
Tel: (607) 587 8655
(Basic equipment)

Ferro Corporation
PO Box 6650
Cleveland
Ohio 44101
(High quality colors)

AP Green Fireclay Ltd
Valentine
New Jersey
*(Extremely plastic heavy iron
fireclay (PXB fireclay)*

Norton Co.
Industrial Ceramics Division
Worcester
MA 01606
*(Kiln furniture and
refractories)*

Kentucky-Tennessee Clay Co.
Box 449
Mayfield
Kentucky 42066
Tel: 502 247 3061

CANADIAN SUPPLIERS

The Pottery Supply House
Box 192
2070 Speers Road
Oakville
Ontario L6J 5A2
Tel: 416 827 1129
*(Wheels, kilns, clays, glazes
and colors)*

Plainsman Clays Ltd
Box 1266
Medicine Hat
Alberta T1A 7M9
Tel: (403) 527 8535
(Wide selection of clays)

The Green Barn Potters
Supply
PO Box 1235 Sation
Surrey
British Columbia
Tel: (604) 888 3411

Blythe Colors Ltd
Toronto
*Glazes, colors and raw
materials)*

Ferro Enamels
26 David Road
PO Box 370
Oakville
Ontario
*(Kilns, glazes and raw
materials)*

AUSTRALIAN SUPPLIERS

Diamond Ceramic Supplies Ltd
50-52 Geddes Street
Mulgrave
Melbourne
Victoria 3170
Tel: 560 4466
also
12 Bridge Street
Rydalmere
Sydney
NSW 2116
Tel: (02) 638 3774

Venco Products
2 Kilburn Way
Kelmscott
Western Australia 6111
Tel: (09) 399 5265
(Wheels and pugmills)

Ceramic Supply Co.
61 Lakemba Street
Belmore
NSW 2192
Tel: 759 3891
(Kiln wheels and pugmills, clays, glazes and colors)

Walker Ceramics
Boronia Road
Wantirna
Victoria
PO Box 208 Bayswater 3153
Tel: (03) 729 4755
(Kilns, equipment and all raw materials)

Pottery Supplies Pty. Ltd
51 Castlemain Street
Milton
Brisbane 4064
PO Box 250 Paddington
Queensland 4064
Tel: (07) 3693633
(Wheels, pugmills, clays, raw materials, tools and colors)

Bendigo Pottery
PO Box 666
Epsom Victoria 3551
Tel: (054) 484404
(All types of clay)

Talisman Potters Equipment
NSW Agent
The Potters Society of Australia
48 Burton Street
Dorlinghurts 2010
NSW
Tel: (02) 3313151
(Wheels, sieves, pugs and clay rollers)

B & L Tetlow
12a George Street
Blackburn
Victoria 3130
Tel: (03) 8774418
(Kilns, wheels, spray booths, ball mills)

Potters Equipment
14 Pitt Street
Ringwood 3134
Victoria 870 7533
Tel: 729 2857
(Tools, clay, wheels, glazes)

NEW ZEALAND SUPPLIERS

Central Ceramics
89 North Street
Box 345
Fielding
NZ 36827
(Clays, raw materials, kilns and equipment)

Cobcrafts
Potters Suppliers Ltd
88a Victoria Street
PO Box 25052
Christchurch
NZ 67229
(Kilns and materials)

Winstone Clay Products Ltd
PO Box 54002
Main Highway
Plimmerton
Wellington
Tel: 33 8029
(Wide range of clays)

WD McGregor Ltd
118 Stoddard Road
Mount Roskill
Auckland 4
Tel: 669 619
(Kilns, shelves, elements, control equipment)

Smith & Smith Ltd
73 Captain Springs Road
Box 709
Te Papa
Auckland
Tel: 661 249
also
213 Tuam Street
Christchurch
Box 22-496
Tel: 64 649
(All pottery equipment and materials)

Screenprinting and Ceramic Supplies Ltd
4 Sydney Street

Petone
Wellington
PO Box 30180
Tel: Lower Hutt 688495
(Clays, glazes and equipment)

Costal Ceramics
124 Rimm Road
Paraparamma
Wellington
(Clays, kilns and equipment)

Mintech (NZ) Limited
Head Office
PO Box 440
Nelson
Tel: (054) 80 092
(Wide selection of raw materials)

Southern Ceramic Import Co.
Main Road
Lornviile N06 RD
Tel: 59 543
(Clays, kilns, tools, equipment and materials)

McSkimming Industries Ltd
George Street
Dunedin
(Clay suppliers)

Western Potters Supply Ltd
18 Clark Street
New Lynn (Private bag)
Auckland
(All pottery materials and equipment)

Furnace Engineering Ltd and Ceramic Supply Co.
10 Ward Street
New Lynn
Auckland
PO Box 15-293 New Lynn
(Kiln equipment and materials)

Stan Lay
6 Exmoor Street
Havelock North
(Pugmills)

Talisman
Potters Supplies
171 Archers Road
TaKapuna
Auckland
Tel: 480 735
(Manufacturers of wheels and other equipment. Suppliers of clays, raw materials, colors, kilns and other machinery)

PYROMETRIC CONES

There is a variety of cones available on the market, but the two most common are Standard Seger cones and American Orton cones. The table below gives temperature conversions from cones to centigrade and fahrenheit.

STANDARD SEGER CONES

Cone	°C	°F
019	690	1270
018	700	1290
017	730	1350
016	755	1390
015a	780	1440
09a	930	1710
08a	950	1740
07a	970	1780
06a	990	1810
05a	1000	1830
04a	1025	1880
03a	1055	1930
02a	1085	1980
01a	1105	2020
1a	1125	2060
2a	1150	2100
3a	1170	2140
4a	1195	2180
5a	1215	2220
6a	1240	2260
7	1260	2300
8	1280	2340
9	1300	2430
10	1320	2410
11	1340	2440

AMERICAN ORTON CONES

Cones	°C	°F
022	600	1110
021	615	1140
020	635	1170
019	680	1260
018	715	1320
017	745	1370
016	790	1450
015	805	1480
014	840	1510
013	850	1560
012	885	1620
011	895	1640
010	895	1640
09	920	1660
08	955	1750
07	985	1770
06	995	1820
05	1045	1910
04	1060	1940
03	1100	2010
02	1120	2050
01	1135	2080
1	1155	2110
2	1160	2120
3	1170	2140
4	1185	2160
5	1195	2180
6	1220	2230
7	1240	2260
8	1265	2310
9	1280	2340
10	1305	2380
11	1315	2400
12	1325	2420

Glossary

Agateware Clay patterns and structures formed by laminating, mixing or inlaying different colored clays, to give an effect like agate stone.

Ball Clay A very fine plastic secondary clay with few impurities.

Ball Mill An enclosed, mechanically revolved cylinder containing flint or porcelain balls which are used to grind ceramic oxides or materials mixed with water.

Bat A slab of highly refractory material used for kiln shelves, or a circular base made of plaster or another material such as wood, used for throwing on. Also used to dry out wet clay by absorbing the moisture.

Bat Wash A mixture of flint and water used to clean drops of glaze from kiln shelves.

Bentonite A fine-grained compound, similar in composition to primary clay. It is used to give plasticity to clay bodies, and extensively in glazes to prevent settling.

Blunger Mechanized container with paddles for mixing clay and water to a fluid slip.

Biscuit or Bisque Pottery which has been fired once to harden it, prior to glazing.

Brogniart's Principle A useful formula for calculating the amount of dry material present in a liquid. The formula is as follows:

$$W = \frac{(p - 568) \times g}{g - 1}$$

W = dry content (in grammes) of 1 pint
p = weight (in grammes) of 1 pint of liquid
g = specific gravity of dry material
The specific gravity is generally taken as 2.5 for all clays, but with glazes the specific gravity varies.

Burnishing Compacting a clay surface or slip coating by rubbing in the leather-hard state with a smooth, hard object to give a polished finish.

Calcine A form of purifying, by heating oxides or compounds to drive out carbon gases or water and to reduce plasticity in powdered clays.

Cast Making pots and shapes by pouring slip into plaster molds.

Casting Slip Chemically induced slip with less water content than ordinary slip.

Celadon Green stoneware and porcelain glaze colors, containing iron.

Chattering An irregular surface caused by blunt turning tools or a coarse grog in the clay.

China clay A pure non-plastic primary clay, used in bodies and glazes.

Chuck Metal or clay shape for holding leather-hard articles for turning.

Chum A metal turning lathe attachment for placing leather-hard hollow ware over to hold it while turning. Also applies to a turned dome of clay, over which leather-hard articles are placed, prior to turning.

Chun Chinese glaze which gives a milky blue coloring when fired.

Clay body A balanced blend of clay, minerals and other non-plastic ingredients which make up the pottery structure.

Crazing Fine cracks in a glaze, sometimes desirable, as in crackle glazes, but not for functional earthenware.

Decorem Photographic method used to apply images to a fired glazed surface, before refiring.

Deflocculent Alkaline substance, such as sodium silicate or sodium carbonate which, when added to a clay with a little water, causes the clay particles to separate and remain in suspension.

Downdraft kiln One in which heat and flames are drawn downwards and out through flues at the base or floor of the kiln.

Dunting Cracking of pottery due to a too rapid cooling after firing.

Egyptian Paste A highly alkaline body with low plasticity and alumina content. The alkali comes to the surface in drying, leaving crystals that flux in firing to give a glazed surface. Coloring oxides are also added to the body.

Engobe A prepared slip which contains clay, felspar, flint, a flux and usually colorants.

Enamels Specially prepared low-firing colors with a high flux content.

Fettling The trimming and sponging of cast articles.

Filter Press Machine into which slip is pumped under pressure so that water is extracted, leaving a stiff plastic clay.

Flocculent An acid material which causes clay particles to adhere together.

Flux Group of minerals which reduce the melting point of silica in the ceramic body to form a glass or glaze.

Footring Raised circle of clay at the base of a thrown article, on which it can stand. The footring is usually turned from leftover clay.

Frit A flux used in glazes, stabilized by melting with other ceramic materials and reground to a fine powder.

Fusion When the fluxes in a body cause the clay to melt and form a solid composition.

Grog Coarse to fine sand or ground clay which has been once-fired. Added to clay bodies to reduce shrinkage and firing temperature of the ware.

Ground-laying Applying an even coat of enamel with an oil medium to a once-fired glaze surface and refiring to a low temperature of approximatley 750°C (1350°F).

Gum Arabic and Gum Tragacanth Water-soluble gums, used as adhesive in glaze or colors.

Inglaze To apply pigment, stain, or glaze to an unglazed or glazed surface so that in subsequent firings the color melt into, and combines with, the glaze layer.

Jolleying Shaping a thin layer of clay over a revolving plaster mould with a shaped template or profile.

Kaolin A pure clay, sometimes called china clay, used in white clay bodies such as porcelain. It is used as a source of silica and alumina in glazes.

Lead Sesquisilicate A high lead content frit with low solubility in weak acid or water.

Leather-hard or Cheese-hard Partially dry clay which is no longer plastic, but will crack if pressure is applied. In a state ready for turning.

Lug Side projection of a pot which acts as a handle for lifting.

Lusters Salts of metals fired a low temperatures, giving a lustrous or irridesecent metallic sheen to a body or glaze surface.

Luting The blending of two clay surfaces, using slip.

Macaloid Brand name for a superior and very plastic form of bentonite.

Matting Agent Ceramic compound used to give matt surfaces when added to glazes.

Maturing Temperature The temperature at which a clay body develops the desirable hardness, or glaze ingredients fuse into the clay body.

Melting Point When a clay, in firing, fuses and turns to a molten glass-like substance.

Mochaware Type of decoration performed at the wet slip stage when a mixture of alkaline liquid and pigment rapidly disperse into the slip giving a fine lattice pattern.

Muffle Refractory chamber inside a fuel-burning kiln which contains the pottery and protects it from direct contact with the flames and gases.

Opacifier Chemical used to make glazes opaque. Generally white in color. Tin oxide is the best opacifier, but other oxides are also used.

Oxidation To fire with an ample supply of oxygen.

Plastic clay Clay which can be manipulated, but still retains its shape.

Primary clays Those clays which have remained in their forming grounds, such as china clay or kaolin.

Pug Mill Machine for mixing and extruding plastic clay.

Pyrometer An instrument for registering the temperature in the kiln.

Pyrometric cones Ceramic pyramids used to measure the temperature in the kiln.

Raku An open sandy or grogged pottery, fired between 800°C and 1000°C (1470°F and 1830°F) and generally glazed with a lead glaze. The ware is taken from the kiln when red-hot and placed in water or a combustible material for reduction or carbonizing.

Raw Glazing Glazing an article while it is still in the unfired clay state.

Reactive glaze One that combines with a harder glaze when fired under or over it.

Reduction To fire with a very reduced air intake, creating instability, and thus changes in the body and glaze.

Refractory Resistance to melting; capable of standing high temperatures.

Saggar A round fireclay box for holding glazed pots in a fuel-burning kiln in which there are no muffles.

Salt Glaze A glaze formed by tossing salt into a hot stoneware kiln.

Secondary (Residual) Clays Primary clays which have been carried away by erosion and earth movements and have combined, in the process, with mineral impurities.

Sgraffito To scratch through a layer of slip to reveal a different colored body underneath.

Silk Screen Nylon mesh used for printing an image onto a flat ceramic surface or onto transfer paper.

Slip Mixture of clay and water. Used for binding clay surfaces, in casting and for decoration.

Soak To maintain a steady temperature in the kiln for some time to allow clay bodies and glazes to mature.

Spacers Hollow sections of a thin-walled clay cylinder, used to glue pieces of pottery together.

Sprigging Plastic clay applied to an article to form a relief decoration.

Squeegee A rubber-edge wooden tool, used to force printing ink through a mesh screen in silk screen printing.

Stains Stabilized coloring oxides used for coloring bodies and glazes.

'T' Material Highly grogged white plastic clay (see suppliers lists.)

Terracotta (literally 'baked earth') An iron-bearing earthenware clay which matures at a low temperature and fires to an earth-red color.

Terra Sigillata A very fine precipitated slip used as a surface coating for burnishing or for decorative treatments.

Toxic Any ceramic material, raw, gaseous or liquid injurious to health.

Tube Line To decorate on a fired or unfired clay body, giving a raised line. The tube line is a mixture of clay, flux and other ceramic compounds.

Twadell Degress Twaddell (°TW). Units used to measure the specific gravity of solutions and suspensions.

Updraft kiln A fuel-burning kiln in which the smoke goes into and through the kiln and up the chimney.

Vitrification The point at which a clay body begins to lose its porosity when firing.

Volatalize To become vaporous. Certain oxides, such as copper, do this at high temperatures and are deposited onto other pots and kiln shelves.

Wad Box A manually-operated machine for extruding cross-sections of clay.

Wedging Method of cutting and reforming plastic clay to make it homogenous.

Wheelhead The circular revolving flat disc, attached to the potter's wheel, and on which the pot is thrown or formed.

Index and bibliography

BIBLIOGRAPHY

BOOKS

The Natural Way to Draw
Kinnon Nicolaides
(Andre Deutsch, London)

William de Morgan
William Gaunt and MDE
Clayton
(Studio Vista)

Shoji Hamada — A Potter's
Way and Work
Susan Peterson
(Kondanska International,
Tokyo, New York and San
Francisco)

The Potters Book of Glaze
Recipes
Emanuel Cooper
(Batsford)

Basic Design
The Dynamic of Visual Form
Maurice de Sausmarey
(Studio Vista)

Tin Glazed Pottery
Alan Caiger-Smith
(Faber & Faber)

Beyond East and West
Memoirs, Portraits and
Essays
Bernard Leach
(Faber & Faber)

American Potters
Garth Clark
(Watson Guptill, New York)

Science for Craft Potters and
Enamellers
Kenneth Shaw
(David & Charles)

Understanding Pottery
Glazes
David Green
(Faber & Faber)

Health and Safety in
Ceramics
The Institute of Ceramics
(Pergammon Press, Oxford
and New York)

New Zealand Pottery
Workbook
Howard Williams
(Beaux Art, Auckland, NZ)

Ceramic Glazes
Kenneth Shaw (Elsevier)

Ceramics in the Modern
World
Maurice Chandler
(Aldus Books, London)

Designing with natural forms
Natalie d'Arbeloff (Batsford)

Artists Workbook
Natalie D'Arbeloff
(Studio Vista)

The Craft of the Potter
Michael Casson
(BBC Publications)

Pottery and Porcelain
Mary Rogers
(Alphabooks/Watson-Guptill,
New York)

Lucie Rie
Houston and Cripps
(The Craft Council)

Pottery Techniques of
Decoration
John Colbeck   (Batsford)

Glazes for the Craft Potter
Harry Fraser
(Pitman)

Ceramics: A Potters
Handbook
Glenn C. Nelson
(Holt, Rinehart & Winston,
New York)

Studio Potter Book
Edited by Gerry Williams,
Peter Sabin and Sarah Bodive
(Van Nostrand Reinhold)

The Potter's Companion
Tony Birks   (Collins)

Stoneware and Porcelain
Daniel Rhodes
(Chilton Company)

Shino and Oribe Ceramics
Ryoichi Fujioka
(Kondansha International Ltd
and Shibundo)

Mellors Modern Inorganic
Chemistry
(Longman)

The Self-Reliant Potter
Andrew Holden
(A & C Black)

Clays and Ceramic Raw
Materials
WF Worrall
(Applied Science Publishers
Ltd)

Kiln Building with Space Age
Materials
Frank Colson
(Van Nostrand Reinhold)

Raku Art and Technique
Hal Riegger

Dictionary of Materials and
Techniques
Frank Hamer

PERIODICALS

Craft Work
Scottish Development
Agency
102 Telford Road
Edinburgh EH4 2NP
Scotland

Ceramic Review
17a Newburg Street
London W1

Crafts
Crafts Council
8 Waterloo Place
London SW1Y 4AT

The Potter
Craft Potters Society of
Ireland
Rion Wynne
Wynne Pottery
Springfield
Sandyford Road
Co. Dublin
Ireland

Kerarnik Magazine
Stein felder Str.
10D-8770 Lohra
Main
West Germany

La Revue de la Ceramique et
du vere
61 Rue Marconi
62880 Vendin-le-Vieil
France

Form magazine
Formingen Svensk
Formingen Box 7404/S 103
91
Stockholm
Sweden

Craft International
24 Spring Street
New York
NY 10012   USA

Ceramics Monthly
Box 12448
Columbus
Ohio 43212   USA

Studio Potter
Box 172
Warner
New Hampshire 03278
USA

American Craft
American Craft Council
PO Box 561 Martinsville
New Jersey 08836
USA

Crafts
Expediters of the Printed
Word Ltd
527 Madison Avenue
Suite 1217
New York
NY 1002
USA

The Alberta Potters
Association Magazine
Subscription from Alberta
Potters Association
PO Box 1050 Edmonton
Alberta 75J 2H1
Canada

Canadian Guild of Potters
Tactile
100 Avenue Road
Toronto
Ontario Canada

Craft Dimensions
Candadian Guild of Crafts
2025 Peel Street
Montreal
Quebec
Canada

Canada Crafts
Circulation Department
380 Wellington Street West
Toronto
Ontario M5U 1E3
Canada

Ontario Potter
Ontario Potters Association
c/o Hamilton Place
50 Main Street
W. Hamilton
Ontario
Canada

Pottery in Australia
48 Berton Street
Dorlinghurst
NSW 2010
Australia

Craft Australia
Craft Council of Australia
100 George Street
Sydney
NSW
Australia

New Zealand Potter
PO Box 12-162 Wellington
North
New Zealand

Lively Ceramic Magazine
La Levista del Ceramista
Quirno Costa 1259
1245 Buenos Aires
Republica Argentina

ACKNOWLEDGEMENTS

Firstly I would like to say that I owe much to the generosity of all those whose work has been illustrated and recorded in this book. Without exception they gave valuable time and knowledge which can now be shared by all readers. My special thanks go to the following potters who prepared and demonstrated their individual skills and techniques — Wendy Patterson, Bob Broughton, Alan Caiger-Smith and his colleagues, Marion Gaunce, Idonia Van der Bilj, Siddig El'Nigoumi, Mary Wondransch, Dorothy Feibleman and Paul Tritton. Apart from overseas contributions, most color and black and white photographs were taken by Ian Howes whose skill and sensibility admirably interpreted the many ceramic qualities I was trying to illustrate. Thanks also to Adrian Halstead and Victor Bryant for kindly vetting specialist chapters, to Gordon Slim at Potterycraft for regularly providing information regarding raw materials and to Dominique Stenning who patiently and cheerfully typed and deciphered my rough drafts. Particular thanks are due to Madeline Dinkel for the excellent and informative page of lettering. Thanks also to the following photographers: Dan Bailey, Richard Ball, David Cripps, Bill Kearns, David Reid and Jessica Strong. Additional thanks to all at Quarto who produced this book, especially to Moira Clinch who designed the complete contents and to Emma Johnson for sympathetic editing. Above all, without the help and support of my wife, Ann, this volume would never have been written.